U.S. ARMY HOSPITAL CENTER 804

U.S. ARMY HOSPITAL CENTER 804

An Account of the U.S. Military Hospitals in the Shropshire/Flintshire Area during World War II

Fran and Martin Collins

BREWIN BOOKS

BREWIN BOOKS
56 Alcester Road,
Studley,
Warwickshire,
B80 7LG
www.brewinbooks.com

Published by Brewin Books, 2017

© Fran Collins, Martin Collins, 2017

Fran and Martin Collins have asserted their rights in accordance with the Copyright, Designs and Patents Act 1988 to be identified as the authors of this work.

All rights reserved. No part of this publication may be reproduced, stored in a retrieval system, or transmitted in any form or by any means, electronic, mechanical, photocopying, recording or otherwise, without the prior permission in writing of the publisher and the copyright owners, or as expressly permitted by law, or under terms agreed with the appropriate reprographics rights organization. Enquiries concerning reproduction outside the terms stated here should be sent to the publishers at the UK address printed on this page.

The publisher makes no representation, express or implied, with regard to the accuracy of the information contained in this book and cannot accept any legal responsibility for any errors or omissions that may be made.

A CIP catalogue record for this book is available from the British Library

ISBN: 978-1-85858-565-9

Printed in the UK
by Bell & Bain Ltd.

Contents

Prologue	7
1. The Friendly Invaders – 304th Station Hospital, Llanerch Panna	9
2. A Superb Job in the Midst of Chaos – 16th General Hospital, Penley	20
3. Mud and Incompleted Buildings – 15th General Hospital, Oteley Deer Park	30
4. Best in the E.T.O. – 82nd General Hospital, Iscoyd Park	35
5. Four Thousand, Five Hundred Purple Hearts – 68th General Hospital, Halston Hall	45
6. Fun for All – 68th General Hospital, Halston Hall	58
7. 6810 (Provisional)/804 Hospital Center	66
8. Carrying its Share of the Load – 83rd General Hospital, Llanerch Panna	74
9. Volunteers and Visitors – 83rd General Hospital, Llanerch Panna	83
10. Return to Duty – 137th General Hospital, Oteley Deer Park	91
11. More than Medicine and Surgery – 137th General Hospital, Oteley Deer Park	101
12. Filled to Capacity – 129th General Hospital, Penley	114
13. Everything is fine in the 129 – 129th General Hospital, Penley	125
14. Detention of Prisoner Patients – 82nd General Hospital, Iscoyd Park	133
15. Haec Olim Meminisse Juvabit – One Day this will be Pleasing to Remember	143
16. A Superior Job Well Done	155
Epilogue: Gone, But Not Forgotten	160
Abbreviations	166
Glossary	167
Appendix 1: American Military Camps in Flintshire/Shropshire area during World War 2	168
Appendix 2: Military Camps in Shropshire during World War 2	177
Appendix 3: US Army Hospitals in UK, August 1944	179
Appendix 4: Army Hospital Centers	180
Appendix 5: Hospital Trains	181
Acknowledgements	182

Prologue

ON 7 December 1941 the events at Pearl Harbor altered the position of the United States with regard to the war in Europe. Four days after Congress had declared war on Japan, Germany and Italy declared war on the United States. America found itself involved in a war in two theatres; this resulted in plans being made to send troops both to the Pacific and to the European theatres of war.

It was decided that the U.S. authorities would make arrangements for the build up of U.S. troops in the U.K. which would serve as a staging area for the expected Allied invasion of Europe. Codenamed Operation Bolero (known to some as the 'Allied Invasion of Britain'), plans were put into motion for the billeting and living arrangements of the large numbers of U.S. service men who would be training in the U.K. prior to the invasion.

From the beginning the U.S. Medical Department were involved in these arrangements. It was necessary for the department to ensure that there was provision for the care of both wounded and ill soldiers. For the period prior to the invasion the army would require a garrison medical establishment to care for its sick and injured during the build up and waiting period as well as additional hospitals for Air Force casualties. After the commencement of the Cross Channel Assault extra hospitals would be required to accommodate the expected flow of casualties.

The responsibility for organising the hospital provision in the U.K. fell largely to General Paul R. Hawley, the E.T.O. Chief Surgeon. He began by requisitioning a small number of established British hospitals for U.S. troops, although the majority of these had already been set aside for British casualties. Hawley then required that the British War Office find sites for 35 station hospitals, which were each to be less than five miles from centres of concentration of U.S. troops in the U.K. The War Office and the Ministry of Agriculture then worked together to select

General Paul R. Hawley (U.S. Archives, NARA)

suitable sites, usually in parks or estates to avoid building on farm land. By August 1942, 33 sites had been located.

Hawley aimed to group the larger general hospitals in groups of four or five units for greater efficiency. He requested that the British find locations with adequate rail connections for hospital trains without disrupting overall traffic patterns. After consulting the railway authorities the War Office decided to place the first three centres in Cirencester, Great Malvern and Whitchurch, and in July 1942 it ordered the construction of fifteen general hospitals in groups of five at the three centres.

Unfortunately, due to poor weather, lack of man power and lack of materials the U.S. hospital building programme in the U.K. fell behind schedule and it was necessary for Hawley to put back his timetable for the shipment of hospital units to the U.K. Despite this the advance parties of the hospital units arriving in Shropshire and Flintshire in the latter part of 1943 and early parts of 1944 found British construction companies still working on site to complete the buildings. On some of the sites construction workers were even occupying the living quarters of the hospital personnel.

This book sets out the history of the five hospital sites in the Shropshire/Flintshire area under the jurisdiction of the 6810 (provisional) Hospital Center: Penley, Llannerch Panna and Iscoyd Park in Flintshire and Halston Park and Oteley Deer Park in Shropshire. It looks at the experiences of the staff and their patients through eyewitness accounts and archive material and the impact of the hospital on the surrounding areas and their inhabitants.

Chapter 1

The Friendly Invaders – 304th Station Hospital, Llanerch Panna

THE MAELOR area, situated on the boundary of England and North Wales to the West of the River Dee, has been the scene of border warfare since ancient times. In the 1940s the region was settled in by friendly invaders, our allies in World War Two. The first settlers to arrive and temporarily live in the area were the American military units which set up camp prior to and after the Allied invasion of France. The second group was made up of displaced Poles, who made the Maelor area their home at the end of World War Two.

During World War Two the area saw a large influx of American servicemen. The majority of them just spent a short time in the U.K. while preparing for D-Day. Towards the end of 1942 British engineers commenced work on the construction of a number of purpose-built U.S. military hospitals. These hospitals were built to care for the wounded from the conflict in Europe, but on the departure of the Americans some would serve as hospitals for sick and disabled Poles.

A cluster of five U.S. hospitals were built on large estates along the Shropshire/Flintshire border. In Shropshire, hospitals were constructed at Oteley Deer Park in Ellesmere and Halston Hall in Whittington. In Flintshire a hospital was erected at Iscoyd Park, Wrexham, and two were built in Penley, Overton-on-Dee. Penley One was built in the grounds of Penley Hall and Penley Two (also called Llanerch Panna or Overton) was constructed in the grounds of Llanerch Panna (meaning Penley in Welsh).

The Maelor area was chosen as a suitable site for military hospitals because of its railway links. Patients could be smoothly transferred by rail from the South coast to stations close to the five hospitals. The two hospitals at Penley were situated near to the railway station at Overton-on-Dee. To give ambulances easy access it was necessary to remove the existing fences around the station. As the Wrexham and Ellesmere lines had been closed to passenger trains since 1940 it was necessary to route hospital trains via Whitchurch.

Both of the hospitals at Penley were built by Robert McAlpine and Sons Ltd, at the cost of around £25,000 each. McAlpine used a predominantly Irish labour force which was bussed in daily from Wrexham, the Wirral and Liverpool. Because of the increase in road traffic during the building of the hospitals, Penley Parish Council found it necessary to request either a resident policemen or extra police patrols in the area during March 1943.

Margery Preston and her puppy (M. Jones)

The construction of the two hospitals at Penley had a substantial impact on the area. Public utilities such as electricity and sewerage were introduced and roads were upgraded. The population of the small rural community was trebled when both hospitals were full to capacity. Local resident, Margery Jones remembers that because of the large numbers of American servicemen in the area a bus service was established from Penley to Wrexham, this meant that, unlike her older sisters, she was able to catch a bus to her secondary school, The Convent, in Wrexham. Margery's family, the Prestons were farmers and an added advantage of having the American camp in the area was that they were allowed to collect the waste from the mess halls at Penley to use as pig swill.

Penley One hospital, designated Plant 4191 by the U.S. military authorities, was built in the grounds of Penley Hall which had been home to the Dymock family since 1842 although they had not lived there since the beginning of the century. The small Georgian mansion was set in a garden with a stable block. The grounds included 95 acres of woodland and 39 acres of parkland.

Penley Two hospital, designated Plant 4190, was built in the grounds of Llanerch Panna (now known as Tudor Court), a half-timbered house with a brick chimney and a red tiled roof. It had been built at

Aerial view of Llanerch Panna and Penley Hospitals. (Penley is situated at the top of the page and Llanerch Panna in the centre) 106/UK1517 May 1946 (Welsh Assembly)

10

Llanerch Panna

the end of the nineteenth century for the Honourable George T. Kenyon and was occupied by Lady Leche when the Americans arrived in the area.

Llanerch Panna was the first hospital site of the cluster to be completed. The 304th U.S. Station Hospital, commanded by Colonel John D. Barnwell, arrived in the U.K. in September 1943. The unit, travelling aboard the British transport ship, Orion, had docked at Greenock in Scotland on the night of 14 September. During the voyage 2nd Lieutenant Sharia G. Wilson, laboratory technician with the unit, had taken on duties in the sick bay of the ship, identifying and treating an outbreak of dysentery on board. For this he was awarded a commendation.

Hospital site under construction at Penley Two (Llanerch Panna can be seen in background) (Author's collection)

Lieutenant Sharia Wilson (JD Wilson)

Colonel Barnwell recorded that having been at sea for nine days:

> "…land was a very welcome sight. The mountains coming down to meet the sea were covered with a vivid green vegetation. It presented a peaceful scene that contrasted with the masts of sunken ships to be seen above the waters of the harbour." (304th S.H. Archives, NARA)

On 15 September the unit was transported in two separate groups to the quayside where the first party boarded a train at 1345 and began the 400 mile rail journey to Overton-on-Dee Railway Station. There were no cooking facilities on the train so the men ate cold C-rations and drank coffee, cocoa and lemonade made with cold water.

On arrival at Overton-on-Dee, shortly before midnight, the unit was met by the advance party, which had travelled ahead of the main group, arriving in July 1943. From the railway station the men and women were transported the three miles to the hospital site by motor transport. The Colonel's first impressions of the camp were that it:

"… was certainly more than had been expected or anticipated in an overseas installation." (304th S.H. Archives, NARA)

Construction site at Llanerch Panna – 1943 (Author's collection)

Construction site at Llanerch Panna – 1943 (Author's collection)

Newly completed hospital at Llanerch Panna, August 1943 (Author's collection)

THE FRIENDLY INVADERS

Wards and key buildings such as Headquarters, X-Ray, Dental clinic, EENT, Operating Theatre, Supply, Boiler Rooms, Mess, Garage, Guard House, ablutions, showers and Chapel were permanent type constructions of brick, tile and cement.

The hospital wards were divided for different types of patients. The Medical Service had six general medical wards for enlisted men, one for male officers and two for female officers. General Surgery had two wards, which were also used for neurosurgery patients; Orthopaedic surgery had nine; Septic cases, EENT and Dental surgery had one ward each. On two occasions it was necessary to open a third ward for female officers for relatively brief periods. Between one and three wards were used for communicable diseases and it was necessary to erect a pyramidal tent between two of the wards to use for sterilising kitchen utensils and bedpans with mobile field units. Six of the wards on the Surgical Service were connected with the Operating Theatre by covered corridors, the remaining surgical wards had open walk-ways, as did all of the medical wards.

The laboratory, under the supervision of Francis B. Vandeloo and Lieutenant Sharia Wilson, was made up of six rooms: a large general laboratory, a waiting room, an office, supply room used for bacteriology and serology and a utility room. The men in this section worked on identifying the causes of diseases and dispensing treatments. A lack of facilities precluded some tests and facilities for research were unavailable while the 304th were at Llanerch Panna.

The Chapel was shared by two chaplains on the base: the Catholic Chaplin, Captain Richard G. Whelan and the Protestant Chaplain, Captain Carl Osaphl. They serviced not only the personnel of the 304th but, at times, those in nearby hospitals and other small military units. On arrival the Chapel already had a lectern, but it was necessary to purchase an altar, flags, vases and drapes.

The operating personnel of the 304th consisted of 37% Protestant, 51% Catholic, 8% Jewish and 4% of no religious denomination. Jewish personnel were provided with opportunities to worship by a visiting Jewish Chaplain and transportation to nearby towns with a Jewish community.

Barracks for officers, nurses and enlisted men were of temporary construction and made of wood and tar paper. Six additional temporary buildings had been erected as living quarters for the workmen building the hospital. One was designated as a P.X. and the other as a detachment dayroom. The dayroom contained a

Captain Carl Osaphl, Protestant Chaplain (P. Osaphl)

snooker table, dart games, phonographs and radios. A library was established in a building opposite the dayroom.

The 304th also had a Recreation Hall and the Special Service Officer, 2nd Lieutenant Emilio P. Ferrari, arranged for movies to be shown there four times a week. Visiting show troupes also used this building. During the 304th's time at Llanerch

Panna there were five U.S.O. shows, four ENSA stage shows and three Red Cross Stage Shows. A group of thirty enlisted men from the detachment also put together a minstrel show which gave two performances in Ellesmere Town Hall for civilians, a performance for the R.A.S.C. depot at Overton and another for the 168th Station Hospital in Cheshire.

Special Service also organised sports activities on the base. A soccer team was established but after a 7-1 defeat at the hands of the 351st Search-light Battalion (British), its popularity died out. The men enjoyed playing other sports on the base such as touch football, ping-pong, volleyball, baseball and horseshoes.

Although the main priority of the 5 American Red Cross workers attached to the 304th was providing recreational activities for the patients, the unit also provided activities for the personnel. The Red Cross had the use of a building named 'The Red Cross House', which contained a radio, phonograph, piano, workbench, snooker table and two ping-pong tables. There was also a supply of books, magazines, checkers and other board games.

Decorations of the Red Cross House varied with the season. For Halloween:

> "... all previous attempts to prevent the house appearing as a barn were reversed and autumn leaves, cornstalks and hay were used to carry the motif for the barn dance. ... Valentine's Day saw hearts hung everywhere and rosy cupids peering from doorways." (A.R.C. 304 G.H. NARA)

Lieutenant S. Wilson (J.D. Wilson)

The personnel of the 304th also found their own entertainment in the locality. Lieutenant Wilson's son remembers that:

> "He loved the people of the U.K. ... and the beer."

Although British beer was somewhat different to the drink that the G.I.s were used to in the U.S. it was still popular. Tec. 5 Thomas McConkey from the nearby 137th General Hospital at Oteley Deer Park described the beer found in the locality, in his letters home:

> "British beer suffers from never having been introduced to that common denominator of every American drink, the carbon dioxide bubble ... and the beer and 'minerals' (soft

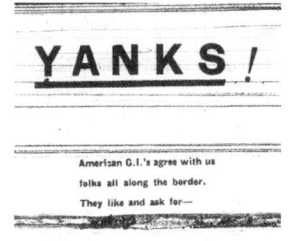

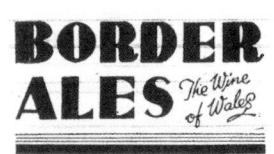

Advert in Wrexham Advertiser and Star 26/6/1944

14

drinks) have rarely made the acquaintance of ice, either. As a result there isn't nearly as much froth. ... It is more difficult, however, to sit all evening long and drink British Beer, you fill up too rapidly. ... It isn't true that English beer is warm either. It is reasonably cold, coming usually from deep, musty cellars far under the inn."

He also noted that although British beer was different in consistency from American beer:

"It all works out in the long run since I get just as destructive and 'lovable' – so the M.P.s say – on the same amount."

The nearest pub to Llanerch Panna was 'The Dymock Arms'. It was the only free house in Maelor, so it often had a stock of ale when the other pubs ran short as it was able to source its supplies from both local firms and those farther afield. It was said that at busy times the landlord removed the traditional pumps and the cellar men were sent to fill large jugs straight from the wood, carrying the pitchers to the top of the cellar steps where they were rapidly emptied and passed down again for refilling.

Dymock Arms, Penley (M. Engelman)

From time to time black engineer units were based at one of the two Penley hospitals. Apparently because of American rules of segregation black soldiers were served in the bottom kitchen at the Dymock Arms, which had its own entrance, while the white soldiers used the main saloon and top bar, which had a piano and dart board.

There was a story that on one occasion a G.I. had pulled a gun on the landlord at the Dymock Arms because 'time' had been called. When the landlord still refused to serve him apparently the soldier emptied the dregs from all the other glasses on the tables into his glass.

During its first few weeks at Llanerch Panna the 304th encountered some 'teething problems'. The first one was that as the unit was designated a 'station hospital' it was staffed as a hospital operating on an established military post – i.e. it did not have the extra man-power that a hospital operating on a 'stand-alone' basis needed. It was necessary to use medical staff for Fire Department, Post-

Nurses of the 304th on parade (J.D. Wilson)

Exchange, Barber Shop, Salvage, interior Guards and coke and coal details. The lack of central heating in the hospital necessitated the use of eighteen men as firemen in boiler room, latrines, wards and mess halls.

The second difficulty encountered by the 304th was the unfamiliar equipment that was provided, much of it not as efficient as that which the men had been trained on. To overcome this problem extra classes were immediately commenced for enlisted personnel. A large group of Medical and Surgical technicians attended the professional classes under the instruction of various nurses. A number of men were given individual training and instruction by their department head and his assistants.

There was also some confusion due to the adaptation of the 110 and 115 volt American equipment to the 230 volt British system. Only the X-Ray room and five other departments had 115 volt transformers and even in these departments the outlets were inadequate. Consequently American equipment such as sterilisers, hot plates and microscope lamps either had to be rewired or the voltage reduced by improvising transformers through the use of bulb series.

The lack of essential equipment was overcome by making a critical shortage list and touring depots to find missing items. During the first week medical requirements such as aspirin and adhesive tape were obtained from the 168th Station Hospital at Warrington, the nearest U.S. military hospital.

The shortage of typewriters on the post meant that they had to be shared between departments; clerks ended up working long hours to complete their work. Two of the officers bought an 'antiquated mimeograph machine' with their own money to help with the administrative work.

Another shortage experienced at the 304th was clothing supplies. All patients transferred from troop transports to the hospital were assigned to the Detachment of Patients. Upon return to duty or transfer to a convalescent hospital patients were required to have a Class A uniform and full field equipment. Unfortunately station hospitals were not authorised to stock and issue clothing and personal equipment. It was necessary for the hospital to try several different channels to source the uniforms and equipment.

Another resource in short supply at the 304th was motor transport. The unit had been allocated two 6x6 2½ ton trucks, one 1½ ton 4x4 dump truck, two jeeps and one ¾ ton Command Car. It also had the use of a Godiva Model Coventry Climax trailer pump with accessories. It was necessary for a representative from the National Fire Service in Wrexham to come to Llanerch Panna to instruct personnel in the use of the pump in the event of a fire.

The vehicles were needed to transport patients to and from the 168th Station Hospital at Warrington, the 52nd General Hospital at Wolverley and the 96th General Hospital at Malvern. It was also necessary for the Transportation Section to collect supplies, rations and mail from three different supply depots: G16 at Wem, Shropshire, G18 at Sudbury, Derbyshire and G20 at Burton Upon Trent, Staffordshire. Coal and coke also had to be collected from the railway stations at Overton-on-Dee and Wrexham.

THE FRIENDLY INVADERS

Trips were coordinated so that several deliveries or collections were made each time a vehicle went out. The 304th instigated a system whereby all routine trips were posted and every attempt was made to combine individual trips with the routine. Even the drive to the nearest petrol pump at Overton, four miles away, was incorporated into a dispatched trip.

A number of the day-to-day problems encountered at the 304th were due to the fact that it was breaking new ground as it was one of the earliest station hospitals in the U.K. that was not connected to an established post or station. Colonel Barnwell noted:

> "A goodly portion of the work was done with tongue in cheek for lack of a definitive established policy." (304 S.H. Archives)

On 19 October 1943 the 304th Station Hospital was officially opened as a 834 bed station hospital, even though it only actually had 714 beds. The first patient, an American Private with a fractured finger, was admitted the next day. As a station hospital the unit took care of the medical needs of servicemen stationed in the area. The Command devised a plan whereby up to 300 patients at one time could be received, admitted to wards, put to bed and definitive treatment commenced, all within two hours. The plan was never tested as the largest number of patients received at one time was 65, who were admitted within half an hour.

The 304th celebrated Christmas 1943 at Llanerch Panna. The U.S. Government had encouraged those with relatives overseas to send Christmas presents early and Chaplain, Captain Osaphl, received his first Christmas cards and packages in October, not long after his arrival at Llanerch Panna.

Christmas V-mail sent by Chaplain Carl Osaphl to his son (P. Osaphl)

The Chaplains, Special Service Officer and Red Cross Unit at the 304th coordinated the Christmas activities at the hospital. A souvenir programme was designed which included a timetable of religious services, the Christmas dinner menu, a rota of the personnel and greetings from the Commanding Officer.

Each ward of the hospital was decorated and had its own tree. Nurses, ward men and patients made improvised decorations out of paper, cotton, card and tin cans. Lady Leche, from the Manor House, contributed armloads of freshly cut holly.

Captain Osaphl had set his heart on a traditional candlelight service in the base chapel for Christmas so he asked his wife to send candles as they were not readily available in the U.K. Apparently the clerk in the Mason City, Iowa store insisted on sending some as her personal gift to the hospital. In readiness the carpenter, Sergeant Holte, made candlesticks and holders to be placed on the altar and brackets to be fixed around the walls. (Candles could not be placed on the windows because of black out restrictions.) One of the civilian employees on the base decorated the chapel with holly branches while a florist from the unit made a large holly wreath to be hung above the altar.

By the afternoon of Christmas Eve the candles had still not arrived, but shortly before the service was about to begin, the Christmas mail, including the candles, was announced. There was just time to set up the sixty-six candles before the service, which was a traditional one with readings, carols and Christmas music.

The Red Cross unit hosted a party on Christmas Eve and on Christmas morning a group of carollers toured the wards, finishing off under Lady Leche's window. During the day there was another service in the Chapel and short services in every ward, the singing accompanied by a field organ, which was carried from ward to ward.

Christmas Day ended with a turkey dinner and all the trimmings. The dining room was decorated with holly and the tables were arranged in a banquet style. Chaplain Osaphl noted:

> "We thought of home, country and Allies as we looked upon Old Glory in the center with Allied flags draped on either side."

At the end of the meal Colonel Barnwell stood up to say a few words and request that the personnel sing 'Happy Birthday' to Chaplain Osaphl and a visiting airmen who shared his birth date.

Because the 304th was the first hospital to be established in the Flintshire/Shropshire area other hospital units, including the 15th and 16th General Hospitals, were billeted at Llanerch Panna while awaiting completion of their own hospital buildings. When 102 enlisted men and five officers of the 49th Collecting Company were attached to the 304th for quarters and rations on 14 February 1944 it was necessary to erect ward tents to accommodate them as the hospital buildings were full to capacity.

In April 1944 the hospital was given notice to leave Llanerch Panna. The Red Cross unit were disappointed at the timing as they were in the middle of Easter preparations for the patients. Kathryn Snyder of the Red Cross notes:

> "Easter preparations and plans soon turned to cupboard straightening and hours of inventorying ... The plasticine eggs covered with papier mache were put away and Easter ideas put aside. Easter found us far away from Easter eggs and candy." (A.R.C. 304 G.H. NARA)

The girls were also disappointed as a number of improvements to the Red Cross building had recently been made. The Grounds Detachment had built a bicycle rack for guests and moved sod from a nearby field to provide a lawn in front of the building. The civilian engineer at the base had recently agreed to pipes with running water in the building and the Special Service Section had put up spotlights and grey and red curtains in the ward that was being used as a theatre. A movie projector had also recently been delivered to the base for use in the Red Cross building.

Around Easter time the Red Cross had been planning a ceremony to dedicate their newly built fireplace in the Red Cross Hall. As it turned out the dedication ceremony took place the night before the 304th left, and the occasion became a farewell party. The Red Cross unit from the 16th General Hospital based at Penley helped to make sandwiches for the occasion and decorated the Red Cross building with daffodils, narcissi and forsythia.

At the event the patients and personnel gathered around the fireplace decorated with flowers while the Assistant Field Director, Eleanor Morris, read out a short history of the unit and then placed it along with a roster tied with red, white and blue ribbon, into a hole prepared by the stone mason who had built the fireplace, She noted:

> "Word had somehow gotten around that we were about to leave and nearly all of our civilian friends, together with friends from other hospitals nearby, managed to get there for a last evening together. The American Red Cross workers for the incoming hospital were also on the Post and we were glad to have the opportunity of introducing them to so many of their new neighbours. We only wish for the new Red Cross unit, that it will be as happy in its work as we were and will get from its organisation something like the sincere interest and enthusiastic help which we have always had from ours." (A.R.C. 304 G.H. NARA)

Miss Morris described Llanerch Panna as the 304th left:

> "The thermometer and the patients population were both rising and warm afternoons found the hillside and nearby gardens dotted with maroon bath robes" (A.R.C. 304 G.H. NARA)

460 patients were left in the hospital when the unit was relieved by the 83rd General Hospital between 3-8 April 1944.

From Llanerch Panna the 304th moved to temporary accommodation in Llandudno for two months before being assigned to Kingwood Common, near Reading in June, where it treated German Prisoners of War as well as U.S. Servicemen. The following year the 304th sailed for LeHavre and then travelled to a site in Deggendorf, Germany, where it established a station hospital.

Chapter 2

A Superb Job in the Midst of Chaos – 16th General Hospital, Penley

THE SECOND hospital to arrive in the Flintshire area was the 16th General Hospital, which moved into Penley, Plant 4191, in February 1944. As a general hospital the 16th had a greater capacity than the 304th: there was sufficient staff to cater for 1084 patients. In the first instance the 16th acted as a station hospital, admitting patients from the U.S. military bases in the area, but after D-Day it took on the role of general hospital, treating wounded from the Allied invasion of the Continent.

The 16th General Hospital had embarked on the troopship, Edmund B. Alexander from Boston Harbor at the end of December 1943. As the personnel were issued with tropical clothing on the voyage they assumed that they were to be sent to the Pacific Theatre of Operations, but in fact they arrived at Liverpool Docks, England, on 8 January 1944. From Liverpool the unit travelled to a staging area at Oulton Park, Cheshire, while it awaited the completion of Plant 4191. Nurse Muriel Phillips was not enthusiastic about her stay at Oulton and described her billets as 'Ye Olde Dustbine' in her letters home. Miss Phillips had been a student nurse when Japan bombed Pearl Harbor in December 1941. She decided to

Nurses of the 16th General Hospital disembark at Liverpool (M. Engelman)

enlist immediately, choosing to be an army nurse, rather than a navy nurse as she wasn't a good swimmer and "would prefer to get killed on dry land".

On 16 January the unit travelled to Flintshire where they were temporarily billeted with the 304th at Llanerch Panna as Plant 4191 was still incomplete. Muriel described Flintshire in her letters home:

> "The countryside is beautiful and all the hills are green ... the cottages are quaint and picturesque, the people very friendly but apologetic for existing conditions in this country."

While at Llanerch Panna some of the nurses worked alongside nurses of the 304th while others were transferred to work on detached service at other hospitals. Miss Phillips remembers that a number of the personnel of the 16th spent some time with the 304th as patients, because they had developed 'the famous English hack' (cough).

Finally, on 19 February the 16th were able to move into their own hospital at Penley. While awaiting the arrival of patients the nurses set to work to make their living quarters home-like. Nurse Phillips recalls creating a dressing table from a packing box and dyeing material to make a table cloth and curtains. One of the dentists from the unit helped her to put together a bureau, while she sewed his insignia on for him.

Aerial view of Penley 106G/UK1517 (Welsh Assembly)

View of the nurses' area taken from the Officer's Club (M. Engelman)

Muriel Phillips – 2nd from right (M. Engelman)

Nurses' area (M. Engelman)　　*Muriel Phillips planting primroses outside the nurses quarters (M. Engelman)*

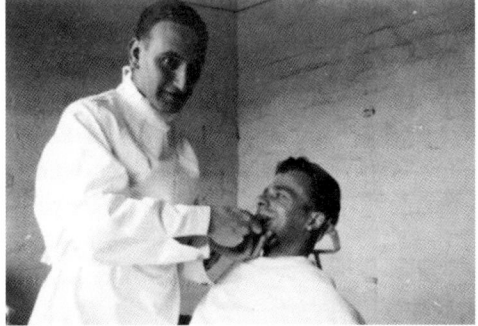

3 Dentists from Hut 5 (M. Engelman)　　*Dentist – Sammy Schneider (M. Engelman)*

Unfortunately Muriel Phillips lost her first month's pay in England because she left the bank notes in her dressing gown pocket. She recalls that the English pound notes were made of 'harsh' paper similar to toilet paper and when she visited the latrine she used them as such. Later she wrote to her family to ask them to post her American toilet paper; when writing to thank them she noted:

"That stuff is very valuable for winning friends and influencing people."

Muriel's family also posted her parcels of cookies and tinned food to supplement her rations. Eggs were in short supply in wartime Britain but Muriel was lucky enough to meet a farmer at one of the pubs near the base. He gave her eggs and then took her and a friend home with him so that his wife could cook them for the girls. Another nurse sharing Muriel's quarters was seeing a local farmer, consequently she was sometimes able to obtain eggs to share with the inhabitants of the hut.

While the hospital awaited the arrival of its patients the Red Cross unit attached to the 16th arranged for personnel to visit various U.K. cities, furnishing them with a list of American Red Cross Clubs where they could stay. On 29 February, 1944, Assistant Field Director of the Red Cross Unit, Alberta Davis wrote:

> "Our first bit of specific service to the nurses came when we left the unit to go to Headquarters in London. We were able to source from E.T.O. Headquarters information regarding the whereabouts of relatives of theirs in the United Kingdom." (A.R.C. 16 G.H. NARA)

Muriel Phillips was one of the nurses who was helped by this information. In her last phone call to her mother before leaving the States her mother had told her about her father's two aunts who had emigrated to Manchester from Russia thirty years earlier.

Muriel Phillips in dress uniform (M. Engelman)

Muriel contacted the Red Cross in Manchester but was informed that there was no-one living there with the name 'Karengold' but there were two families called 'Craingold'. When Muriel wrote to the two addresses she was given she was surprised to receive a letter confirming the fact that Craingold was a derivation of Karengold. The two ladies had changed their name to 'Anglicise' it when they arrived in England.

It was decided that Muriel would meet one of the daughters of the family, fourteen year old Pam, at Manchester Railway Station. Apparently her mother, Gertrude, had instructed her to 'walk on by if she doesn't look proper'. Fortunately for Muriel, Pam didn't 'walk by'; she escorted Muriel to her home where she met the rest of the family. Pam's ten year old sister, Shirley, remembers that she thought that Muriel was 'the cat's whiskers' as she looked so smart in her uniform. The meeting was the beginning of a long and happy relationship between the two families who are still in contact today.

As well as making arrangements for the personnel of the 16th to sight-see in various cities the Red Cross also established links in the local community; servicemen and women were invited to concerts, theatre parties and sports events as well as dances in the area around Penley. Muriel Phillips had the opportunity to attend a dance held in a hall near the hospital. She was dismayed to find that the venue smelt of horse manure but was amused by the elderly trumpet player whose toupee bounced up and down when he played jazz numbers. In April, Muriel and the nurses in her hut travelled by truck to a dance at a U.S. Engineer's base in the area. Unfortunately, due to the blackout restrictions, the driver got lost on the way home. The party eventually arrived back at the base at 3.45 a.m. Needless to say the nurses overslept and were late for their duties the following day.

In addition to organising events off base the Red Cross provided recreational facilities on base in a building which was open 8.30 a.m. until 9.00 p.m. The hall, which was located outside the Patient's Mess, incorporated: a games room, craft shop for the

Army Rehabilitation Programme, a library and a movie theatre, which doubled as a theatre for travelling shows to perform in. The building was ready for use in April with the help of detachment personnel. The floor was painted to add colour and keep the dust down and a bright red border was painted along the walls. The girls acquired four rickety chairs, which had come from an old ship, as well as two small cabinets, card tables and game tables. The furniture was sanded and varnished and the chairs were upholstered with curtain remnants. Cupboards were built to house the games and craft supplies.

Until the hospital was officially opened to patients the ward men spent some of their off-duty time in the craft workshop making items such as mail boxes, ashtrays and foot lockers. The men repaid the Red Cross by building items needed in the Recreation Hall and also helping them to create a small garden outside. Before the arrival of the patients the Red Cross carried out two 'dry runs' in the Recreation Hall with the hospital personnel playing the part of the patients. Jesse Halle, the Senior Recreation Worker noted that:

> "… they appreciated the Red Cross games, music and reading programs, almost as much as real patients do." (A.R.C. 16 G.H. NARA)

During working hours the personnel of the 16th spent this period preparing the hospital for the arrival of its patients. On 10 April Muriel Phillips noted that she was kept busy from 8 a.m. until 5 p.m. unpacking and scrubbing instruments. Once the patients started arriving at the end of April 1944 the hospital was fully prepared.

One of the first patients to be treated at the hospital was an unusual case. Miss Phillips remembers sitting outside in the sunshine on one of her Sundays off in April, watching the commotion that took place because of an injured dog. (Because Muriel worked in O.R. and was on call at night she was given every other weekend off.)

A nurse in the hut next door to Muriel's had taken her dog out for a ride in a basket on her bike, when it had jumped out of the basket and been run over by a truck. The nurse had phoned the post and an ambulance with two doctors was sent to bring the dog back. A vet from another base in the area came to Penley to treat him. Fortunately he had suffered no broken bones, just a prolapsed rectum. Muriel noted in a letter home:

> "Everyone in the camp has been to see him and they talk in hushed voices just as though he was a real patient."

Another unexpected patient at the 16th was one of the nurses who sustained a broken arm. She, along with the other nurses, was unused to the civilian water closet used at the time in the U.K. Muriel Phillips described them in her letters home as:

> "…a large rectangular water-filled box suspended close to the ceiling with a pull-down chain dangling from it."

The nurse in question pulled on the chain too vehemently and brought the box crashing down onto her arm. Muriel commented in her letter home that she didn't think she would receive a Purple Heart Medal for that injury.

The 16th General Hospital was designated a Z.I. Hospital: it was a staging hospital for those awaiting transportation to the Zone of the Interior (U.S.A.). Patients were 'Z.I.ed' if they would not recover from their injuries within a given time frame (the time period fluctuated at different stages in the war) or if treatment would be more effective for the patients in the U.S.A. Patients awaiting transportation home were known as 'Z.I. patients'.

For the non-Z.I. patients the hospital ran a full rehabilitation programme in order to return most of the patients to duty, either in the combat zone or in a non-combatant role such as truck driver or cook. In a meeting with the nurses in April 1944 the A.F.D. of the Red Cross unit attached to the 16th, explained how she saw the role of the Red Cross at Penley with regard to the rehabilitation process:

> "The Rehabilitation Program has as its purpose the return to duty of service personnel recovered from disease or injury in the best possible physical and mental condition through the use of leisure time in educational pursuit designed to effect a greater realisation of personal importance and produce a more informed soldier." (A.R.C. 16 G.H. NARA)

She hoped that both the Red Cross casework and recreation programmes for bed and convalescent patients at Penley would meet the needs of the patient and ultimately make better soldiers of them. She explained that:

> "A misconception is that the Red Cross coddles patients, we definitely try to avoid that and our aim is to strengthen the patients' will to get well. Patients who are worried or bothered do not respond to medical treatments as do those with peace of mind. ... We are here to help them get over fears about hospitalization, diagnosis, treatment and prognosis. After all, there are many men with injuries of such a type that it will involve a great change in their life plans." (A.R.C. 16 G.H. NARA)

The Psychiatrist at the 16th referred some of the patients with 'combat exhaustion' or concerns about home situations to the Red Cross Social Worker. She was able to contact Red Cross Chapters from the home-town of the serviceman or patient to carry out home visits if necessary. In June 1944 the social worker managed to arrange the reunion of a seriously depressed patient with his brother, who was stationed in the U.K.

Another problem patients encountered on their arrival at Penley was their lack of possessions. As one of the patients commented:

> "The medics were so busy getting us patched up in time to save our lives and get us back to the hospitals they didn't even have time to toss our garments or

field jackets with our money and stuff on to the litters, and none of us cared."
(A.R.C. 16 G.H. NARA)

The Red Cross was able to supply the patients with some comfort articles but it was more difficult to supply them with cash. The majority of the patients arrived with no money at all, a small number had some French Franc notes which were rapidly acquired as souvenirs by the other patients. There was a substantial delay before the patients' service records reached the hospital and the Finance Officer would not issue pay without them. The patients applied to the Red Cross for loans which resulted in the Red Cross having to submit two appeals to Red Cross Headquarters for extra funds.

Alongside the arrival of the battle casualties, came the additional problems of finding accommodation in the small village of Penley for the relatives and wives that came to visit. It was decided that brothers of patients would be quartered with the enlisted men on the post while three families in the village offered their spare bedrooms for the wives and female relatives.

Once patients had been admitted to the 16th regular inspections were carried out. Nurse, Muriel Phillips, wrote home that she believed that:

> "Half of the army officers in the E.T.O are inspectors I guess and just go from post to post looking for things to find fault with. By gosh, no matter how perfect you are they'll always find something wrong. Have to salute them indoors, outdoors, everywhere except the latrine. So when we see brass on the post we turn around and go in another direction so they can't tell us our salute is a 47 degree angle instead of 45."

Major Quintus Nicola of the 82nd General Hospital at Iscoyd Parks tells the story in a letter home of the visiting inspector who was turned back twice by the M.P.s at the gate of the 82nd because he was not correctly dressed. When he did finally carry out the inspection Major Nicola felt that he 'was just as unreasonable' and it was all he could do to 'keep from telling him how we felt.'

As well as the visiting inspectors, the hospital held regular Friday morning inspections carried out by the Commanding Officer, Colonel Kubin. Before the imminent inspection Muriel remembers that floors were swept, scrubbed and polished to such a high degree of gloss that their silhouettes were mirrored in them. The nurses even wrapped newspapers around their feet so that they wouldn't mark the floor just prior to an inspection. Apparently the patients were warned not to complain or wrinkle their sheets while the Colonel was there.

The Colonel wore white gloves for the inspection, which he swept under mattresses and around beds. If he found an offending speck of dirt on the O.R. ward, he would look accusingly at Nurse Phillips, who was the head nurse on the ward. He would also flip coins on the empty beds in the wards to check that the sheets were flat. As the Colonel walked through the ward he did pause at a few beds to inquire about the

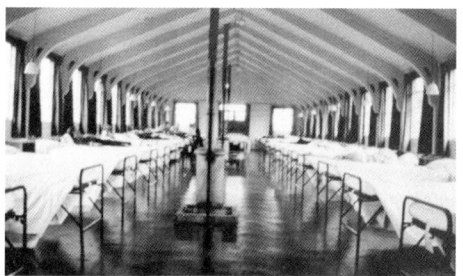
Ward ready for inspection at the 16th (M. Engelman)

Receiving and Discharge Office and Surgical wards (M. Engelman)

patients' health, but Muriel felt that he was more interested in the state of the ward than the patients in it.

In June the battle casualties from Normandy started arriving at the 16th. Jesse Hall, the Red Cross Recreation Worker, reported:

> "We, at the 16th General, swung into full operation almost overnight. In a week's time we jumped from a few hundred patients to hospital capacity. It was a mad scramble for a few days trying to visit and equip new wards as they opened with games, magazines and a few books. We were reminded of the staff in Washington who had told us: 'You'll walk miles until you think you can't move another foot and you'll keep on walking between wards'. We did, our only regret being that there weren't enough hours in the day to do all we'd like to do." (A.R.C. 16 G.H. NARA)

During the day the Red Cross worked with patients on the wards, evenings were spent in the Recreation Hall, working with the ambulatory patients. Miss Davis, the A.F.D., noted that the two recreation workers were:

> "… doing a superb job in the midst of chaos." (A.R.C. 16 G.H. NARA)

To spread the load a little the Red Cross enlisted the help of the local branch of the British W.V.S. One of their ladies came in to catalogue and card the library books, helped by the rehabilitation patients. The W.V.S. also collected bottles for specimens and made gauze masks for the doctors. They gave the hospital some large castors which the Red Cross were able to put to good use on the book cart that a Danish Merchant Marine patient had made. This meant that the books, which had been donated by the British Red Cross, could be transported around the wards.

The Red Cross unit at the 16th were also responsible for booking travelling shows to entertain the patients. Two A.R.C. troupes ('The Harmony Four' and 'Two Girls and a Guy') and a U.S.O. troupe performed at the hospital in May. The A.R.C. troupe 'Sweet and Swing' visited in June, as did Joe Louis, the well-known heavy weight boxer, which particularly delighted the black patients at the 16th. When a Welsh male voice

Joe Louis, visiting a hospital 'Somewhere in England' (NARA)

choir visited the hospital the patients were sceptical as 'there were no girls', but once the singing began the hall soon filled out and it was necessary to open the windows so that those outside and on the wards could hear. Other visitors to the 16th included a group of A.T.S. girls who came to play games and provide dance partners at a tea dance.

The Red Cross also organised parties for the patients at the 16th. On D-Day they held a 'fudge party'. One of the patients remarked:

> "After all this is about the best way to celebrate a day that will bring us home sooner by doing something that reminds us of home." (A.R.C. 16 G.H. NARA)

Later on in June the girls organised a '48 States' themed party. The starter game involved collecting autographs from men from as many States as possible (the winner got 33). The patients played a number of games such as races with paper horses and ring tossing. Winners of the games earned coupons that could be exchanged at the counter for prizes. Refreshments consisted of cocoa, sandwiches and doughnuts from a nearby 'Donut Dugout'. One evening in June the Recreation Hall was closed to patients as the girls had organised a 'Monte Carlo' themed party for the enlisted men of the detachment.

The Red Cross also established a craft programme for the patients. Small wooden dolls were made to send to a nearby crippled children's convalescent home. Along with the dolls the men sent their cookies, candy and gum rations. The A.R.C. planned to take some of the patients to visit the children. As Mother's Day approached two of the patients sketched portraits of the other patients to send to their loved ones and one of the nurse patients cut out silhouettes of the men to make Mother's Day cards with. In June some of the men opted to make 'ditty bags' out of some spare black-out material. The recreation Worker, Jesse Hale, noted that:

> "The men are learning to make small enough stitches so that articles no longer fall out." (A.R.C. 16 G.H. NARA)

Partly because the hospital was a Z.I. hospital and a large number of patients were 'killing time' while awaiting transportation back home, crafts were popular. The Red Cross found that their craft supplies were being used up very quickly. When a Mosquito aeroplane crashed on the hospital site on 4 June 1944 the Red Cross salvaged some of the metal and Plexiglas for the patients to make items such as rings, bracelets, lockets, hearts and cigarette lighters. The patients also used British coins such as threepenny bits to make jewellery.

At the beginning of July 1944 the 16th were alerted to prepare for movement. On 11th July, with only two hours' notice, the unit moved out. The Red Cross Staff Aide, Miss Lavington, had not passed her physical assessment to move so she remained to help orient the incoming Red Cross unit and forward any documents that had been left behind in the rush.

The 16th entrained to Bridport, Dorset, where they stayed for one month before sailing for France and eventually setting up a hospital in Liege, Belgium. One of the nurses from the 16th, Sylvia Johnson, was to return to the U.K. at the end of the war to marry the legendary British Spitfire pilot and T.V. presenter, Raymond Baxter.

Parade in Chester shortly before leaving Penley. 2nd Lieutenant Muriel Phillips is the Platoon leader, saluting the reviewing officer (M. Engelman)

Chapter 3

Mud and Incompleted Buildings – 15th General Hospital, Oteley Deer Park

PLANT 4189 at Oteley Deer Park, one mile East of Ellesmere in Shropshire, was the third hospital to be occupied by the U.S. Army. The hospital, which stood in the grounds of Oteley Manor, had been built by Henry Boot and Sons with the capacity of 1084 beds and an operating unit of 650 personnel. Oteley Manor House was a large country house built in 1826 for Charles Kynaston Mainwaring. The land had been used as a deer park since the fourteenth century but the park and gardens were developed in the

Oteley Manor House (Author's collection)

Oteley Deer Park – Manor House can be seen in distance overlooking the camp (J. McConkey)

Ornamental gardens of Oteley Manor overlooking Ellesmere Lake (Town of Ellesmere can be seen in the distance) (J. McConkey)

mid-nineteenth century to accompany a rebuilding of the house. (The 1826 house was demolished in 1960 replaced by the building that now stands in the park.)

The 15th General Hospital, under the command of Colonel John P. Bachman, arrived at Oteley Deer Park in March 1944. (At this point the Mainwaring family, who owned the park, were living at Lee Hall, a boy's college, just outside Ellesmere.) The unit had left America aboard the R.M.S. Queen Mary on 1 March 1944 and after the usual zig-zag journey across the Atlantic Ocean the ship arrived in Gouroch, Scotland. Because the Queen Mary could move at speed she had sailed alone, rather than as part of a convoy.

Oteley Deer Park (Author's collection)

After a long train ride the 15th arrived at Oteley Deer Park by moonlight. The men and women were given a warm welcome by the unit's advance party that had prepared a hot meal for the tired servicemen and women. The next morning the personnel were less than impressed by what they saw in the light of day:

"Mud and incompleted buildings" (A.R.C. 15 G.H. NARA)

The buildings were not completed until 15 March when the contractors signed them over to Colonel Bachman. Meanwhile the Colonel decided to adapt some of the temporary buildings which had been used as billets for the builders to make day-rooms for the men. The day-rooms were furnished through the combined efforts of the Red Cross and the Special Service Officer. An Officers' Club was opened in the building which had been originally designated as a Nurses' Mess.

Shortly after the arrival of the main body of the 15th at Oteley Deer Park the attached A.R.C. unit rejoined the unit once they had completed orientation

Lee Hall, home of Mainwaring Family during the war (J. McConkey)

in London. They arrived as the signing over took place. The hospital site was now complete and the Red Cross had more favourable first impressions than the main body of the unit. On her arrival Alice Merton, the A.F.D., reported:

> "We were charmed by our location and amazed by the comfort of our living quarters which were all ready for us." (A.R.C. 15 G.H. NARA)

The Red Cross Unit decided to utilise the time until the first patients arrived on 6 May by exploring the locality and looking for resources. They also visited other Red Cross units in the area such as the ones attached to the 304th Station Hospital at Llanerch Panna, the 16th General Hospital at Penley, and the 19th and 90th General Hospitals in Malvern, to see how Red Cross units at working hospitals were organised. As two of the girls succumbed to nasopharyngitis during this time they spent a short time at Penley as patients.

The girls also set about acquiring extra Red Cross resources. They managed to borrow two pianos and set up a library consisting of about 500 books. They also opened up a hobby shop where the men could make items such as ashtrays, inkwell stands and key racks. During this time preparations were commenced for the first anniversary party for the 15th. The girls auditioned enlisted men for a variety show and helped to put together a dance orchestra. One of the newly opened wards was decorated as a dance hall.

In May there was an E.T.O. order that ward space was to be used for beds only; presumably this was in anticipation of the large influx of patients after D-Day. It was necessary for the Red Cross, along with the Chaplain, who was also leading a nomadic existence, to move into the building which had been originally designated as the Officer Patients' Mess. (In the middle of June the Chapel was completed and the Red Cross had the building to themselves.)

In May the girls organised a 'May Birthday Party' in their new building for those on post with a birthday in this month. They decorated the room with flowers arranged in large grocery store canisters that had been bought at local auction. (For each party during the summer months the girls took a weekly excursion into the countryside around the hospital to collect wild flowers. Patients who had helped the Red Cross during that week would accompany the girls as a reward for their time.) The girls spent a considerable amount of time the day before the party decorating the centre stove and its pipe to resemble a Maypole. When they arrived at the building the next morning they found that all of the stove pipes had been removed the night before so that a movie could be shown in the hall. Fortunately the girls were able to find a suitable piece of wood to take the place of the decorated stove pipe in time for the start of the party.

As the patients arrived at the May event they were given a piece of 'glamour girl' cut from Esquire Magazine. Their challenge was to make up the jigsaw puzzle by finding others with a piece of the same girl. This activity established the teams for the evening. Later in the evening each team dressed one of their group as a May Queen using crepe paper, a head scarf, needle, thread and scissors. The most glamorous 'queen' was the winner who was selected on the volume of applause, cat calls or wolf whistles. The winner was crowned with a wreath of fresh flowers and allowed to sit at the 'banquet table' with those who were celebrating May birthdays.

In June the Red Cross organised an 'Italian Fiesta' inspired by a spaghetti dish served in the Mess Hall. For this party the girls poised a series of challenges for the patients such as darts, quoits, throwing pennies and threading a needle.

As well as being entertained on the post the personnel and patients also spent off-duty time in Ellesmere and the surrounding area. The Town Hall had a cinema on the ground floor and held dances on the first floor (sixpence hops). Usually music was provided by records on a radiogram, but occasionally there was a live band such as The Billy Gibbons Band. The Fox Pub and fish and chip shop were also popular with the G.I.s from Oteley Deer Park.

St. Mary's Church, Ellesmere (J. McConkey)

Shortly after the initial invasion of the Normandy Beaches the first battle casualties were received at the 15th. Ambulances were sent to collect from Ellesmere Station the men who had travelled by hospital train from the South coast. Upon their arrival at the hospital ambulatory patients were met by the Red Cross team in the Red Cross building and given hot chocolate. Due to the lack of space it was not possible to do the same with litter patients who were admitted directly to the wards.

The arrival of the large number of battle casualties increased the work load for the Red Cross. Frances Macdonald, the Senior Recreation Worker, reported that:

> "We came back wearily from dinner after receiving the patients, to clean up the mess and found the hall already full of recreation-seeking patients and our library disappearing under our eyes. From that moment on we have hardly had time to catch our breath." (A.R.C. 15 G.H. NARA)

A large number of the patients arrived with no shoes so the Red Cross designed a slipper pattern to be made out of felt and linoleum. Miss MacDonald noted that:

> "This has been our major craft project of the month ... and we have felt rather like a slipper factory at times. The men are delighted to make those slippers and patients who have both arms will make them for those who have both feet. Some

of the patients have elaborated our basic pattern by monogramming the slipper, or decorating them with tassels and fancy stitching." (A.R.C. 15 G.H. NARA)

In early July 1944 the 15th General Hospital was given notice to prepare for overseas movement. On her departure the Assistant Field Director of the Red Cross admitted that the girls had found their time at the hospital in Shropshire challenging. She reported:

> "This has been a trying time for the Red Cross Staff. All but the Assistant Field Director are new to the Red Cross, to Army life, to hospital work and to the complete lack of privacy. Add to this an unfamiliar country and separation from home, work under confusing and highly pressured circumstances in an entirely new field of activity and getting used to new personalities." (A.R.C. 15 G.H. NARA)

1300 patients had been admitted to the 15th General Hospital during its two months of operations at Plant 4189. From Oteley Deer Park the 15th travelled to the staging hospital at Blandford, Dorset. In August the unit sailed to Normandy and eventually established a hospital in Liege, Belgium.

Chapter 4

Best in the E.T.O. – 82nd General Hospital, Iscoyd Park

ISCOYD PARK, which means the park beneath the trees in Welsh, was the fourth hospital site to be occupied by American servicemen. The park had originally been gifted to Queen Eleanor by Edward 1st in the fourteenth century. A fifteenth century house which had been owned by the descendants of the royal Lorweth Foel family, preceded the eighteenth century house that stood in the park when the Americans arrived. The Godsal family, who had made their fortune building horse-drawn carriages, had bought the house in 1843 but because of business interests in other parts of the country they had not lived there for some years. A tenant lived in the house until the 1930s when it was requisitioned for the use of the young ladies of St. Godric's Secretarial College, who were evacuated to the country at the beginning of the war.

The 82nd General Hospital, under the command of Colonel John W. Rich, arrived in Liverpool on 10 March 1944, having left the New York Port of Embarkation on 28 February on U.S.A.T. Uruguay. From Liverpool it proceeded to the hospital staging area of Llandudno, where it met up with the advance party of three officers and forty men, led by Major Quintus Nicola, (later to be promoted to Lieutenant Colonel). This group had arrived in the U.K. on 28

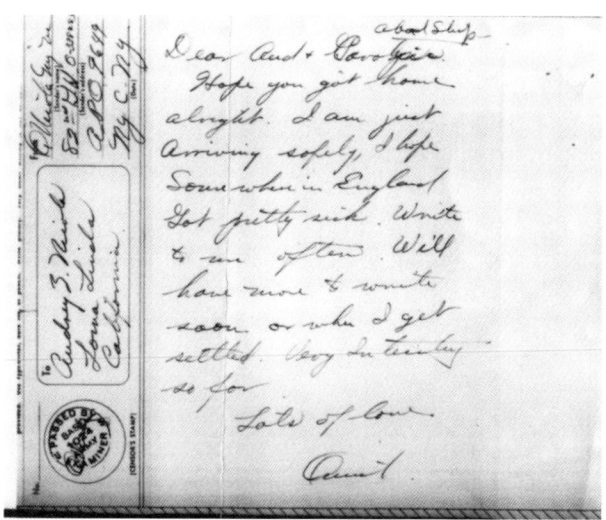

V-mail letter sent by Executive Officer Major Quintus Nicola while aboard the ship to England (Q. Nicola)

Nurse Angela DeGioia (A. Weiss)   *Major Quintus Nicola, Executive Officer (Q. Nicola)*

February 1944. While in Llandudno the unit underwent training consisting of physical exercises, road marches, gas mask drill, lectures and professional conferences. The training programme for nurses covered subjects such as physical exercise, close order drill, the wearing of the uniform, military etiquette, conservation of material, chem-

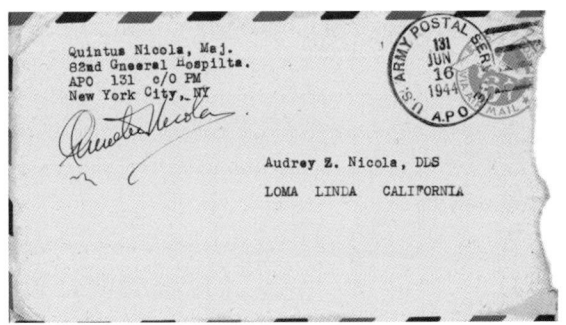

Letter home from Major Nicola (Q. Nicola)

ical warfare, care of equipment and keeping records in the European Theatre.

Nurse, Angela DeGioia remembered that the nurses were boarded with local families in Llandudno. However she told her daughter in later life that the Welsh families were not happy about having the nurses living with them. She recalled that the nurses attempted various means to make friends with their hosts, including bringing food stuffs from the base camp that were unavailable or rationed such as butter, eggs, coffee and toilet paper, but they still found it very difficult to establish a rapport.

On 20 March the advance party were detailed to proceed to Plant 4192, Iscoyd Park, Flintshire, to prepare the hospital for occupation. Upon their arrival the only building ready for use was the Officers' Mess, the other buildings were in various stages of completion. Major Nicola recorded his first impressions in a letter home:

"This is a nice place to live for scenery and countryside etc, but the rest of the set-up is not so hot. It has really been a very pretty and beautiful spring here, with all the flowers and leaves and grass changing colour. Of course this is the best time of the year, but there may be rain any minute of the day and the next minute, sunshine."

Aerial view of 82nd General Hospital 106G/UK 1517 (Welsh Assembly)

The remainder of the unit arrived on 28 March and promptly established Headquarters, Dispensary, Mess and a Guard. The personnel were all designated billets, although it was necessary to put in an extra requisition of mattresses for the enlisted men's quarters. There were shortages of other items. Major Nicola found that eleven out of the nineteen typewriters belonging to the 82nd had been damaged in shipment.

Nurse Angela DeGioia remembered that the nurses were always cold in the Quonset huts and many developed chilblains. She recalled that each hut had a pot-bellied stove but the heat only radiated out about six feet so just the people sleeping near the stoves felt the warmth.

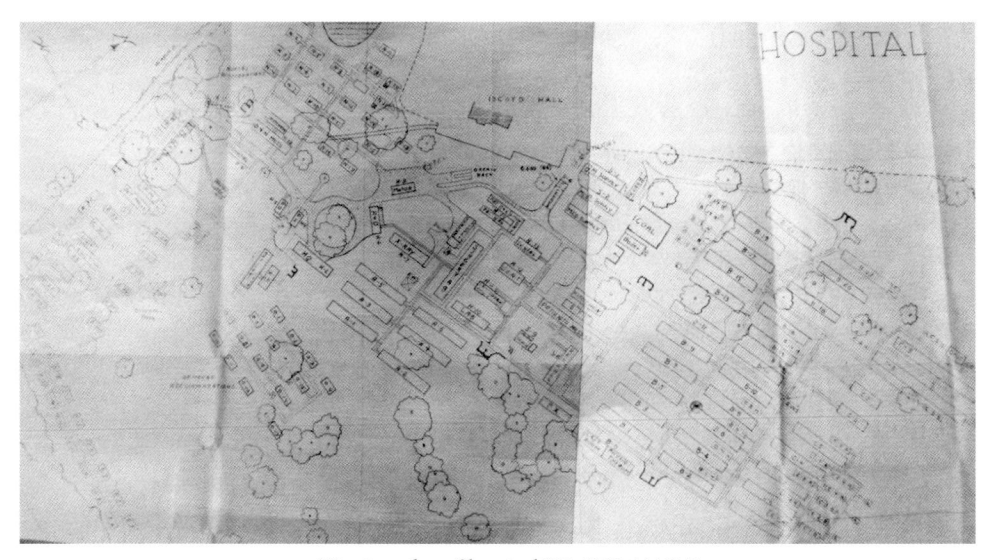

Wartime plan of hospital (82. G.H. NARA)

Major Nicola wrote home that the stoves were:

> "... always too hot or out. We are not supposed to have fires in our huts between 0700 and 1700 (my orders) to try and save fuel. We may be out next winter if we do not save it now."

One day a group of nurses found a tiny black puppy wandering around obviously lost or abandoned. The girls adopted it as a mascot but were not sure of its sex. Nurse DeGioia told them that if you run your hand down the puppy's belly and you come across a bump then it's a boy. The dog became known as 'Bumpy' and lived in the Nurses' hut where he slept next to the stove.

Angela DeGioia also recalled that there was a small river on the property (Iscoyd Brook) that she was told was the official border between England and Wales. At one point where it was quite narrow and shallow the nurses would stand with a foot on either side and say that they were 'straddling the border'.

On 31 March British and American authorities attended a formal board meeting concerning the hospital area at which time the 82nd assumed control of all post buildings and installations. By this time the building work (commenced in 1942) was judged to be 90% finished. The contractors agreed that the site would be completed in 21 days. The hospital had about 158 buildings and requested that six more to be built. At the meeting the Commanding Officer remarked that he found the physical layout of the post satisfactory, except for the placing of the Physiotherapy Clinic, X-ray Laboratory and the Patients' Post-Exchange, which were situated on the outskirts of the hospital plot, rather than centrally where they would be more accessible to a greater number of patients.

Nurse Gough and companion, 82nd General Hospital

The non-commissioned officers adapted a building that the contractors had left on site into a club. Major Nicola noted in a letter home that it looked like a "Hollywood dive with nudes and all." Apparently they had bribed some of the British contractors to get furniture and fittings for the club with 'liquor and tobacco and whatnot'. The officers of the detachment had their own club which was opened in May.

A maintenance department of fifteen enlisted men along with the British Foreman of Works and his staff of seventeen civilians were given the task of up-keeping the buildings and site. However Colonel Rich felt that:

> "... there never were enough men to properly attend to the multitude of tasks presented. This situation was made particularly acute by the fact that the hospital was built on the 'Austerity Scale'. Construction was rushed and

performed by British labor, from which many of the best craftsmen had been drafted into war plants or the Armed Forces. Consequently maintenance was a pressing problem." (82 G.H. NARA)

Major Nicola mentioned in a letter home that:

"Material is scarce and the British hate to give us anything and it takes three weeks just to get the smallest bit of repair of building approved."

In a subsequent letter he noted:

"Civilian help here is worse than nothing but the workers get less than two pounds a week which is not much. ... Relations are none too cordial."

Records show that a total of over 1,184 separate requests for maintenance repairs were submitted and dealt with over a period of 30 weeks. This included the replacement of 297 windows, the unblocking of 298 sewers, the repair of 130 stoves, 209 leaking pipes and 23 leaking roofs. In May Executive Officer, Major Nicola, noted in a letter home that:

"… every toilet leaks and it either runs on the floor or outside thru a pipe they build for it cause they know it is going to leak when they build it. They said if it runs down the hole then no one will stop the leak, but if it runs out on the floor then someone will fix it, and thus save water."

He goes on to describe an incident where a maintenance man was bracing himself on the brick interior wall while repairing a toilet when he fell through the wall onto the man in the adjacent cubicle 'wrecking the man and the seat both'. Major Nicola had the responsibility of sourcing a new toilet seat. (Incidentally on one occasion a member of the Major's family sent him a letter written on toilet paper so that it could be recycled for its original purpose.) As he was writing a letter home in May 1944 one of the officers brought him a note reporting that the ceiling was in the process of falling down in the Officers' Surgical ward.

Excerpt from letter from Major Nicola, May 1944 (Q. Nicola)

The 82nd also had some problems with the British 230 volt electrical systems that were in place in the buildings. American apparatus used 115 volts hence it was necessary to use transformers in order for American equipment to work.

As far as possible maintenance was assigned to the British employees, while authorised construction changes were handled by the detachment personnel. In many cases it was necessary for the enlisted men to adapt buildings and equipment so that they were fit for purpose. The detachment even made equipment for the gym and physiotherapy department. Numerous construction changes were accomplished by the extensive use of salvage and scrap metal.

It was noted in the official records of the 82nd that the enlisted men:

> "… gladly gave their unstinted efforts and endeavoured to supply every request made to them. They were the ones who worked twenty-four hours a day when necessary to pack and move and supply the organisation, worked half the night in the rain on electrical poles to provide lights and did the hundreds of other little tasks cheerfully and conscientiously that have gone to make this hospital the best in the E.T.O." (82 G.H. NARA)

The maintenance detachment also worked on landscaping the grounds. Colonel Rich commented that the men had:

> "… converted a desolate, colourless area into an interesting, bright and well demarcated post." (82 G.H. NARA)

A telephone with an outside line was made available to the 82nd pending completion and installation of the unit's switchboard and securing a staff of civilian personnel. By the end of 1944 ninety British hand phones and eight field phones were located in the hospital.

The only equipment the unit possessed on arrival at Iscoyd Park was a partial requirement of military vehicles. A number of vehicles had been received while the 82nd was at Llandudno (one ¾ ton Command Car, one ¼ ton jeep, two 6x6 Cargo Trucks, one 2½ ton dump truck, six ¾ ton ambulances and three trailers) but upon arrival at Iscoyd Park the number of vehicles was found to be insufficient so requests for additional vehicles were made. On 9 June the unit received three additional Command Reconnaissance vehicles and two 1½ ton trucks.

It was necessary for the 82nd to borrow thirteen vehicles from the Rail Transportation Officer of a nearby supply depot to collect 'Bolero Stores' (Post, camp and station equipment) from the depot at Overton eight miles away.

The 82nd was one of the first units in the U.K. to be supplied entirely with American equipment. Over 300 truckloads of supplies were loaded, delivered and sorted in the space of three and a half days. It was necessary to collect coke for the hospital from a railway siding four miles away, however coal was delivered by British civilian trucks directly to the 82nd. In the period from March to December 1944 925 tons of coal and 1650 tons of coke were received and utilised for cooking and heating of water and buildings.

All of the physical structures, installations and grounds of the hospital were completed in time for the official opening of the hospital on 29 April. The first patient, Private Wilbur E. Dixon, a member of the command, had actually been admitted to the hospital on 27 April. On 1 May, 286 patients from the 91st General Hospital at Headington, Oxford, were transferred to the 82nd because of staff transfers at the 91st. The first surgical operation was performed on 10 May. Before D-Day surgery at the 82nd consisted mainly of haemorrhoidectomies, appendectomies, herniorrhaphies and venous ligations. Major Nicola noted in a letter that:

> "Expanding so rapidly from just taking care of ourselves to taking care of a gen. hosp. full of patients in about a week's time really shows the weak spots."

After the first group of battle casualties had been admitted to the hospital on 18 June, surgery consisted predominantly of secondary closures, application of casts and skin grafts. The largest section of battle casualties was admitted to the orthopaedic ward; the majority of these cases had some type of bone injury in addition to soft tissue damage. The busiest month for the surgical section was August 1944 when 631 operations were performed.

Nurse, 2nd Lieutenant June A. Reny by ward tents at 82nd 12/7/1944 (82 G.H. NARA)

Convoy of ambulances awaiting arrival of hospital trains at Malpas Station (82 G.H. NARA)

As the majority of the hospital admissions were surgical four of the five junior doctors in the Medical Section were charged with the treatment of chest wounds and established a thoracic ward that earned a written commendation from the Senior Consultant in Medicine E.T.O.U.S.A., following an inspection visit of the hospital.

Until August 1944 the Medical Service was still admitting and treating 'station hospital' type patients from the U.S. units local to the hospital. It had also been necessary to treat one third of its own nurses, who were found to be anaemic, with

Nurse Angela DeGioia (A. Weiss) *Sketch of Angela DeGioia made by a patient (A. Weiss)*

iron therapy. It was concluded that the deficiency was due to their dislike of the food high in iron that they had been given in the Mess Hall (powdered eggs, pork and green vegetables).

Five days after the arrival of the first battle casualties the bed capacity of the hospital was expanded from 1084 to 1634 by the setting up of hospital tents on the ends of wards to extend them. Between 18 June and 30 September 1944 ten train and five air convoys of patients were received at the hospital. Patients included members of the U.S. Army, U.S. Navy, U.S. Merchant Marines, British Armed Forces, Free French Forces and civilians. Four patients died at the hospital during this time, two indirectly due to battle injuries. One of the patients Nurse DeGioia nursed had been an artist. He was badly injured but offered to sketch the nurses. Her daughter believes that he was one of the patients who died.

The influx of patients at the 82nd increased the need for transportation and further requests were made for more vehicles. In early November 1944 another truck was assigned to the unit while the dump truck was recalled and replaced by a less efficient British tipper. Shortly after this, one of the trucks was transferred to an ordnance depot because of its poor mechanical condition. The six ambulances also suffered mechanically because they were in constant use. One particular evening they were called to assist in the evacuation of patients to three different hospitals from three different railway stations.

As many of the vehicles were in constant use during the daytime personnel of the Motor Pool Detachment at the 82nd were required to service and repair vehicles 'after hours'. Colonel Rich noted that:

> "… much credit was due the Motor Pool Detachment staff for their untiring efforts in 'keeping them rolling'." (82 G.H. NARA)

Cyclist at 82nd General Hospital (Q. Nicola)

Major Nicola records in one of his letters home that there were about 200 bikes on the post, he had managed to acquire a tandem for himself. It was necessary to register the bikes with the Provost Marshall with a number painted on the back fender.

Once patients at the 82nd had received surgical or medical treatment they were given Physical Therapy. The building that was originally designated for this was found to be inadequate in space and inconvenient in location. Better facilities were secured with the assignment of one half of the building that was intended to be an Officer Patients' Mess. This building was more conveniently located near the orthopaedic wards and provided a separate room of 1200 square feet as a clinic. All exercise equipment was used in the main clinic until an adjoining room was converted to a gymnasium by the rehabilitation patients. The gymnasium could be used both for physical therapy and rehabilitation. Major Nicola felt that he needed to find a new mess hall for the officer patients as soon as possible as there were 'a couple of M.D.s [doctors] among them and also a couple of eagles' [colonels].

The Rehabilitation Programme was established in May 1944 and was available to all patients. In some cases orthopaedic and other surgical patients commenced rehabilitation and reconditioning on their first day at the hospital. Rehabilitation included remedial and physical exercises, gymnastics and recreation. Full emphasis was placed on military drill and restoring the individual to duty status in the minimum period of time. Research showed that rehabilitation and reconditioning programmes were responsible for reducing the length of the patients' stay in the hospital and minimising the number of deaths. At any one time there were around 150 patients in the Reconditioning Section of the hospital, these patients had completed their medical or surgical treatments and were undergoing exercise to be returned to full fitness.

Rehabilitation patients also attended lectures organised by the Red Cross Unit. These were sometimes given by patients and sometimes outside speakers came to the base. The lectures dealt with current political and economic issues as well as combat experiences. The lectures were not compulsory, but attendance was usually good – two to three hundred patients each afternoon. Sometimes the discussion groups took place on the wards and were attended by patients from other wards. To round off the evening cocoa was made on the stoves in the buildings.

The Red Cross organised other activities for the rehabilitation patients. They planned nature walks, arming the patients with bird and tree books. The walks became a contest with a prize for the patient who could identify the most birds and floral life. The Red Cross also set the rehabilitation patients the task of creating a miniature golf course for the other patients to play on. In addition to this, recreational activities were organised by the Red Cross for all of the patients at the 82nd. A Recreation Hall was furnished and equipped by: improvising seats from packing boxes; borrowing benches from the Mess Hall for watching shows on; and making a ping-pong table from a mess table.

Major Nicola, the Executive Officer with the 82nd wrote home that he had managed to get some ping-pong tables by 'begging and bribing' a salvage officer at the Liverpool docks. The tables had been taken out of a cruise ship during refitting as a troop ship. The Major wrote:

> "The guy did not want us to take them but after a couple of packages of cigarettes and lipstick and powder for his wife etc. we got that and more too."

In July easy chairs, writing tables and lamps were delivered to the hospital for use in the Red Cross Club and in August the new furniture was put to use when about twenty W.A.A.F. girls stationed nearby came to the newly furnished recreation hall for a party. The furniture was set up in 'café-style' and Coca-Cola and cakes were served.

Unfortunately the Red Cross Unit's days at Iscoyd Park were numbered and on 10 October 1944 they were withdrawn from the 82nd due to a change in use of the hospital.

Chapter 5

Four Thousand, Five Hundred Purple Hearts – 68th General Hospital, Halston Hall

THE FINAL site to be established as a U.S. hospital and complete the cluster of five hospitals in the Maelor area was Plant 4188, Halston Hall in Whittington, Shropshire. This camp was constructed in the grounds of a Grade 1 listed building which had been built in 1690 for the Mytton family. The family lived in the house until John 'Mad Jack' Mytton died penniless in prison in 1833. During the 1940s it was owned by Mrs Patricia Eccles.

Halston Hall c1891

Plant 4188, Halston Hall when still under construction, August 1943 (Author's collection)

The 68th General Hospital, under the command of Colonel Stanley W. Matthews, left New York on 1 March 1944 aboard the H.M.S. Queen Mary. The ship docked in Scotland and the unit entrained to the hospital staging area in Llandudno, North Wales, where they awaited the completion of the hospital buildings. On 7 April Detachment A, consisting of 15 officers, 13 nurses and 123 enlisted men, under the command of Lieutenant Colonel Sterret E. Dietrich, was assigned to a station hospital in Londonderry, Northern Ireland, to replace the U.S. 9th Field Hospital.

Meanwhile, on 5 April Detachment B, which included forty enlisted men and acted as an advance party, departed Llandudno for Halston Hall. Upon their arrival they found contractors still at work and a number of unfinished buildings. The civilian contractor was instructed to complete the more urgently needed buildings first. Local British Barracks officers were contacted and plans were made for the collection of beds, pillows, mattresses and mess equipment. It was necessary for the hospital's two trucks (one large and one small) to collect the items from a British depot some miles away. Unfortunately because of the Easter bank holiday the depot was closed for a few days so the supplies were delayed. Eventually, five days prior to the arrival of the main body, the advance party was able to collect the supplies and set up the billets and mess halls. It was necessary for the crews of men to work from 0730 to 2230 daily to finish the task.

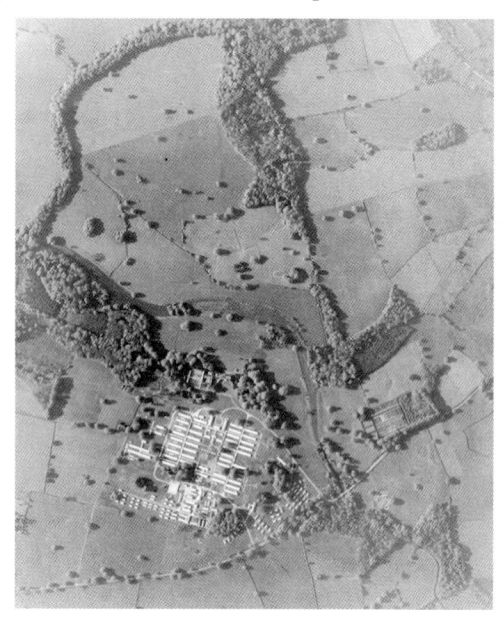

Aerial view of Plant 4188 G/UK.151717 (Welsh Assembly)

Collecting the supplies was also problematic for the Transportation Detachment of the 68th:

> "Lack of shop facilities, lack of equipment, lack of road signs and the lack of most everything formerly taken for granted, had to be overcome. Narrow, twisting roads cluttered with livestock, carts and bicycles and many such obstructions was by no means an aid to driving." (68 G.H. NARA)

During 1944 vehicles from the Transportation Department were involved in ten traffic accidents, three requiring major and seven requiring minor repairs. There was one fatal accident in September 1944 when the driver (Private Hermes H. Hanebrine) lost his life and six others were hospitalised.

On 14 April the main body of the unit travelled by rail to Halston Hall. 1st Lieutenant Alton G. Grube recorded:

> "After the arrival of the main body matters became more or less routine; attempts were made constantly to speed up the construction of wards, clinics and the patients' mess, but it was soon learned that the British had only one speed – SLOW." (68 G.H. NARA)

Motor pool at 68th General Hospital (Author's collection)

Noticeboard made by Utilities Department (Author's collection)

Despite all pleas for rapid construction it took until early September 1944 for the camp to be fully completed. Meanwhile the Utilities Department set to work making racks, cupboards, shelves and equipment for the hospital from lumber that they had salvaged.

Once settled at Halston Hall it was necessary for the Medical Supply Department to put in a requisition for the appropriate medical supplies and equipment. This was transported by train in 65 goods wagons to the railhead at Whittington, about a mile from the hospital. The 68th's trucks were able to collect it from there.

It was also necessary for the hospital to contract out services required by the hospital personnel such as shoe repair and laundry. At the beginning contracts were awarded to organisations located some distance away from the hospital. (In one case a round trip of almost three hundred miles was taken for enlisted men's laundry and dry cleaning.) By July 1944 more local contractors had been sourced.

On 10 May 1944 the hospital was officially opened for patients, but with a limited bed capacity of 300 beds, as a number of the wards were still not in use. The first patients of

Parade in front of Halston Hall (Author's collection)

Award of Purple Heart Medals at 68th General Hospital (Author's collection)

Award of Purple Heart Medals at 68th General Hospital (Author's collection)

the 68th were 64 members of the detachment who were admitted two days previous to the official opening. They had been struck down with gastroenteritis (food poisoning) caused by something they had eaten in the mess hall.

On 11 May Lieutenant Colonel Dietrich, who had been on detached service in Londonderry with Detachment A, returned to the main group and immediately assumed control of the hospital due to the sudden illness of Colonel Matthews, who had been in command of the 68th since August 1943. Colonel Matthews was admitted to the 83rd General Hospital at Llanerch Panna and was subsequently transferred to the Zone of the Interior. On 18 May at 1900 hours the first trainload of patients for the 68th (275 patients) arrived at Gobowen train station.

30 May (Memorial Day for the U.S. troops) saw Detachment A return from Northern Ireland and rejoin the main unit. At 1600 on that day a formal flag raising ceremony and retreat parade was held in front of the Post Headquarters. 350 Good Conduct medals were presented to the enlisted men of the command by Captain Samuel G. Trask. Lieutenant Colonel Dietrich read out a farewell letter from Colonel Matthews to the members of the command at the ceremony.

During June 1944 only a small number of patients were received at the hospital. Lieutenant Grube recorded:

> "It was a month of house cleaning and shaking down for the hospital. The 700 acres of land and the 152 buildings were cleaned over and over, each time improving the general appearance." (68 G.H. NARA)

The hospital also had the opportunity to lay cement bases for 29 ward tents and seven latrine tents. Tents were then erected and wired, thus completing the 'tent expansion programme'.

Admissions Block at 68th (Author's collection)

U.S. ARMY HOSPITAL CENTER 804

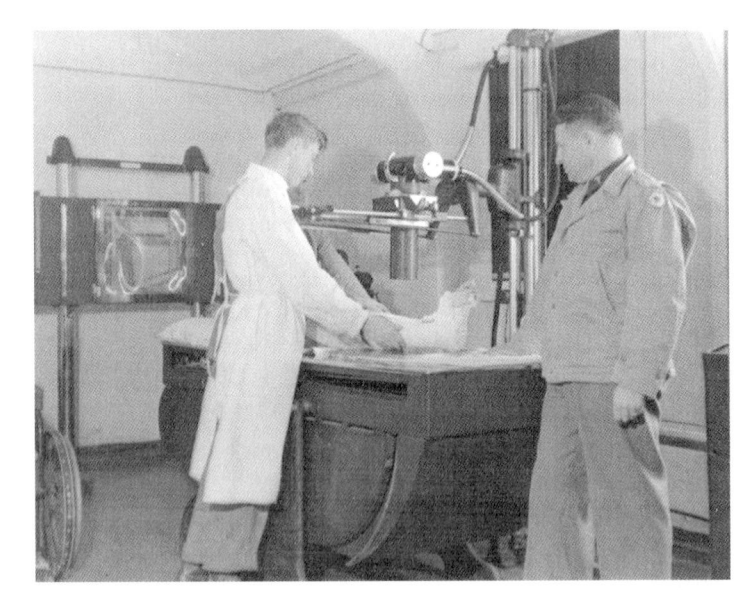

X-Ray Department (Author's collection)

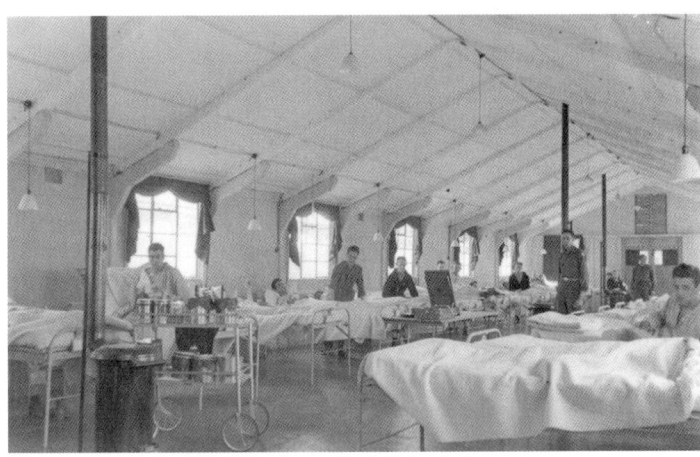

Ward at 68th General Hospital (Author's collection)

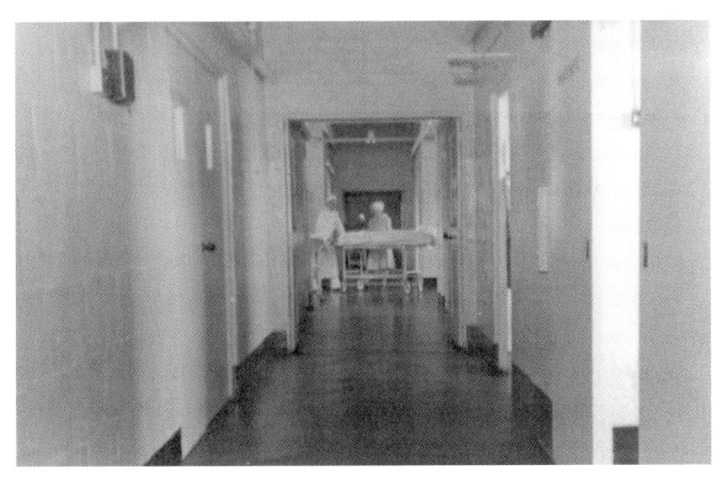

Corridor in ward building (Author's collection)

FOUR THOUSAND, FIVE HUNDRED PURPLE HEARTS

Laboratory (Author's collection)

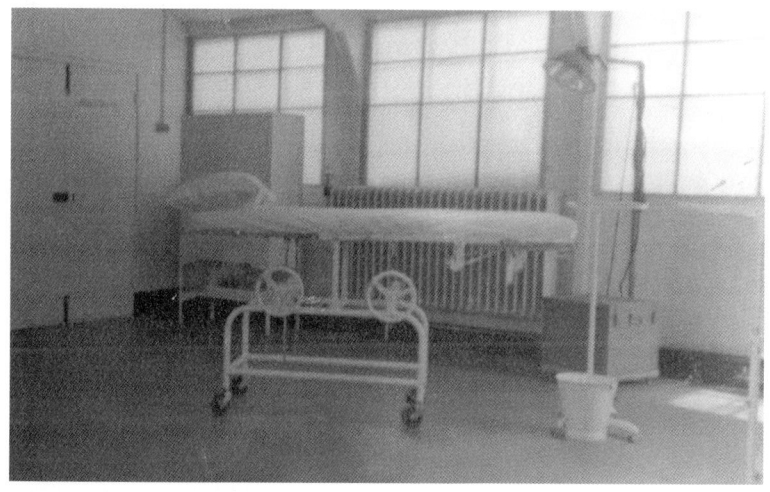

Operating Theatre (Author's collection)

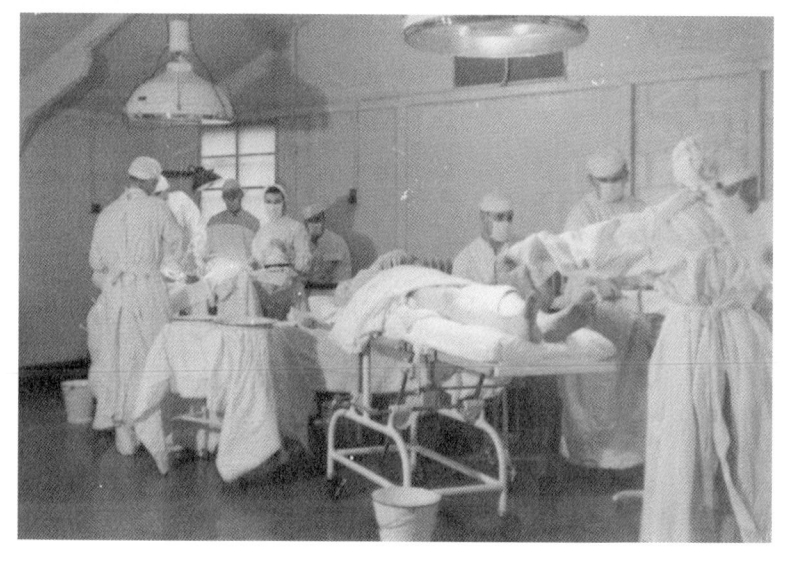

Operating Theatre (Author's collection)

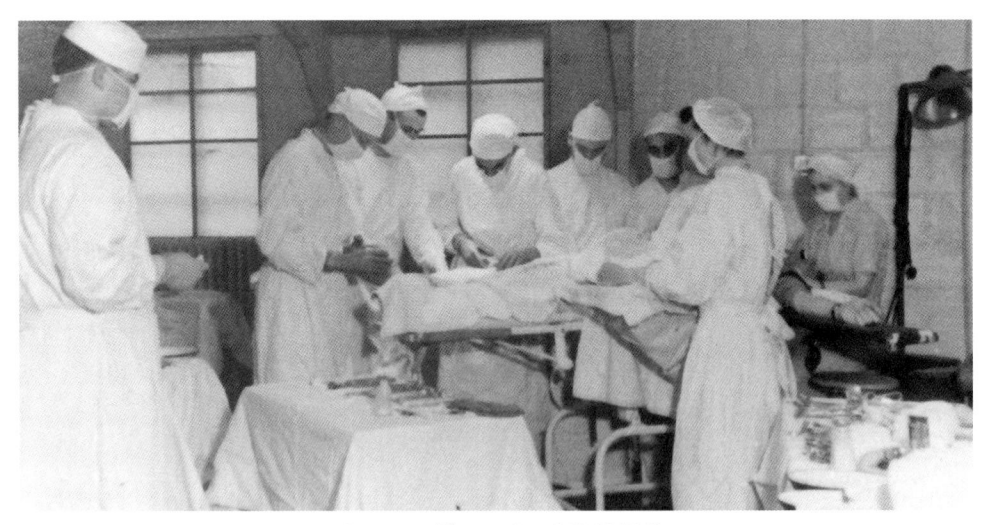

Operating Theatre (68 G.H. NARA)

Around this time a number of the personnel were transferred to other organisations. Pfc Fletcher, Pfc Harry Hawryluk and 1st Lt. Frank J. Davis Jr. were put on detached service at the 305th Station Hospital, but then became the first members of the 68th to see action when they were assigned as medics on an L.S.T. for the D-Day invasion. Unfortunately on their second trip to the coast of Normandy the L.S.T. struck an enemy mine and was sunk. Lt. Davis received a compression fracture of lumbar vertebrae and spent the month of June as a patient of the 185th General Hospital. Pfc Fletcher was also sent to a hospital in the U.K. but Pfc Hawryluk was uninjured and returned to the 68th on 19 June.

3 July saw the first mass admissions of patients to the 68th by air from the battlefields of France. Within a period of nine days more than 900 patients had been admitted in groups of 150-250 each flight. On 4 July several patients wounded in the morning were received that same afternoon. The patients arrived by C47 at Rednal Airfield, six miles from the hospital. They were met at the airfield by transportation from the 68th along with the 571st Ambulance Company which was attached to the 6810th Hospital Center.

The 68th established a procedure for new patient admissions. When the number of patients arriving was known, ambulances in sufficient numbers were sent to the airfield or railway station. Once patients were received at the hospital by the ward surgeons they would be sent to the appropriate departments. If possible the patient would be made comfortable, given a bath and food. The Medical Officer would check the wound and report his diagnosis to the Chief Surgeon. At this point decisions could be made about the type of surgery that would be necessary.

During July 1944, 1545 patients were admitted to the 68th, 1252 of them had been evacuated to the U.K. by air. The hospital quickly became full to capacity and it was necessary to use the tent expansion wards that had been used earlier for convalescing patients. Of the sixteen deaths at the 68th (fifteen U.S. Army and one prisoner of war) thirteen occurred during the months of July and August. During this period the relatively new drug, penicillin, was used in large quantities. By the end of the year the hospital had used approximately 300,000,000 Oxford units of the anti-biotic.

During August the number of admissions fell off, only three main admissions were recorded. Among the patients received were soldiers of the Free French Army who had become casualties in the first engagement in battle by Free French Forces in France since 1940. The average number of patients at the hospital during August was 1,000.

The high spot of the social activities during the month was the celebration of Lieutenant Colonel Dietrich's birthday party on 26 August. The Officers' Club was set out for a buffet supper with cocktails served before the meal. Tables were covered with cloths and decorated with candles, flowers and ferns. The unit orchestra, dressed in sailor suits, played dinner music followed by a dance. After the meal Colonel Dietrich cut his birthday cake after a few remarks about the work of the unit and his hopes for the future.

In September there was only one mass admission at the hospital which occurred on the 27th of the month. On 18 September fifteen repatriated American Prisoners of War arrived at the 68th. None of them required medical attention although they were to be repatriated because of physical disabilities. On 19 September they departed for the States. During this month the patient census decreased and the average number of beds occupied was 744. The command took advantage of the light patient census to deliver extra training.

Also during September five hospital ships platoons were attached to the unit pending movement orders. Each platoon consisted of two officers and fifteen enlisted men who were quartered in tents on the site. While at Halston Hall the men were used to supplement understaffed departments of the hospital. When possible, duty assignments included providing technical training to enlisted personnel. In October there were two mass admissions by train of 286 and 293 patients as well as numerous smaller admissions.

In Europe the Battle of the Bulge was taking a heavy casualty toll. As the wounded were received at Halston Hall a number of detachment personnel were relieved of their assignment with the 68th and sent to the 12th Ground Force Replacement Depot at Tidworth for combat training. In contrast some of the patients who had finished their treatment at the 68th but were unable to join their combat unit were reassigned to non-combatant units such as hospitals.

Five enlisted men from the 68th were fortunate enough to be offered:

> "… perhaps the best duty which could be offered to an overseas soldier – a trip home." (68 G.H. NARA)

The men were assigned as attendants on a hospital ship back to the U.S. where they would be able to enjoy a ten day furlough at home before they returned to the U.K.

Also in October 1944, the Unit Correspondent to the 68th, Tec. 4 George Moffat, visited Sergeant John Kerr, radio announcer on the American Forces Network in

London, and as a result the unit received mentions on the U.S. Radio programme: 'Duffle Bag', Tec. 4 Moffat was also given the opportunity to submit 40 press releases for publication in papers in the United States.

In November the 68th was designated as the Center Hospital for treatment of Trench or Immersion Foot cases, 68 patients were admitted to this section this month. The General Medical Section under Major Burger was given the task of treating these cases. An effective system was put into place so that the majority of the trench foot patients could be returned to duty in eight weeks. A small number of more serious cases were returned to the U.S. for treatment; others were returned to limited service assignments. Two hospital trains of 263 and 289 patients respectively arrived at Ellesmere Station for the 68th this month. About half of these patients were battle casualties, most of the remainder were suffering from diseases, while a small contingent were non-battle casualties.

In November it was also necessary to winterize the ward tents which had been attached to the ends of the wards. This process was carried out by the 1325th Engineer Regiment, a black unit, who were housed in empty wards on the post. The procedure involved construction of four foot high walls to the height of the skirt and doors of the tents.

December 1944 was one of the busiest months for the 68th. The 6th Hospital Group informed the hospital that it was necessary to increase the bed census by 250 beds, consequentially requisitions for extra beds, mattresses and blankets were submitted. Five hospital trains of patients were received in December, one arriving on Christmas Eve. By the end of December the bed census was 1767 and every bed on the post was being used. By the end of 1944 the Unit Supply had issued 4500 Purple Heart medals and 500 Oak Leaf Clusters to patients.

One of the patients received at the 68th on 1 January 1945 was Tom Morrissey, who had received a leg injury in France. Morrissey had originally come to the U.K. to be attached to the U.S. 1st Base Post Office, which was based in Sutton Coldfield, Warwickshire. In the second half of 1944 a large number of the postal clerks were being replaced with G.I.s who had been wounded and then reassigned to a limited assignment role. In turn the clerks were assigned to the Ground Force Training Center at Tidworth, to be retrained for combat.

Morrissey was one of those sent to Tidworth. After combat training he went over to France, arriving around the middle of September. From Omaha Beach Morrissey was transported to Carentan where he boarded a freight train for the journey to the front. After several days travelling in the discomfort of the freight train, which travelled at about ten miles per hour, the men were awakened by a loud bang. The jarring of the car sent some of the equipment flying and Morrissey was hit in the face with a metal helmet that had been hanging on the ceiling.

The train had been in a head-on collision with another train, apparently due to an act of sabotage. Several G.I.s in the forward cars had been killed and Morrissey's platoon leader, Lieutenant Kraus, had suffered a broken jaw from being hit in the mouth with the butt end of a rifle. The lieutenant was taken away in an ambulance but Morrissey, who had been given a black eye, was taken with the others to an encampment.

The following morning the men were transported by truck to a barracks near Nancy where Morrissey was assigned to the 26th Infantry Division and issued with hand grenades and rifle ammunition. He set off to join his new division by truck but once it got dark he was dropped off to continue the journey by foot. At this point he could hear the sound of the 155mm 'Long Toms', America's largest artillery piece, up ahead. After spending the night in a barn, Morrissey was introduced to the men who would be in his platoon. By this time it was the end of October. He recalled:

> "That evening non-coms met with the Company Commander Captain Stanalius. He welcomed the new members and told us what he expected of us. He described the plan of attack for the next day and when he finished shook hands with each one of us."

A few weeks later, on 17 November, the men of the 26th, who believed that they were due to have a rest period, were sent to fight in Luxembourg where Morrissey was wounded. Tom recalled the moment:

> "On November 18 my squad led an attack on a small town in Luxembourg. While crossing a very green farm area we drew machine gun fire on our left flank. We were closest to the gun. It's hard to describe how it felt to be the direct target of a gun firing 1200 rounds a minute. Mortars and 88 artillery followed and many of us were hit with no place to cover."

Sometime later the medics evacuated the wounded. Morrissey was sent to the 104th Evacuation Hospital in Nancy and after a few days he was transferred to a tented hospital in Verdun where he received treatment until 16 December. While there he wrote to his mother to inform her that he was wounded but 'still in one piece' and also to let her know of a chance meeting with a former neighbour. He found that the neighbour had already written to his relatives about the meeting. Sadly, this man was killed in action on 28 November.

Morrissey was evacuated from Luxembourg on Christmas Day 1944 and on New Year's Day he was flown from Paris to the U.K. aboard a C47. On his arrival at the 68th General Hospital he remembers seeing single-storey ward structures which were set back about four hundred yards from a country lane where buses travelled to and from Oswestry. On the opposite side of the road was a field where G.I.s played softball. He also remembers concrete walkways with

Tom Morrissey – photo taken in Oswestry (T. Morrissey)

roofs supported by columns eight to ten foot high. He recalled that "on windy days the elements overruled the roof protection".

During Morrissey's convalescence from his leg wound the nurses on night duty reported that he was having disturbing nightmares. He remembers:

> "After several doctors examined me I was diagnosed as having combat fatigue. General Patton didn't allow people to have combat fatigue but it was a fact of life and many had it. It was somewhat comforting when doctor, Major Albert Clark, who cared for me the whole time, advised me I was no longer fit for combat duty."

Morrissey continued his convalescence treatment at the 68th so that he could be fit for a limited assignment in the military. He remembers being wheeled across the hospital grounds in a wheelchair to visit the Red Cross Club and the Recreation Hall for dances or movies. Eventually his leg injury healed enough to be allowed off base and he remembers enjoying sing-songs at a quaint country pub where the men were accompanied on the piano by a British civilian and a G.I. patient. He also travelled into Oswestry to have his photograph taken at Petersons. He wanted to send something home to his mother and fiancée that would show that he was returning to health. After undergoing convalescence at the 68th Morrissey was assigned to Assembly Area, Command H.Q. in Mourmelon, France, to classify and ready troops for the Pacific Theater of War or return to the States.

Of his time in hospital he writes:

> "I could write pages about the beautiful people I met at the 68th who spread smiles, shared laughter and a bit of sadness. I'm grateful for having been there."

On his eventual return home a friend of the family commented:

> "Tom the boy went away and Tom the man returned."

In March 1945 only two hospital trains were received at the 68th but in this month the hospital also admitted a group of five U.S. airmen who had come from a plane that had crash-landed in North Wales.

The B24 Liberator of the 856th Bomb Squadron had taken off from Harrington in Northamptonshire at 2000 hours on 18 March for a night cross-country training flight. It had proceeded on a course to Overton Heath and then on to Cinderford. At 2115 hours while flying at 2100 feet in the vicinity of Llangynog on the Cinderford to Shrewsbury leg the aircraft struck the side of the Berwen Mountain Range approximately fifty feet from the summit of Disgynfa. The aircraft appeared to be flying up the valley when it struck the ground a glancing blow on the incline of the slope, this served to lessen the force of the impact and prevent a more serious accident.

The nose and waist sections of the aircraft absorbed most of the crash and were completely crushed. Large portions of the fuselage in this section were torn completely from the aircraft, carrying with them the Bombardier Navigator and both waist gunners, who were killed instantly.

The force of the crash threw Sergeant David Blanton, the tail gunner, out of his turret backward and he landed in the middle section of the aircraft. He was uninjured apart from shock and bruises so he was able to climb out of the aircraft through the waist window and assist Lieutenant Julian Bradbury, the Co-pilot, in getting the remainder of the crew out. Lieutenant Bradbury, who was suffering from a fractured leg, minor bruises, lacerations and abrasions, had managed to climb through the window of the plane and check there was no danger of fire or explosion.

The two men were able to break open the upper turret where Sergeant James Green, the engineer was trapped. He had come off lightly and only suffered minor bruises and lacerations. Together they were able to assist the Radio Operator and Pilot to climb out of the escape hatch. The Radio Operator, Corporal John F. Mattingly was suffering from a broken pelvis and Lieutenant Randolph Sheppard had sustained fractures of his right thigh and skull and serious abrasions and lacerations to his scalp and forehead.

It was decided that Lieutenant Bradbury and Sergeant Blanton should go for help while Sergeant Green remained with the injured men. Before they left they tore up some parachutes to make bandages and used the others to keep the men warm and dry as it was raining.

The two men started out in different directions, but after a while Blanton turned back as he was unable to find help. Fortunately, eventually Bradbury came across a shepherd's hut. The shepherd, Thomas Davies, sat Bradbury on the handlebars of his bike and rode down to the Home Guard Headquarters. A search party was organised but the weather was causing limited visibility. Fortunately Sergeant Mattingly had managed to find a flare gun and flare in the wreckage which he fired before he collapsed. The rescue party located the survivors and managed to get them down the mountain and to a nearby civilian hospital. From there they were transferred to the 68th.

Three of the five men were able to return to flying with their squadron after treatment at the 68th but the injuries of the other two men took longer to heal. Flight Officer Lieutenant Schaeffer, Sergeant Kauser and Pfc Volata had been killed on impact and were buried with full military honours at the American Military Cemetery at Cambridge on 23 March 1945.

In April the 68th received two more trainloads of 269 and 288 patients respectively.

> "The patients were in quite bad condition and all departments began to function at a faster pace." (68 G.H. NARA)

On 3 May the last trainload of predominantly surgical patients were received at the 68th. It was necessary for the operating team to work overtime to complete the necessary surgical work for this group.

Chapter 6

Fun for All – 68th General Hospital, Halston Hall

The detachment personnel, officers and nurses of the 68th had a demanding job to do but Lieutenant Grube, the Adjutant, noted:

> "…there was still time for fun for all." (68 G.H. NARA)

Several buildings on the post were assigned for off duty time and recreation. Officers and nurses had the use of the Officers' Club which had been decorated by Captain James Ross on a nautical theme. Ross had acquired ships' fittings such as lights, life preservers and a helm to place around the room, and portholes and ocean scenes to put on the walls. The enlisted men had their own dayroom with tables, chairs and a bar. Parties were held monthly at each club.

Special Service Officer, Lieutenant Alfred Skepinkski, had the task of organising recreational activities for the personnel on the post. At the beginning he was not impressed with the facilities at Halston Hall:

> "Upon our arrival at our permanent ground in the earlier part of April things did not look too good in general. There was a lack of field space for outdoor activity and a lack of building space for dayroom or indoor activity. … A very rough field was used for baseball and softball, there was always the danger of breaking one's legs. Special Service equipment was very slow in coming and it wasn't until July we received a projector for theatre entertainment." (68 G.H. NARA)

A couple of months after this was written a building was turned over to Special Service to use as a dayroom and N.C.O. Club.

A number of sports activities were organised at the 68th. Softball games were played between officers, nurses and the enlisted men of the command. The enlisted men's team won the most games. On 6 April there were two inter-unit softball games. The officers'

FUN FOR ALL

Recreation Hall at 68th (Author's collection)

team was beaten 5-4 by a team from the 93rd General Hospital (based in Malvern) but the nurses' team beat the 93rd's nurses' team by 10-5. On 22 May the non-commissioned officers of the 68th beat those of the 83rd General Hospital from Llanerch Panna 2-1.

The American Red Cross unit attached to the 68th also played a part in organising events for the personnel's off-duty time, although its main task was providing recreational and social events and activities for the patients. On arrival at Halston Hall the Red Cross used one of the vacant wards as an office but with the arrival of the

Softball being played at 68th General Hospital (Gary Bedingfield's Baseball in Wartime Collection)

Softball being played at 68th General Hospital (Gary Bedingfield's Baseball in Wartime Collection)

patients it was not possible to utilise the wards in this way. On 17 May, the day before the opening of the hospital, the Red Cross was given the theatre building to use for the organisation of recreational activities. Unfortunately, at first the girls found that:

> "… it was not too adequate as there was neither office or storage space and every time there was a movie the building had to be cleared of furniture and chairs. Partitions were finally built and little by little we acquired odd bits of furniture, hung curtains and added a bit of paint to brighten up the place." (A.R.C. 68 G.H. NARA)

By Sunday 21 May the Recreation Hall was ready for use and was officially opened by the 68th General Hospital Band. In July partitions were established, creating two offices and storage space. Outside of the building a tent was erected that could be used as a craft shop.

On 4 July the patients celebrated American Independence Day in the Recreation Hall, which they had decorated in red, white and blue for the evening. The girls

Day Room at the 68th (Author's collection)

organised a number of team games such as 'Find the Name of the State' and 'Bounce the Ping-Pong ball through the crack in the Liberty Bell', but the highlight of the evening was a 'Miss America Beauty contest'. Each team was given a musette bag containing a house coat, crepe paper, pins, newspaper, make-up and other miscellaneous articles to dress the chosen team member. After twenty minutes the three queens paraded across the stage while the judges chose 'Miss America'. The party concluded with hot dogs and cokes.

Also in July plans were made to move the Red Cross to a different building so that the Recreation Hall could be used solely as a theatre building. This would mean that the task of setting up and taking down chairs several times a day could be avoided. The Red Cross were happy to move to a more suitable building but Claire Sweeney, the Assistant Field Director realised:

Theatre building (Author's collection)

> "... that its permanency depended on whether or not our new home is suddenly needed by some other department. Our philosophy must be 'It will be fun while it lasts'" (A.R.C. 68 G.H. NARA)

On 1 August the Red Cross moved to a building that had originally been designated as an 'Officer Patients' Mess and Recreation Hall'. The girls put up curtains, put down lino and painted. They planned a 'Grand Opening' of the new building for 3 August and contacted the Red Cross Field Director to order a delivery of doughnuts for the big event. Unfortunately, the doughnuts never arrived and the girls had to make do with cookies. Later they found that the doughnuts had been delivered to one of the other hospitals in the area by mistake. They were re-ordered for the next Sunday for an 'Open House' event and this time the delivery was successful.

The new Red Cross building had a separate craft room and the girls were able to offer a number of different crafts to the patients including woodwork, clay modelling, leather work and bedroom slippers made of felt, linoleum and string. The slippers were very popular, particularly with the patients who had arrived at Halston Hall with no shoes.

Also in August the girls organised a 'Baby Picture Contest', 600 pictures of the patients' children or nieces and nephews were entered and posted on a bulletin board in the Recreation Hall. Two of the doctors and a nurse were given the task of choosing a winner. The little girl who won was sent a ten shilling note with a first prize ribbon, while her proud uncle was given a box of cigars. The second prize winner received a money order and the father a carton of cigarettes. The event was so popular that the patients requested a 'Big Baby' contest for photographs of wives and sweethearts which took place the following week.

In September the Red Cross organised a dance for the patients. The patients themselves decorated the hall and planned the entertainment; helped with the refreshments; and cleared the place up afterwards. Transportation was sent for a group of A.T.S. girls and the patients were allowed to invite their own dates if they registered the girl's name in advance so that a pass could be issued. The detachment orchestra played and a patient acted as a Master of Ceremonies. Every other dance was either a spotlight dance, a waltz, a jitterbug contest, or an 'Excuse Me Dance'. Prizes were lipsticks, fancy soap and cigarettes. Patients in wheelchairs and those on crutches were also able to join in.

Halloween was celebrated at the 68th with several parties. The Officers' Club was decorated with leaves and straw and the 'dress code' was fatigues with paper hats and accessories. A British R.A.F. orchestra from Rednal furnished the music. There was also a fancy dress party at the N.C.O. club. On 23 November the 68th celebrated Thanksgiving with a half holiday and a complete turkey meal. Menus, which included the history of the unit, were printed for all the messes.

For Christmas the hospital was decorated accordingly. The Recreation Hall had a large tree with electric lights and home-made ornaments. The contest, which was held to determine the best decorated ward, was won by Ward 25 led by Ward Officer, Major Samuel Greenberg. The Red Cross gave each ward a Christmas Party with cocoa, cookies and ice-cream, but the winning ward had an extra party as a prize. Refreshments for the party were supplied by the Mess Department which also

Christmas decorations in the Mess Hall (Author's collection)

made Christmas cookies and candy for the patients.

Souvenir Christmas booklets, which contained greetings from the Commanding Officer, Red Cross and hospital staff; the Christmas menu; the schedule of activities for the week; and the words for a number of Christmas carols which were to be sung on each ward, were distributed to each patient. The covers of the booklet were block printed in red or green using a design from one of the patients.

One of the mess halls at the 68th, decorated for Christmas (Author's collection)

One of the mess halls at the 68th, decorated for Christmas (Author's collection)

On the Sunday before Christmas a Welsh male voice choir sang carols on all the wards. In the evening an English stage company was due to put on Dickens' Christmas Carol in the theatre but was unable to get to the 68th because of the dense fog.

On the Friday afternoon a children's party was held in the Red Cross building. Around forty children aged six to twelve from a nearby school came to sing carols and play games around the tree. The Red Cross girls noticed that:

> "...the men enjoyed most the informal period after the program when they had time to get acquainted with the children." (A.R.C. 68 G.H. NARA)

The children received 'patient-made' gifts of stuffed toys, wooden toys and model aeroplanes.

On Christmas Day church services were held by the Protestant and Catholic chaplains. Two Santas made rounds of the hospital wards and presented each patient with a gift courtesy of the Red

Christmas decorations in the Enlisted Men's Mess (Author's collection)

Cross. Outside agencies also provided entertainment for the patients of the 68th. The manager of one of the local E.N.S.A. companies arranged visits to the 68th on a regular basis and in August 1944 Ivy Benson and her orchestra visited the base. A British serviceman, Corporal Jimmy Silver, regularly came to entertain the patients on the wards with his accordion and a thirteen year old local boy, George Humphries, also visited some of the wards with his guitar to sing for the patients. In November 1944 a group of twenty children ranging in age from six to fourteen came to play their home-made instruments to the ward patients. The patients, particularly those with younger brothers and sisters, enjoyed listening to the children.

Ivy Benson and her all girl band

A group of A.T.S. girls from a local battalion visited the base every Saturday night for a party for the patients. (One of their captains, Margaret, known as Peggy, met Major Samuel Trask one of the officers from the 68th, on one of these occasions. Their friendship developed into love and in 1946 she was to fly to the U.S. to marry him and begin life as an army officer's wife at Fort McArthur in San Pedro, California.) The A.T.S. also brought flowers for the wards. Another organisation to donate flowers to the Red Cross for the Recreation Hall was Oswestry Rotary Club.

The Red Cross were constantly looking for sight-seeing opportunities for the rehabilitation and Z.I. patients who were 'filling' time while awaiting transportation either to a replacement depot or home. Recreational transport for the patients was a problem. The Assistant Field Director noted in her report:

> "… these opportunities are few and far between for we have to depend on the Hospital Center for transportation. We used trucks for a while but this was very unsuccessful because of the distances and the weather." (A.R.C. 68 G.H. NARA)

A number of the patients and personnel visited the local town of Oswestry in their off-duty time.

The Special Service Section was able to make some helpful contacts to provide sight-seeing trips in the local area around the base. The Rotary Club agreed to organise visits to Chirk Castle in Denbighshire, courtesy of Lord Howard de Waldron. The men travelled to the castle by bus and were given a guided tour by the butler. Some of the men even had the opportunity to meet Lord de Waldron. After the tour of the castle the men visited a nearby abbey then had tea at a tea room.

A local hotel offered to provide an evening party for a group of thirty men and personnel from a nearby British camp offered their Garrison Hall for dances for the men. In November 1944 thirty patients had the opportunity to watch an American

Farmer's market in Oswestry (J. McConkey)   *Chirk Castle (J. McConkey)*

football game and another group was the guest of the British Council at an English professional football match.

The Red Cross also sourced resources in the local area. The British Red Cross and a local private school loaned the hospital some French books for their French patients and householders in the local community saved their jam jars for the use of the Laboratory Service who needed a uniform container to collect specimens. The response was so great that the excess jars were donated to other hospitals in the area.

A British Red Cross volunteer came to the hospital once a week to visit the British and Canadian patients. She wrote letters, brought in supplies and contacted their families. In addition she was able to arrange billets in the nearby town for visiting relatives. She also co-ordinated a group of volunteer seamstresses who made ditty bags out of black-out material. When filled with toothpaste, shaving cream, soap, razor blades, cigarettes, chewing gum and an airmail envelope, they could be distributed to new patients on their arrival.

Although the Red Cross worked together to achieve much for the patients at the 68th it appears that all was not running as smoothly under the surface and problems between the personnel caused a number of staff changes. The Field Supervisor, Olive Kestin, made an inspection visit at the end of September 1944, she noted:

> "Although the Assistant Field Director is not too pleased with the type of work being done by the Secretary the office has been quite well set up and is very orderly in appearance." (A.R.C. 68 G.H. NARA)

The fact that Miss Sweeney was not happy with the secretary is obvious from the official A.R.C. records. The A.F.D. notes in the archives that the job of making phone calls had fallen to the Staff Aide who was already busy with her own duties.

> "We had thought that some of the telephone work could be done by our secretary, but her South Carolina accent has made this impractical." (A.R.C. 68 G.H. NARA)

In December the Secretary applied to leave the 68th and carry out Red Cross Club work instead. The 68th were sent a replacement but unfortunately, before she got chance to commence her duties she slipped on the ice and broke her leg, consequently she couldn't take up the post.

In October 1944 the Chief Recreation Worker, Mae Louise Fuller, was given a transfer to a unit in France as she wanted to work nearer the front line. Before she left on 23 October she was given a buffet supper at the Officers' Club when the guests wished her luck in her new venture. She was replaced by a new Recreation Worker.

In January 1945 the Field Supervisor, was again called to visit the A.R.C. unit at the 68th. This time Miss Sweeney was having problems with the Staff Aide, Faye Dietz. She complained that Miss Dietz was not carrying out the case work that had been assigned to her. Miss Kestin reported:

> "It was Miss Sweeney's impression that Miss Dietz is very resentful of supervision, that she has a difficult personality in social as well as professional relationships and that she (Miss Sweeney) has had complaints … from the other girls in the Red Cross Staff who live in the same hut with her." (A.R.C. 68 G.H. NARA)

For her part Miss Dietz complained that Miss Sweeney was very negative and she did not feel that the criticism given her was constructive.

> "She did not know whether it was a personality clash between her and Miss Sweeney (If so, this would be entirely on Miss Sweeney's part) or whether Miss Sweeney had developed a dislike for her on some other basis." (A.R.C. 68 G.H. NARA)

The Field Supervisor concluded that the two girls should discuss the matter and sort it out between themselves. In the end Faye Dietz did leave the 68th and in February 1945 she was replaced by a new Staff Aide who caught a severe cold and was admitted to the 129th General Hospital at Penley for two weeks before she could commence her duties at the 68th.

In January the Red Cross also lost the services of the enlisted man who was cleaning and doing odd jobs for them. He was sent as a replacement to the combat zone. In February the girls were able to hire an English woman who assisted with the cleaning each morning and brought flowers for the Recreation Hall for the remaining months of the 68th's occupancy of Plant 4188.

Chapter 7

6810 (Provisional)/ 804 Hospital Center

ONCE a number of general and station hospitals had been established in the U.K. Higher Headquarters decided to open 'hospital centers' to deal with the administration and to act as a headquarters for groups of hospitals. The 12th and 15th Hospital Centers were established at Great Malvern and Cirencester respectively to act as a headquarters for the hospitals in the Malvern and Gloucestershire areas and the 6810th (Provisional) Hospital Center was inaugurated in Flintshire.

The primary function of the 6810th (Provisional) Hospital Center was to act as headquarters for the five hospitals in the area – at Llanerch Panna, Penley, Oteley Deer Park, Iscoyd Park and Halston Hall. It was to:

> "… correlate and coordinate their activities; take responsibility for administration and supply; supervise reception and evacuation of patients; and through regular inspections assist them in maintaining a high degree of professional, administrative and training efficiency." (6810 H.C. NARA)

One of the tasks of the hospital center was to prevent duplication of administration and allow the individual hospitals to spend more time and effort in professional duties. The 6810th also acted as a centre for the evacuation of Z.I. patients back to the States.

The concept of the 6810th began with a letter to the Office of the Surgeon, Headquarters, Western Base Section, dated 20 May 1944 and entitled 'Provisional Hospital Center, Whitchurch Group'. It stated:

> "A site in the Whitchurch area will be available on or about 28 May 1944 for the Headquarters Medical Department Concentration Center and the Convalescent Section of the 12th Hospital Center. The Commanding Officer appointed by this office will be Lt. Colonel Francis Wadsworth, Commanding

Officer of the 1st Medical Department, Medical Concentration Center until such time as Headquarters, ETOUSA appoints the permanent commanding officer. This group will operate as a Provisional Hospital Center in the near future." (6810 H.C. NARA)

From this letter it can be seen that the 6810th was originally intended to be the Convalescent Section of the 12th Hospital Center based in Great Malvern.

The 6810th was activated on 25 May 1944 at Gwernheylod Hall, Overton, Flintshire, it was located near to the two hospitals at Penley. Gwernheylod, a manor house built around 1600 and remodelled in the 1830s, had been sold by the Lloyd-Fletcher family in 1938 to Major Peel of Bryn Y Pys who amalgamated the two estates. Gwernheylod remained unoccupied until it was requisitioned in October 1939 for 'the quartering of soldiers'. From July 1940 it was occupied by soldiers of the British Royal Artillery and in May 1944 the 329th Regiment of the 83rd U.S. Infantry Division was billeted there while undergoing combat training in Wales in preparation for the conflict in Europe. (This regiment landed on Omaha Beach on 18 June 1944.)

Gwernheylod Hall (Jill Burton)

On 1 June three officers and twelve enlisted men of the 6810th were assigned to Gwernheylod. A further ten officers and 106 enlisted men were attached to the unit. Lieutenant Colonel Wadsworth assumed command of the Hospital Center on 1 June but unfortunately, on that very evening, he was taken ill and admitted to the 16th General Hospital (Penley), as a patient and it was necessary for Major Peter J. Doering M.C. to take command of the 6810th.

Work was commenced immediately to prepare the grounds of Gwernheylod for use as a holding camp for patients awaiting evacuation to the Zone of the Interior. The work was carried out by the personnel of the 6810th with assistance from British engineers. While construction work was ongoing in the grounds, plans were made for the administration headquarters inside the building.

The general hospitals already functioning in the area (15th at Oteley Deer Park, 16th at Penley, 68th at Halston Hall, 82nd at Iscoyd Park and 83rd at Llanerch Panna) were attached to the 6810th on 13 June 1944. Visits were made to all the hospitals by the Commanding Officer, Adjutant and Receiving and Evacuation Officer to present the plans and purposes of the Hospital Center and to determine the needs of the hospitals. The Center requested that the hospitals furnish the Receiving and Evacuation Officer with a plan of the hospital sites, a list of all available transportation and a daily transportation schedule so that administrative activities could be coordinated.

Rednal Aerodrome. View of C47s unloading wounded to waiting ambulances, taken from control tower (Rednal Airfield)

Arrangements were made with the U.S.A.A.F. Composite Command for the use of a small area of land adjacent to Rednal Airfield for the purpose of establishing a medical detachment to engage in the evacuation of patients by air. On 11 June a detachment of one officer and thirty enlisted men was directed to proceed to 61st O.T.U. R.A.F. Rednal to open the site as an evacuation area. Tents were erected on the site so that if ambulances weren't immediately available patients could be unloaded and planes could be cleared for departure. Three officers and eighty enlisted men from the 571st Ambulance Company were designated to aid in the reception and evacuation of patients to and from the hospitals of the Center. Individual hospitals were instructed to have teams available for loading and unloading patients from trains and planes. Arrangements were also made for hospitals to receive patients from planes landing at Tilstock, Seighford, Hixon and Burtonwood airfields.

On 17 June 1944 the Center received its first hospital train carrying 203 patients. On 20 June the first air evacuation for patients from the Center took place at Rednal Airfield. Two C47 U.S.A.A.F. planes evacuated 28 patients. 20 June also saw the first rail evacuation from Ellesmere Station. 65 patients were transported by ambulance from a number of different hospitals to be loaded for evacuation back to the U.S.

Casualties arriving in U.K. brought back from a beachhead in Northern France by C47s of a 9th Air Force Evacuation Unit (U.S. Archives, NARA)

Towards the end of June work ceased on the expansion of the Gwernheylod site and personnel began the search for a more appropriate building. Broughall School in Whitchurch was chosen. Broughall School had been built as a secondary school to replace a school in the area whose building had been condemned. It was almost complete when war was declared in September 1939. The school, which still stands today, is made of red brick and its design incorporates three open courts. The offices and various sections of the building were joined by covered ramps. At the outbreak of war it was immediately requisitioned and turned over to the British War Office. (This meant that the school it was built to replace was forced to remain open even though the building was in a delapidated state.) Until 1944 it housed British troops and then the 11th (U.S.) Replacement Depot used the building as Headquarters.

On 7 July 1944 the majority of the personnel of the 6810th moved to the new site; a small detachment was left during the handover. Gwernheylod was then temporarily used by the 930 and 633 U.S. Hospital Ship Platoons.

The intention of Higher Headquarters was that Broughall School should act as a Holding Center for Class IV patients who were awaiting evacuation to the U.S., 67 hospital tents with concrete slab floors were erected in the grounds and plans were submitted for latrines, ablutions, a kitchen, water supply, sewage disposal, garbage racks and cinder paths. The Hospital Center was to supply its own labour with

Broughall School in the 1970s (then known as Sir John Talbot School) (D. Broad)

Army Post Office 209, Whitchurch (U.S. Archives, NARA)

supervisory assistance from engineers on electrical wiring and plumbing. A courier service was established from the school to the five surrounding hospitals with two runs made daily to deliver and pick up mail and messages.

On 17 July the 15th and 16th General Hospitals were released from attachment to the 6810th Hospital Center because of their imminent departure for France. The 16th was replaced by the 129th General Hospital at Penley and the 15th was replaced by the 137th at Oteley Deer Park. Also in July other hospitals in the surrounding areas were attached to the Hospital Center: 10th Station Hospital in Lancashire, 168th Station and 109th General Hospitals in Cheshire and 157th General Hospital in Merseyside. On 23 September the 33rd, 36th and 312th Station Hospitals at Lichfield were assigned to the Center.

On 11 August one officer and 25 enlisted men of Detachment A, 286th M.P. Company were attached to the 6810th to patrol towns and villages in the area so that medical personnel who had taken on M.P. duties could be released for hospital duties. On 15 August the 1st Medical Demonstration Platoon, consisting of one officer and thirty enlisted men, replaced the 571st Ambulance Company which departed 21 August 1944. On 8 September notification was given that the Holding Camp for this Center would not be needed so all work on the project ceased. The tents were taken down and returned to the supply depot.

On 22 November 1944 the 6810th (Provisional) Hospital Center was designated 804th Hospital Center under the command of Colonel Neville H. McNerney. It was also known as 6th Hospital Group.

The Medical Supply Section of the 804th, under the direction of 1st Lieutenant Alfred Chance, was responsible for all requisitions of supplies for all the hospitals attached to the Center. As it was the largest hospital, 129th General Hospital at Penley held an emergency supply of certain reserve items. It had ample storage space and refrigerator capacity for certain biologicals; in addition to this it was located centrally for the hospitals in the command. A blood bank was also maintained at Penley.

The Medical Inspector, Major Charles Cataldo, and his office carried out regular inspections of the hospitals. All deficiencies were reported to the commanding officers who were expected to take the required action to correct them. The inspection team:

"… always kept in mind its primary mission – to ensure for the sick and wounded soldiers entering into our hospitals every advantage for a speedy recovery, with a military atmosphere that promotes the feeling of confidence in the medical officers, nurses and enlisted men. A dirty hospital, poor administration and an unmilitary, inadequately disciplined Medical Department certainly does not breed confidence in our Medical Corps set up. … The result of all these endeavours has produced a group of hospitals worthy of praise." (804 H.C. NARA)

The Medical Inspectors' Office developed a procedure involving coordination between the ward, baggage room and supply systems handling soldiers' clothing and baggage, which was to be returned to the Zone of the Interior. Missing baggage had been causing the requisition of extra clothing which was in turn, causing dwindling stocks of clothing in the Center.

The Chief Nurse of the Hospital Center, Major Ivy M. Wadsworth, coordinated the duties appertaining to the nurses of the hospitals in the group. She ensured that various nurses with specialities were transferred to hospitals where they would be of most value. On 23 February Colonel Florence A. Blanchfield, Chief Nurse of the U.S. Army and Lieutenant Colonel Danielson, Chief Nurse of the United Kingdom Base, visited the Headquarters of the Hospital Center. Each hospital in the Center sent their chief nurse to meet them. All nurses that could be spared that evening also attended a meeting where they discussed the various nursing techniques they had found on their tour of the hospitals, pointed out deficiencies to be corrected and efficiencies to be shared.

The Transportation Section of the 804th coordinated transportation within the Center so that the necessary vehicles could be drawn on with a few hours' notice from any of the hospitals for evacuation or reception of patients. This section worked alongside the Rail Transportation Officer, 1st Lieutenant Daniel Walsh, who was based at Whitchurch. Civilian buses and other forms of non-military transport were also used to transport patients, supplies and rations. A garage was requisitioned in Whitchurch for maintenance work on the vehicles. During inclement weather in the winter months vehicles could be stored in the garage.

Colonel Blanchfield, Chief Nurse of the U.S. Army (U.S. Archives, NARA)

The Receiving and Evacuation Office, under the supervision of Lieutenant David Anton, coordinated the movements of approximately 60,000 patients during the months from January to June 1945. During the Battle of the Bulge it was necessary for Lieutenant Anton to organise procedures to obtain the extra beds (30,000) needed in order to accommodate the larger numbers of patients than expected arriving at the

804th. Other factors, such as sewage, personnel and supplies were also taken into consideration by the Receiving and Evacuation Office when anticipating the arrival of large numbers of patients.

Since the activation of the 6810th it had been necessary to transport large convoys of Z.I. patients to Liverpool Docks for passage home. This journey was taken by a combination of train and truck until January 1945 when it was decided to load each ship from one large motor convoy. This procedure was decided upon to eliminate the need to load trains at Malpas Station and it meant that the patients would only require one movement from the hospitals concerned. Each planned convoy could move up to 981 patients. Ambulances and buses met at Broughall where they were sorted into class and placed in the convoy. British and Canadian drivers assisted in this procedure, furnishing up to an additional thirty vehicles when required.

Malpas Station

The vehicles carrying patients set off towards Liverpool, at Birkenhead additional ambulances were amalgamated into the convoy from hospitals North of the group headquarters. After this the convoy proceeded without interruption to the Port of Embarkation at Liverpool, where patients were unloaded and placed on the ship. This procedure took two hours and fifteen minutes and was carried out with the aid of the British R.A.M.C. at Liverpool Princes Dock.

The 804th also organised the evacuation of patients by air from hospitals in the center. Patients were flown from Tilstock to the station hospital at Prestwick in Scotland, from where approximately 2500 patients were flown to the U.S. each month.

The Receiving and Evacuation Office also instituted a Card Locator Section containing the names and data of all personnel in the hospitals in the center. Records were kept on the disposition of each patient through the use of daily Admission and Disposition sheets submitted by each individual hospital to Headquarters. The Locator system was useful to other departments such as the Army Post Office, which could locate the recipients of mail more efficiently.

On 10 April 1945 it was decided that the Western District Headquarters at Chester would be closed and relocated to Broughall School, and on 11 April Colonel Bronson arrived to take control of

U.S. troops at Princes Dock, Liverpool (U.S. Archives, NARA)

Headquarters Western Area. On the same day the American Red Cross Field supervisor, Miss Elizabeth I. Lynth and Miss Doris Buck, her secretary, were assigned to Broughall School to coordinate all Red Cross activities within the hospitals of the center.

As well as its official procedures the school also had recreational facilities for the personnel serving there. There was a spacious dayroom in which regular movies and an occasional dance were held. This room also held a large library, a Special Service radio and two ping-pong tables which:

> "… have been in almost constant use during off-duty hours." (804 H.C. NARA)

Stage shows were presented on the auditorium stage, which was equipped with lighting effects and screens. The men at Broughall also participated in the softball league run within the Center in their off-duty time. In addition to the facilities on site there was a bus which ran to Chester at least once a week, which the personnel made use of.

Colonel McNerney concluded his report for 1945 stating:

> "The mission of the 804th (U.S.) Hospital Center had been to coordinate both the administrative and the technical functions of the hospitals in the Center. Medical Department Units, prior to their departure to the Continent, have been staged for their departure and orders and directives from all higher administrative Command have been carried out. … The technical administration has been ably handled by the coordinators and other staff sections. Numbered memorandums have been continued to be used to a great advantage in outlining the policies as procedures for all hospitals and medical units under this command. The main feature of this has been consolidated lists of reports to be made by each hospital and listed specifically the number to be rendered as well as the channels in which each should be directed. In addition regular meetings have been held which included the commanding officers of each of the fourteen hospitals in the command including 8 general, 6 station and 1 field hospital." (804 H.C. NARA)

Broughall School was relinquished back to the Education Authority in 1946 and after some extra building work was used for its intended purpose as a school. Whitchurch Secondary Modern School, as it was known, was opened in 1947. In September 1978 the Secondary Modern and Grammar School amalgamated and Whitchurch Secondary Modern became St John Talbots Lower School. The school closed as a secondary school in the 1990s and is currently (2017) a nursery school.

Chapter 8

Carrying its Share of the Load – 83rd General Hospital, Llanerch Panna

ON 1 APRIL 1944 the 83rd General Hospital, commanded by Colonel F.G. Norbury, received orders for assignment to the installation at Llanerch Panna operated by the 304th Station Hospital. The 83rd had crossed the Atlantic on the Britannica, as part of a convoy, in March 1944. It was staged at the hospital staging base of Llandudno until the 304th had had notice to leave Llanerch Panna. Meanwhile Detachment A of the 83rd was assigned to temporarily operate a plant at Orangefield near Belfast, Northern Ireland. The main body of the 83rd left the staging post at Llandudno for Llanerch Panna in three groups between 4 and 8 April, while Detachment A left for Northern Ireland in two groups between 3 and 6 April.

Upon arrival at Llanerch Panna the Assistant Field Director of the Red Cross unit attached to the 83rd described Plant 4190 in the Red Cross records:

> "The location is very scenic as we overlook a charming dingle and rolling hills. … Adjoining the hospital is an estate with beautifully landscaped gardens. We and the patients are welcome guests there and the hostess (Miss Leche) is generous with her flowers." (A.R.C. 83 G.H. NARA)

The personnel of both the 304th Station and the 83rd General Hospitals worked to make the transition of the 450 patients from one hospital to the other as smooth as possible. The Royal Army Ordnance Depot at Overton-on-Dee commanded by Colonel F.A. Martin, also supported the hospitals during the changeover.

The 83rd took control of the site at Llanerch Panna on 8 April and the former 750 bed station hospital became a 1084 bed general hospital. This changed it in status from a hospital that catered for the needs of soldiers training in the locality into a hospital that would take wounded soldiers from the combat zone. The shift from station to general hospital required increased professional activity, greater utilisation of material on hand and the arrival of expansion units of equipment.

Because of the transfer of Detachment A to Northern Ireland, the 83rd were understaffed to operate as a general hospital so 12 officers and 83 enlisted men of the 304th remained temporarily on detached service with the 83rd. They were also able to help with the orientation and coordination of activities. From 26 April officers from the 15th General Hospital (at Oteley Deer Park) and the 99th General Hospital arrived on detached service to bring the 83rd up to required operating strength. Over a period of time the men of the 304th were withdrawn to their own unit. Although the living quarters became more crowded it was still possible to billet the extra personnel on site.

In the period up to D-Day the hospital served the dual function of station and general hospital as patients were received from units in training and staging areas as well as by transfer from other hospitals. Major A. James Gordon, Executive Officer of the 561st Field Artillery Battalion which was stationed at Doddington Park in April 1944 notes in his diary that a fellow officer, Chestnut, became ill on the day after his arrival at the base. Gordon took him to the 83rd General Hospital where he was operated on for a ruptured appendix. After nearly a month at the 83rd he was transferred to the 77th Station Hospital, near Bromsgrove, to convalesce. On 31 May Detachment A returned from Northern Ireland to work alongside the parent unit; the personnel from the 99th left shortly after this.

On 9 June Major William R. Lipscomb, the consultant in Neurosurgery for Northern England, Scotland and Northern Ireland, joined the command as Chief of Surgery. The 83rd was designated both a Neuro-Surgical Center and a Primary Treatment Center for Neuro-Psychiatry in the 804th Hospital Center. The unit became the principal hospital in the group for specialised treatment of 'Combat Exhaustion' with narcosis insulin and abreaction procedures (Transcriptions of battle sound recordings were made as a part of the abreaction treatments.) As a result of this there were a number of transfers of neuro-surgical, neuro-psychiatric and urological patients from other hospitals.

By the time convoys of battle casualties were received in mid-June the command was running efficiently. The first group of patients that arrived at the hospital were in a poor state. Some had not shaved for nine days and most arrived without funds or equipment. Local people remember watching the lines of U.S. ambulances making their way to Llanerch Panna or Penley from the railway station at Overton-on-Dee. One resident recalls seeing the muddy boots of casualties through the rear windows of the ambulances.

As the patients arrived at the hospital the Red Cross gave out cigarettes and comfort articles which they obtained from the P.X. or 'borrowed' from the 15th General Hospital, which was on standby to move out at the time. Thelma Menzer, the Assistant Field Director of the Red Cross Unit attached to the 83rd, commented that:

> "… most appreciated by the battle-worn and scarred were the doughnuts and coffee served from 2.00-4.00 a.m. as they came to the hospital. … For several

days our whole staff worked all hours performing errands, making loans, distributing reading material and comfort articles, providing treats and entertainment and doing whatever we could to help the wounded soldiers. The arrival of these patients seems to have stimulated the entire community. Everyone wants to help. A neighbour sent six baskets of freshly picked strawberries, others are providing flowers. Our volunteer, Mrs Allchurch, has returned to a regular schedule of two days a week. She has been very helpful with the new patients, sewing, writing and filling other requests. Mr Jones of the British Red Cross in Denbigh sent 72 more books, including some from his own library." (A.R.C. 83 G.H. NARA)

Nurse, Althea Rawlins worked on a ward of Z.I. patients. She reminisces:

> "… The morale was high on this ward. These soldiers knew they were going home, but they didn't understand the extent of their injuries, particularly the paraplegics. Many of them would be permanently paralyzed. There were some who would be able to regain the use of their legs but many of them had no feeling beyond their shoulders and most couldn't use their hands."

Nurse Althea Rawlins (wearing a flight nurse uniform in this photo)

She also remembers giving the men penicillin injections for infection. She remembers that the penicillin was in liquid yellow form given hypodermically intramuscularly, which could be very painful. She remembers waking a patient to give him an injection one night; he stirred and even spoke to her so she assumed he was awake. However when she gave him the shot it woke him up and his reaction was to come up fighting. She was scared but did manage to calm him down and remove the needle.

One of the patients arriving at the hospital in June 1944 was 19 year old Steward 2c John Noble Roberts, a black steward serving on one of the landing crafts that had taken the G.I.s to Omaha Beach on D-Day. Roberts had been drafted into the Coastguard and had arrived in the U.K. on 27 January 1944. His duties included preparing for and running errands for the officers on board.

On D-Day Roberts was aboard LCI (L)-93, which was ferrying G.I.s to Omaha Beach. On the first shuttle to the beach one of the men

Steward 2/c John Roberts

CARRYING ITS SHARE OF THE LOAD

U.S.S. LCI (L)-93 aground on Omaha Beach
(US Coast Guard photo # 2395 from the collections of the U.S. Coast Guard Historian's Office)

refused to disembark once he had seen the chaos on the beach; Roberts was ordered to take his name. On the second trip to the beach the tide was going out and the craft became stranded on a sandbank off the beach. Roberts was given a message to carry down to the engine room, but as he made his way there a German shell struck the stranded vessel. The explosion took off Robert's lower right leg from the knee down and badly injured his left. He managed to hop down off the ladder he was climbing and get onto the deck where he called for help. Pharmacist's Mate, Charles Mudgett was able to apply a tourniquet to the leg and save Robert's life.

While Roberts was waiting to be taken off the landing craft the boat shifted a little and hit a mine. Roberts was showered with sand and water. It was necessary to evacuate the whole crew via a Higgins Boat. Roberts was transferred to the

U.S.S. Doyle (DD-494)
(U.S. Navy Bureau of Ships photo NARA)

77

U.S.S. Doyle (DD-494), where he was given emergency surgery. Later he was transferred to another ship for transport back to the U.K. where he recalls that American patients were in bunks on the one side while German patients, who had also been taken off the beaches, were on the other side.

Once in the U.K. Roberts was transported to the 83rd General Hospital where he received treatment for six weeks. While at the 83rd, he took advantage of invitations to visit some of the local people. He also received his Purple Heart medal during his stay at the 83rd. At the end of July he was sent back to the U.S. where he spent some time in a Naval hospital in Philadelphia until he was discharged at the end of January 1945. Once in the States no mention could be found of his Purple Heart Medal on the paperwork. This is because while he was at the 83rd it was believed that he was in the Navy, rather than the Coastguard and the incorrect paperwork had been filed. Once Roberts had recovered from his treatment, he devoted his career to developing prosthetic limbs and orthotic devices.

From D-Day onwards the Neuropsychiatric ward received a number of patients suffering from combat exhaustion. On a selective basis, the N.P. patients were sent to the Red Cross building for an interview with the A.F.D. or Social Worker. It was thought that a more relaxed atmosphere prevailed in the Red Cross Office than the ward. One patient explained to the Red Cross Social Worker that he:

> "… needed a long rest."

He had already taken part in the African, Tunisian and Sicilian campaigns when he was evacuated from one of the D-Day beaches, having been found unconscious after helping a wounded friend. He told the Social Worker that his worst experience was when his pack was shot through during the Tunisian Campaign. His hand was constantly shaking with nerves and he said that he felt that he couldn't take any more combat. He also commented that he:

> "… had a cousin who was in the last war and still carries the marks of his experience." (A.R.C. 83 G.H. NARA).

Towards the end of 1944 the Red Cross found that their case-work had taken a new turn. Patients who had suffered the amputation of limbs were coming to terms with the loss but found it difficult to inform their families of the situation. Thelma Menzer noted:

> "They seem to find a considerable relief in talking this through and in having a letter sent to the home chapter requesting that the extent of the injury and reactions of the patient be interpreted to the family." (A.R.C. 83 G.H. NARA)

Major Lipscomb also encouraged the Red Cross unit to organise programmes to occupy the Neuropsychiatric patients. One day a week the Red Cross took craft

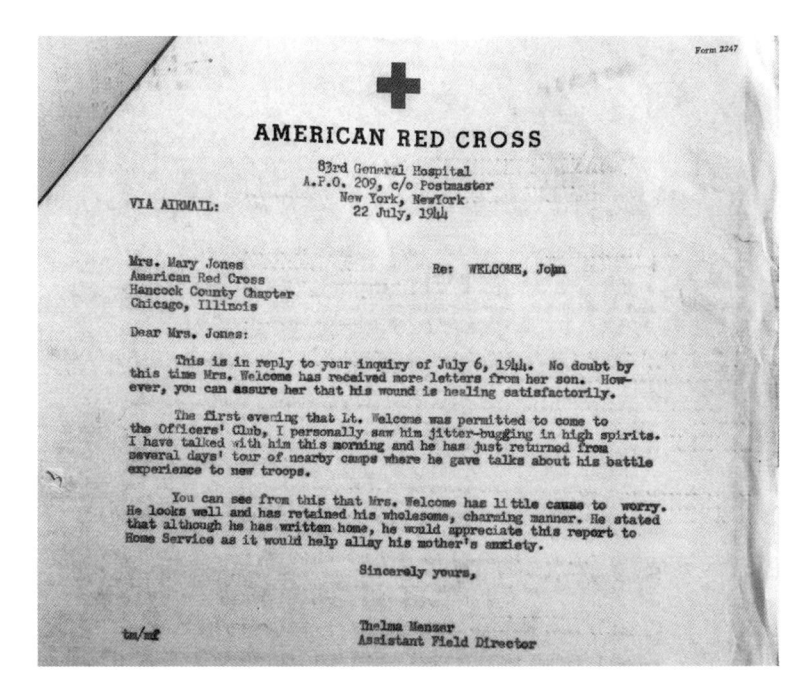

Letter written by the Red Cross at 83rd regarding one of the patients (A.R.C. 83 NARA)

materials to the ward and taught both the patients and the ward men craft so that the programme could be continued during the week at the hands of the ward staff. One of the patients from another ward was a skilled gardener so he was given the task of creating a garden project for the N.P. patients.

Initially the N.P. patients who had completed their treatment and were awaiting disposition to the U.S. were visited by two of the Red Cross girls on the ward three times a week but it was difficult to transport the materials and equipment to the ward so:

> "A plan was worked out whereby for two hours each morning, when the recreation room and workshops were closed to other patients these people came in, accompanied by the nurse and wardmen. They are free to use the games, books and some craft materials" (A.R.C. 83 G.H. NARA)

Rehabilitation had a prominent role at the 83rd. Patients commenced reconditioning training while still bed-bound; they were placed in a group in the Recovery Detachment as soon as they were ambulatory. The name 'Recovery Detachment' was given the detachment for psychological reasons. Two of the large wards along with five ward tents in the surgical part of the hospital were set up for rehabilitation. A salvaged building was also established as a remedial gymnasium. Convalescent officer patients were selected for administrative and training phases under the supervision of 1st Lieutenant Philip Smith, the Rehabilitation Officer. Weapons, field equipment, athletic equipment and training aids were gathered for the use of this group. Because the rehabilitation patients had a full programme of training the Red Cross was allotted limited times when they could work with them on recreational and craft activities. Colonel Norbury noted:

> "They are not allowed to forget that they are soldiers." (A.R.C. 83 G.H. NARA)

The Recovery detachment was given the task of repairing the bicycles that the 83rd had inherited from the 304th. The Red Cross unit supplied the tools to work on the bikes in the hope that the men would be able to put the bicycles to use as part of the Red Cross programme when they were in working order.

The men from the Recovery Detachment were often issued new uniforms and passes simultaneously. One of the patients made an ironing board and Frances Hardy from the Red Cross noted:

> "We feel it would do the heart good of many a harried mother to see her son painstakingly putting razor edged seams on trousers and pleats on blouses. One of the officer patients, not to be outdone by the G.I.s, wished to take advantage of the ironing privilege, even though he had only one pair of trousers. Imagine our amazement when he disappeared into our vacant office and came forth arrayed in our rainbow coloured afghan draped sarong-fashion about his waist. He gleefully ironed his one pair of trousers exclaiming meanwhile, 'Ah, thees Red Cross ees wonderful.' (Incidentally he is a member of the Free French Army.)" (A.R.C. 83 G.H. NARA)

In December 1944 a stream of Trench foot and Frostbite patients began to arrive at the 83rd. These patients were made the subject of a special study and a clinical meeting at the 804th Hospital Center was held to discuss the findings from the 83rd. The Recovery Detachment reached its greatest number of patients (284 on 16 February 1945) at the height of the convalescence period of Trench foot cases.

The 83rd were also involved in pioneering work in manufacturing acrylic eyes. A number of casualties had arrived at the 83rd with facial injuries that required false eyes. Lieutenant Colonel Lloyd Barger and Captain Matthew I. Steel designed two devices which:

> "… have saved many man hours and aided in producing a better looking eye." (A.R.C. 83 G.H. NARA)

The two officers worked alongside 2 N.C.O.s: Tec. 3 Carl D. Shammo and Tec. 4 Raymond Warren, who aided the officers with their engineering and drawing skills.

The first device was a lathe that cut out a recess in the eye blank which would receive the painted discs for the iris and pupil. The device was designed so that the recess could be cut out in fifteen minutes.

The second contraption cut discs out of X-ray film used for the iris and pupil. When it was set up the piece of film could be placed between the plunger and die after assembling in the frame, a tap of the hammer would then cut out the disc, another tap would cut the hole using a second plunger.

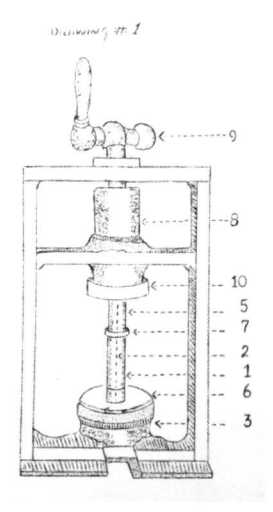

Meanwhile various milestones were celebrated at the 83rd. On 7 August 1944 there was a flag raising ceremony when Colonel McNerney, Commanding Officer of the 804th, reviewed the parade and presented the flag to the guard. On two occasions in August Colonel Frederick Herr, Commanding Officer XXVII District, presented Silver Star Medals to two of the officer patients.

On 25 September 'Activation Day' was celebrated with a programme of entertainment in the theatre on base. Officers and members of the detachment wrote and produced skits depicting various features of the hospital's life during the past year.

On 6 December the bed capacity of the hospital was increased to 1374 and at the end of the month Colonel Norbury noted in his monthly report:

> "It is felt that the 83rd General Hospital is carrying its share of the load. It should. Nothing else would do." (A.R.C. 83 G.H. NARA)

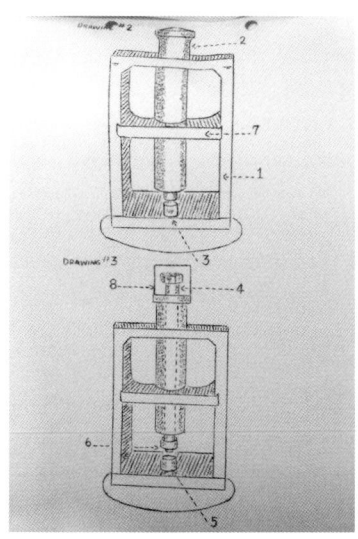

1st device for cutting out recesses in eye blanks (83 G.H. NARA)

1st device for cutting out recesses in eye blanks (83 G.H. NARA)

2nd device for cutting discs to use for iris/pupil (83 G.H. NARA)

Device for cutting discs (83 G.H. NARA)

Device for cutting discs (83 G.H. NARA)

The first few months of 1945 were the busiest. The high point was 2 January when the bed capacity was 1380. By 17 March the bed status was restored to the former level of 1134. One of the patients to arrive at the 83rd in February 1945 was Captain Howard Rosenblum of the 80th U.S. Infantry Division. He had been wounded in the back and left leg in Luxembourg.

This was the second time he had been wounded as he had previously been hit in the face by shrapnel. Rosenblum had been patrolling a fort with his patrol sergeant when both men were hit by a mortar shell. The captain was evacuated to the 10th Evacuation Hospital in Luxembourg where plaster casts were applied. From here he was transferred to the 83rd where he was examined and had his wounds closed. He underwent rehabilitation but it was decided that he should be discharged from the service and sent back home.

Another patient arriving during this period was Captain Gilbert Fuller, whose father, a veteran of World War One, had actually been born in Wales. Fuller, a seasoned veteran who had taken part in the campaigns in North Africa and Sicily and fought on Omaha Beach and then through France and Belgium, received his fourth wound in the Hurtgen Forest, just outside Aachen, Germany.

He had been part of the first unit to cross into Germany and had been dubbed by the Associated Press the 'Honorary Mayor of Aachen' (the first German city to fall to the Allies). His achievements were recorded by Hayle Boyle (a war correspondent who later won the Pulitzer Prize for his military journalism). He had been promoted to Captain for his bravery and received four Purple Heart medals, two Bronze Stars (one with V for Valour) and the Silver Star.

While at the 83rd he met and fell in love with Nurse, Lieutenant Johnna Ferguson. After his wounds had been treated he was sent to the Officers Convalescent Hospital at Bromsgrove (833rd Station Hospital). On 12 March 1945 he travelled back to Flintshire to be married to Miss Ferguson in Penley Parish Church. After spending the honeymoon in London, Captain Fuller was sent back to the front lines. On his way back he had the opportunity to visit his nephew, David Williams. Because he was staying over night with Williams' unit on the way to the front he was asked to share the officers' billets. His reply was that if he could fight alongside enlisted men he could definitely sleep in their billets. Shortly after his return to the front lines the war in Europe ended. His last official duty was to liberate a concentration camp in Austria.

Just before Christmas 1944 another nurse from the 83rd had also been married at Penley Parish Church; Nurse, Lieutenant Betty Hendrik had married G.I. Donald Elder.

In the first few weeks of April 1945 the patient load lightened but then increased again as Recovered Allied Military Personnel (ex-Prisoners of War) and other casualties were rapidly evacuated by air from Germany. On 2 April German prisoners of war quartered in a stockade on the grounds of 129th General Hospital at Penley, were made available for duties at the 83rd.

Chapter 9

Volunteers and Visitors – 83rd General Hospital, Llanerch Panna

ON THE 83rd's arrival at Llanerch Panna the Red Cross was allocated a Recreation building. Once they had unpacked their equipment the girls commenced painting the walls of the hall, which had faded badly. This task was soon taken out of their hands:

> "Almost every man who entered the building was soon wielding a hammer or paintbrush and before long we found ourselves in fatigues atop ladders painting the walls and rafters along with officers, enlisted men and patients." (A.R.C. 83 G.H. NARA)

Both personnel and patients worked into the early hours to finish the decorating. One patient with local contacts surprised the Red Cross Girls one evening with several eggs, so stopping work at Midnight, the girls threw a 'fried egg and coffee party' for the helpers. Once the room had been painted the girls included into their handicraft programme: repairing and painting furniture; upholstering chairs; and building shelves and cabinets. In July the girls purchased a number of milking stools which could be upholstered for use as seats or painted for use as footstools for those with legs in casts.

One of the patients contributing to the décor at the 83rd was Manny Barrios, a member of the 506th Parachute Infantry Regiment, 101st Infantry Division. He was admitted to hospital in mid-June after being evacuated from Normandy. Several large pieces of shrapnel were embedded between the two tendons at the front of his ankle. By the time he reached the 83rd the wound had become infected and the doctors wanted to amputate the injured leg. After much protestation from Barrios the consultant decided to try cutting away the dead tissue around the wound, a very painful procedure.

After the operation Barrios was confined to a wheelchair and in an attempt to relieve the boredom he learnt to paint with the help of a British volunteer. Once it was seen that he had a talent for painting he was asked to create a mural depicting a naked girl above the bar in the N.C.O. Club. He carried out this task but unfortunately the chaplains on the base took offence to the picture and threatened to have the place shut down if he didn't return and paint some clothes over the figure. He compromised by drawing a semi-transparent veil over the lady. Apparently everyone was happy with the final result.

When Barrios's division was alerted for the invasion of Holland in September 1944 those that were fit enough were recalled from the various hospitals. Barrios felt that he was fit, however the doctor insisted that he could only take on light duties. Unfortunately, once he had been discharged and sent back to his unit, he leapt from the tailgate of a moving truck outside his base, fell awkwardly and reopened the wound on his foot. He was sent straight back to hospital.

The Red Cross Recreation Hall was used for a number of different activities for patients and detachment personnel. One evening a week it was kept open after hours so that the officers and nurses could enjoy listening to classical records while relaxing in the candle and fire light. (The 83rd were able to take advantage of the fireplace built by the 304th before them.)

There was room for the Red Cross to run a craft shop in the Recreation Hall. Patients enjoyed making cigarette lighters from empty shells, lipstick tubes and even aspirin bottles. Picture frames made from leather, plexiglas, string and plastic were also popular. Some of the men were interested in linoleum cutting and the girls planned to utilise this enthusiasm to make greeting cards for the patients to send home.

After D-Day German souvenirs mounted in plastic became the favourite thing to make. A number of the patients had lost their division patches between leaving Europe and arriving at the hospital; the Red Cross was able to supply the materials to embroider new patches when a fresh delivery of craft materials arrived in February 1945. One officer spent the afternoon making his division badge which he wore to a dance at a neighbouring hospital that evening. After embroidering divisional patches some patients branched out into more complex projects, some stitching French landscapes.

Model aeroplanes were also popular craft items in the early part of 1945 but the most popular craft activity on the wards was mat making. The Red Cross reported that:

> "An accident has brought about even more variety in the colour combinations, for interesting flecks of green are appearing in exactly the right places. One of the patients accidentally spilled a can of green paint into one of our boxes of yarn as he was painting. We managed to clean most of it with gasoline but now and then a bit of Irish hue pops up to remind us of the great day. Of course not one drop landed on the green yarn." (A.R.C. 83 G.H. NARA)

May 1945 saw another 'accident' that affected the Red Cross supplies. This time the water tower, which was used for storage by various departments including the Red

Cross, had a burst pipe due to the heavy rain. A large number of supplies were damaged beyond repair although the girls did manage to dry some items out in the sunshine the following day. It was necessary to discard chewing gum, playing cards, cardboard games, Plaster of Paris and cases of matches and cigarettes.

Like the Red Cross units attached to the other hospitals, the 83rd received support from local people and agencies. The W.V.S. was willing to help the girls with any sewing projects and was also able to advise the girls of local resources in the neighbourhood. Sir Charles and Lady Lowther, County heads of St John and British Red Cross came to visit the hospital to see what they could do to help. After a tour of the buildings, the couple had tea with Colonel Norbury. The British Red Cross were able to supply books for the library.

The Red Cross girls made personal visits to the local A.T.S., NAAFI and Women's Land Army headquarters to invite their members to dances organised by themselves and the enlisted men. In June the girls invited a group of A.T.S. girls to tea in the Recreation Hall:

> "After some games and refreshments (typically English) many left the building in small groups to walk around the grounds. Some patients were anxious to show the visitors their own wards, just as one would take friends through a new home." (A.R.C. 83 G.H. NARA)

In July a group of A.T.S. ladies were invited to tea on the grass outside the Recreation Hall and in August the favour was returned when 25 patients visited the A.T.S. hostel. After tea the girls taught the Americans to play cricket.

In October a group of W.A.C.s were invited to the Recreation Hall and the Red Cross noticed that there was a different reception from the patients for this group:

> "American girls here in the E.T.O. always receive a warm reception, but certainly no more heartfelt one than that which these patients gave them, and they returned in kind. After the dance, when clearing up, we found one pair of crutches and two canes lying discarded on top of some furniture piled up in one corner – definite proof that three patients had improved overnight." (A.R.C. 83 G.H. NARA)

Another special guest who visited the 83rd in June 1945 was Joe Louis, the heavy weight boxer. However even more popular with the patients than Joe Louis, were the eleven puppies born on the base in May. The Red Cross took one of the puppies on a tour of the wards.

This had the desired effect as:

> "One patient who had been seriously ill was laughing so uproariously that the ward officer came in to investigate – he said it was the first time the patient had even smiled since his arrival." (A.R.C. 83 G.H. NARA)

In July a group of civilian women from the local area were invited to come and look around the hospital. A number of them expressed an interest in volunteering at the 83rd. The Red Cross decided to train the ladies to take the book carts around the wards, serve in the Recreation Hall as hostesses and package Purple Heart Medals to send home. One lady was an excellent pianist and was able to play for the patients on the ward. Another, who used to be a school teacher, taught the patients craftwork.

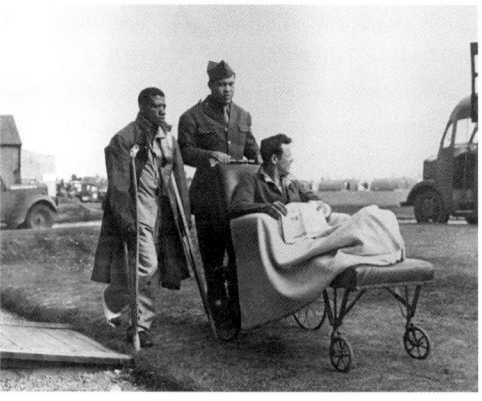

Joe Louis with patients at a hospital 'somewhere in England' (U.S. Archives, NARA)

By November 1944 the number of local people volunteering at the hospital had risen to 25. Thelma Menzer noted that if the local bus was too full for the ladies to get on it they would go to the expense of hiring a taxi, rather than let the patients down.

> "They are very helpful to us and their sincere devotion to the patients and the work is very gratifying. They bring gifts of flowers and fruit from their gardens. If they hear a patient express a desire for 'home-made apple pie' the next time they come they bring the pie." (A.R.C. 83 G.H. NARA)

In August local people started to invite patients to their homes for supper. Recreation worker, Frances Hardy, noted:

> "At one home when the patients were gathered around a tastefully decorated table thrilled with the experience of sitting down once more to the luxury of white linen and shining silver they waited expectantly for the hostess to start eating because they had forgotten which knife to use." (A.R.C. 83 G.H. NARA)

Other activities were organised on and off base by the Red Cross for the patients. On 4 July 1944 there was an Independence Day picnic and Treasure Hunt. The patients congregated outside the Red Cross building, which was decorated with red, white and blue streamers, flowers and giant paper crackers. The first trail of clues was given to the patients, which eventually led them to the baseball diamond where they enjoyed a game and a picnic.

Fishing trips were also popular with the patients; the neuropsychiatric patients were particularly enthusiastic. In August local resident, Captain Williams, ran the event fortnightly. Fortunately there was no shortage of patients volunteering for 'worm detail'. Miss Hardy noted:

> "Though we have brought back very few fish it means a great deal to the men to spend a day on the river bank with hooks and line. …by the end of August

their catch added up to a number of eels, a minnow and a frog." (A.R.C. 83 G.H. NARA)

With the arrival of the better weather the Red Cross were able to organise more trips such as conducted tours of Chester and Colwyn Bay followed by a supper. The patients also had the opportunity to attend the dog races at Chester. The girls organised picnics on the River Dee and Mrs Williams, the owner of the 900 year old Boat Inn, invited ten patients each week to tea. A large group of patients were invited to an August Bank Holiday fair where their team won the tug-o-war. Apparently a British resident was heard to say: "That's what spam'll do for you."

Boat Inn, River Dee

Thomas McConkey, from the 137th General Hospital at Oteley Deer Park wrote home about a village fair he attended where there was a tug-o-war. He informed his family:

> "It was my first opportunity to see a lot of Englishmen and their families gathered together, informally, having fun."

The announcement that there would be a tug-o-war between the British and Americans was immediately followed by the announcer enthusiastically encouraging the U.S. soldiers to line up and then pressing a rope into their hands. McConkey was surprised to learn later that this was the vicar. He described the scene to his family at home:

> "We Americans felt keenly our responsibilities to uphold our national honor, so in short, in a highly disorganised huddle before the battle we tried to organise our attack. Since only one of the G.I.s present had ever been in a tug-o-war (apparently a much neglected sport in America) his mumbled, incoherent instructions about rhythm and team work had little effect so we went into action badly prepared.
>
> However, on sizing up our opponents I felt better. They were almost all 'home guardists', middle aged men, smaller than we, and certainly insignificant looking in any test of brawn. Half of our boys were infantry men, conditioned by months of training; the rest medics, who, while perhaps lacking the brawn, should at least have strong legs from the daily stint of 12 hours on ward duty.
>
> The captain shouted 'Ho' and we started to strain. Because I'm fairly large, and solely on this basis, I was anchor man on the American team, giving me a particularly advantageous position to watch our debacle. It took the little

Englishmen a while to dig in, to get their balance and then they began to exert pressure on our line, as the communiques say. It came in gradual surges and it was felt on our side by a gentle rocking to and fro. We would try to get the 'fro' to come our way but somehow our raw strength couldn't stop that confounded rhythmic pressure. Finally it reached a crescendo, which pulled my feet out their little fox-holes and took me half sprawling, half sliding on my newly cleaned G.I. pants across the dividing line. So they won! As Dad used to say, 'You can't beat the British!'"

In the early part of the following year there was an opportunity for a group of patients from the 83rd to visit some coal mines. The Red Cross workers noted that:

"The coal mine trip was a vigorous one and those that went came back thoroughly exhausted and grimy, but enthusiastic. One patient, who had been a mine foreman in civilian life, went back another day by himself to learn more about British mines." (A.R.C. 83 G.H. NARA)

At the end of the summer the Red Cross organised more events on the base. In September 1944 a pin-up girl contest was held in each ward. Miss Hardy recorded:

"The patients pinned up their choice and a committee of two detachment men and a nurse went through the wards choosing 'Miss Ward …'. Then on Sunday the Pin-Up girl winners in each ward competed for 'Miss 83rd'. One of the judges dropped out so we selected one of the patients from the Free French Forces who speaks no English. We decided that, as a Frenchman, he should be a good judge of beauty, and being unable to speak English, his vote would not be influenced." (A.R.C. 83 G.H. NARA)

At the beginning of December 1944 Christmas preparations at the 83rd commenced. The Red Cross planned to invite a group of orphaned children to the base for Christmas Day. With this in mind one patient drew up plans to scale for a two-storey colonial type dolls house. Sadly he left before he could start on the model but another patient continued the project and others started making furniture.

The Red Cross distributed Christmas trees to the wards.

"Each ward had its own tree no matter how small and of course the decorations had to be improvised. We started by giving each ward an envelope of decorations which consisted of balls made from construction paper and daubed with gold paint, crepe paper twined with tin foil strips that had come as packing in P.X. boxes … By cutting tin cans with curved tin strips we produced shining icicles. Cracked ping-pong balls took on new life with coats of paint and hung from trees." (A.R.C. 83 G.H. NARA)

For the two weeks prior to Christmas the craft programme was centred entirely on Christmas decorations. Some patients made candles from cigarettes and one group produced a string of lights from flashlight bulbs and wire scrounged from 'unknown parts'.

Most of the wards had paper chains or garlands of fringed tissue paper as a background for their decorative schemes. Windows were sprinkled with 'snow' which consisted of cotton, Epsom salts, beer, G.I. scouring powder or soap flakes whipped with an egg beater. Other windows were covered with cut-outs of angels, skiers, trees, bells and Santa Claus.

Large cotton snowballs hung from the roof struts in some wards while others were decorated with large cut out letters spelling 'MERRY CHRISTMAS', 'HAPPY NEW YEAR' or 'NEXT CHRISTMAS AT HOME'. Fireplaces complete with mantle pieces, candles and stockings were featured in several wards. Some patients made wooden frames from packing boxes and some covered tables with red tissue paper and painted on the bricks.

The Red Cross appointed a team of six judges from the enlisted personnel and a husband of one of the British volunteers became the seventh judge. At one time he had judged the gardens of British railway stations so the girls:

> "… felt he was very competent to deal with such an important assignment."
> (A.R.C. 83 G.H. NARA)

Two wards tied for the prize for the best ward which was an ice-cream party and movie. One of the Red Cross staff had been sent an ice-cream mix from home, so after borrowing freezing trays from the Pharmacy, Laboratory and Medical Supply, the ice cream was produced. Chocolate sauce and nuts received in packages from home went to create ice cream sundaes.

The Recreation Hall was also decorated for the season with greens from the estate and Christmas wreaths in every window. At one end of the room one of the Red Cross workers painted two Christmas murals on brown paper: one of Santa and his reindeer and one of angels and a chapel. There was a tree decorated with lights, candy canes and silver icicles and also a snowman made from a huge tin can wrapped in cotton batting. On either side of the door were two large candles made of wrapping paper painted red, in the top were cans which held four real candles, giving the impression of one large flame for the candle.

The British volunteers at the 83rd were invited to a Christmas party in the Officers' Club where small presents such as cans of fruit wrapped in Christmas paper were displayed under the tree. Colonel Norbury, who had contributed to the Christmas gifts, dropped in and chatted with each volunteer while two patients provided the entertainment, singing and playing guitars.

On Christmas Eve a Welsh male voice choir visited the hospital to sing carols in some of the wards and a female choral group, which had arrived at the hospital by mistake, sang in other wards. After the singing the Red Cross workers distributed

Christmas boxes throughout the wards, placing the presents under the trees in each ward. In one ward patients had hung up their stockings at the end of their beds, these were duly filled.

On Christmas Day about fifty orphaned children aged three to eleven arrived at LLanerch Panna from a neighbouring town. Each patient entertained a child for the afternoon. Santa, who was one of the patients, dressed in a patient-made Santa suit, distributed the presents, then one of the nurses put on a marionette show. The Mess Hall provided sandwiches, cocoa, cookies and apples and at the last moment, a box of marshmallows was found in a gift box from home, so there was a marshmallow for each cup of cocoa.

The children visited the hospital again at Easter in March 1945. The Red Cross girls managed to procure enough eggs from the Mess Hall and volunteers between them so that there was one for each patient and the thirty orphans. The patients spent the day boiling and decorating their eggs with dyes from the pharmacy that were usually used in medicines. Designs varied from geometrical designs to portraits of Hitler.

The Recreation Hall was decorated with daffodils, and cut-outs of chicks and rabbits were stuck around the walls. A cross of Calla lilies and ferns secured to plexiglas was placed on the mantelpiece with cherry blossoms around its base.

On Easter Sunday an Easter parade consisting of nine patients adorned with Easter bonnets was held through the wards. One man wore:

> "… a beautifully draped turban fashioned from a G.I. towel and trimmed with fresh flowers. The fact that its wearer continued to smoke a big black cigar throughout the show didn't detract from its daintiness. One 'lovely' wore a mop for a wig topped with a mess kit and trimmed with a red flannel bandage, knife, fork and spoon. Another beauty wore a stocking cap adorned with a hypodermic syringe, ribbons and flowers. The crew strutted through the wards to the tune of 'Easter Parade'." (A.R.C. 83 G.H. NARA)

When the children arrived at the hospital they were paired up with patients who had signed up to be 'big brother' to begin an Easter Egg hunt. After a few noisy games the children were given tea and piled into the bus loaded with gifts from the patients.

The next major event to be celebrated at Llanerch Panna would be V.E. Day.

Chapter 10

Return to Duty – 137th General Hospital, Oteley Deer Park

THE 137th General Hospital, under the commanding officer, Lieutenant Colonel Harry E. Caldwell, replaced the 15th General Hospital at Oteley Deer Park in July 1944. (In February of the following year, Caldwell was promoted to colonel.) Tec. 5 Thomas McConkey, secretary to the Information and Education Officer, Captain Spencer, recorded his first impressions of the area in his letters home:

> "England is delightful and exactly as I have long pictured it, the low, undulating hills, the tiny cottages with the bright red roofs huddling in long rows of uniform design, are certainly the prettiest towns that I have ever seen. I had anticipated narrow twisting lanes running between hedges of verdant boxwood

Tec. 5 Thomas McConkey, 137th General Hospital (J. McConkey)

Tec. 5 Thomas McConkey, 137th General Hospital (J. McConkey)

Enlisted men's billets at 137th (J. McConkey)

and I found them. The charm wasn't exaggerated. There are hundreds of tiny gardens intensely cultivated and carefully tended lying behind every cottage. They have the feeling of being there for generations."

In a later letter McConkey describes a not-so charming feature of England – the rain:

"It is without question ... the most constantly annoying feature of life in the E.T.O. It rains almost every day and it usually gives not the slightest warning, often throwing drops down through shafts of sunlight on a clear airy morning just when people are beginning to thaw out. Mostly the rain doesn't want to wear itself out too soon, so it comes down very gently, often not more than a mist for hours on end – in this way it can spread itself to last for weeks. After some weeks of this sort of thing you automatically wear a raincoat or carry an umbrella, but although we have long since learned to wear raincoats, we have yet to develop the psychological immunity to rain that the English possess. Centuries of living in this spray has hardened them to it so they can take it in its course."

McConkey discovered that British people did not let the weather spoil their social life. One evening he and his friend were due to meet up with two WAAF friends, but when there was a severe storm that knocked out the telephone lines they decided to call it off. Later they discovered that the two girls had cycled the five miles to town in the storm and then had to cycle back when their dates didn't turn up.

Tec. 5 Thomas McConkey on bike (J. McConkey)   *Tec. 5 McConkey with Florence Bright (J. McConkey)*

Within two weeks of arriving at Oteley Deer Park the hospital was treating 1000 patients. It was soon necessary for ward tents to be fixed to the end of wards to increase the bed capacity to 1517. Another large influx of patients took numbers up to 1840 by the end of 1944.

The hospital devised an efficient system for receiving new patients. When the hospital was alerted for the arrival of a train of casualties, a train boarding party comprised of medical officers and representatives from the Registrar's Office proceeded to Shrewsbury to board the train in order to process the patients during

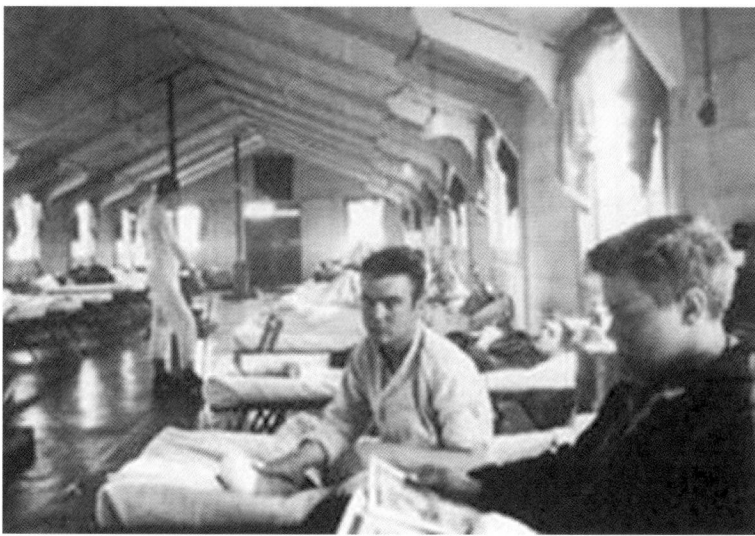

Ward at 137th (J. McConkey)

the last part of their journey to Ellesmere. Before the train arrived at its destination all patients had been classified and assigned to wards. The patients were detrained at Ellesmere and transported by ambulance to Oteley Deer Park where they could be admitted to the previously assigned wards within 25 minutes of arriving at the railway station.

Because of the large number of patients admitted to the hospital, staffing became an issue. To make the staffing shortage worse, skilled personnel from the 137th were sent for combat training to be replacements in the conflict in Europe. The medical personnel were replaced by ex-combat soldiers who had recovered from their wounds but had been classified for limited assignment duty. Few of these men possessed the technical skills required for work in a hospital unit.

Fortunately personnel from six Medical Hospital Ship Platoons were temporarily attached to the hospital for a few days at a time and technicians from the 131st Evacuation Hospital and 81st Field Hospital were attached to the 137th from January to March 1945. The personnel from the latter two hospitals were invaluable for the smooth running of the hospital during the time when it was full to capacity.

The hospital wards were divided between the Medical and Surgical Services. The Surgical Service used seven wards of around thirty beds in addition to winterized tentage of 120 beds. Its function was:

> "... to care for the surgically sick and wounded of the Armed Forces of the United States as well as emergency treatment of Allied personnel." (A.R.C. 137 G.H. NARA)

The department was divided into six sections: General Surgery, Thoracic, EENT, Urological, Physical Therapy and Anaesthesiology.

The 137th was designated a 'Thoracic Surgical Center' for the 804th Hospital Center. It also provided a consultation service for the other hospitals in the group. In most cases the Thoracic Section carried out a rehabilitation programme for its patients which commenced one or two days after surgery with breathing exercises. The first objective was the complete expansion of the lung and this was achieved by an intensive

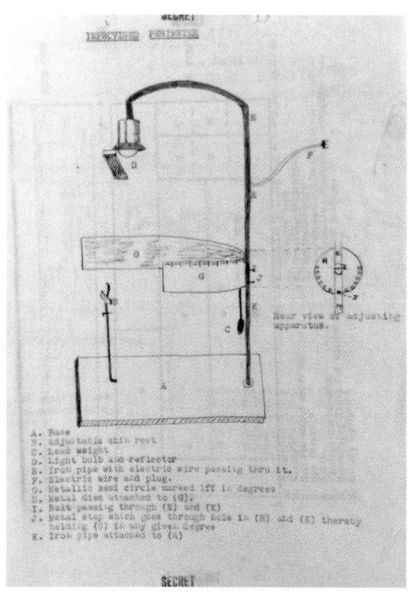

Improvised perimeter designed and made by Optometrist of the 137th (137 G.H. NARA)

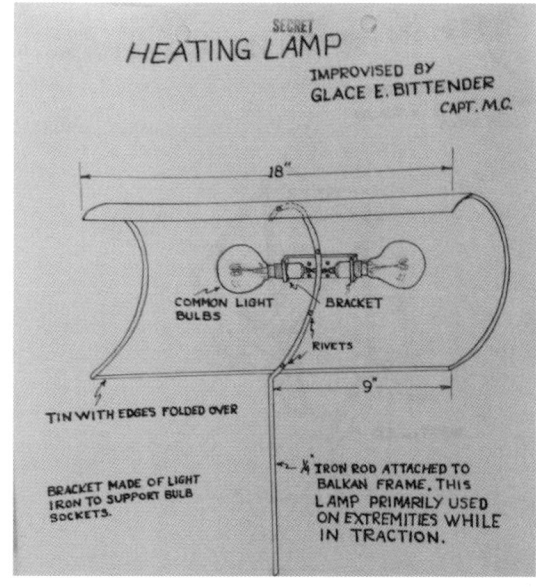

Heating Lamp designed and made at the 137th (137 G.H. NARA)

programme of thoracic exercises to develop the muscles of the chest and fully expand the lungs.

The EENT section of the Surgical Service was composed of two medical officers and five enlisted men. In addition to the equipment provided by the Medical Supply the optometrists of the clinic designed and made a perimeter tangent screen, visual acuity charts and portable ward treatment which were used in the section. The perimeter mapped out and charted the field of vision. It was constructed from salvaged material including pieces of wood and iron. The total cost of manufacturing it was about 10 cents, giving the U.S. Government a saving of $199.90

The Orthopaedic Section took care of fractures and joint injuries as well as general orthopaedic lesions. Specialist wards were established to care for certain types of injuries in order to standardize and facilitate the surgical and nursing care. This section specialised in the treatment of compound fractures of the humerus with skeletal traction by means of a kirschner wire through the olecranon. Either overhead or side arm traction was used depending on which position provided better alignment of the fragments. Captain Glace E. Bittenbender designed a portable radiant heat generator for this section as well as a special frame which fitted on the operating room stretcher for transportation of the patient to and from the operating theatre.

The Physical Therapy Department, which was run as part of the Orthopaedic Section, had the use of a clinic and a remedial gymnasium. In addition to the authorised equipment improvised exercise apparatus was constructed by the enlisted men of the department.

One of the patients to be admitted to the Surgical Section at the 137th was Pfc John Sweeney of the 16th Infantry Regiment, 1st U.S. Infantry Division. He arrived at Oteley Deer Park on 3 October 1944 for the treatment of an injury sustained on 25 September (Sweeney had previously been injured in the arm and leg on D-Day on Omaha Beach.)

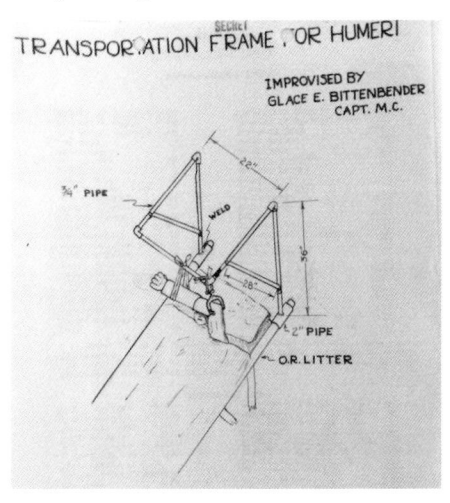

Transportation frame devised by personnel of the 137th (137 G.H. NARA)

On 25 September the regiment was launching a night attack on Germany when Sweeney fell into a bomb crater and injured his knee. He was unable to take part in the attack and spent the night in a deserted German uniform factory waiting for a jeep to pick him up and take him for medical attention. After spending a few days at the battalion aid station Sweeney was transferred to a hospital in Southern England. From there he travelled to the 137th where he received treatment until 26 January. From Oteley Deer Park he was transferred to the 10th Replacement Depot at Pheasey Farms from where he was assigned to the Air Force Replacement Pool.

Another patient to be treated by the Surgical Section was Pfc Melvin Truman who arrived at the 137th on 31 December 1944 by C47 via Rednal Airfield. Truman, a truck driver, had arrived in France on 1 December. He had driven in a convoy across France to Luxembourg where the Germans were making a big push. Strafing from German planes on route lost the convoy three trucks and eleven men. On 20 December the men drove to Arlen, Belgium to take part in the Battle of the Bulge. Truman was wounded on Christmas Eve and taken to the 102nd Evacuation Hospital in Luxembourg City. On 29 December he was evacuated by air to the 104th General Hospital in Paris and then on the 31st to the 137th. He remained at the 137th until 18 April when he was also sent to the 10th Replacement Depot. On 22 April he was returned to his outfit in Nuremburg.

Troops from the 3rd Battalion, 16th Infantry Regiment and 1st U.S. Infantry Division take a rest on Omaha's eastern extremity, shortly after H-Hour (U.S. Army Signal Corps Archives, NARA)

Medal of Honor recipient, Paul J. Wiedorfer, who also took part in the Battle of the Bulge, was admitted to the 137th in March 1945. Twenty-three year old Wiedorfer with his unit, 318th Infantry Regiment of the 80th Infantry Division, was sent to rescue American troops trapped in Bastogne. On 25 December 1944 he and his platoon were advancing across a clearing in the forest near Chaumont when machine guns began firing at them from two camouflaged emplacements. The soldiers dropped to the ground behind a small ridge, pinned down by the German attack. Wiedorfer ran in to the open clearing and threw a grenade into one of the emplacements, killing the remaining Germans with his rifle. He then turned and attacked the second gun emplacement. One of the German gunners was wounded and the other six immediately surrendered. Shortly after this both the platoon leader and sergeant were wounded so Wiedorfer assumed command of the platoon, leading it forward until the mission was accomplished. He was subsequently promoted to Staff Sergeant.

Melvin Truman

Two months later, when crossing the River Saar in Germany Wiedorfer's unit came under mortar fire. The soldier next to him was killed instantly and Wiedorfer was struck by shrapnel. The blast injured his legs and a hand. He was evacuated to the 137th where he was placed in traction.

Iscoyd House (M. Collins)

Emblem of 82nd General Hospital (Q. Nicola)

View of 82nd General Hospital from water tower (Q. Nicola)

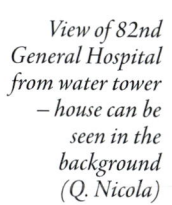

View of 82nd General Hospital from water tower – house can be seen in the background (Q. Nicola)

i

View of 82nd General Hospital from water tower (Q. Nicola)

Another view of 82nd General Hospital from water tower (Q. Nicola)

Medical Supply building (Q. Nicola)

Fire truck at Fire station (Q. Nicola)

82nd G.H. buildings (Q. Nicola)

*Trees in grounds of Iscoyd Park showing carvings by American soldiers
(as well as some by Poles carved later) (M.Collins)*

Black engineer unit working on winterizing tents at 82nd General Hospital (Q. Nicola)

Patients in open walkways outside wards (Q. Nicola)

Playing tennis at Iscoyd Park (Q. Nicola)

German prisoner patients being unloaded at Malpas Railway Station (Q. Nicola)

Prisoner patients arriving at Iscoyd Park (Q. Nicola)

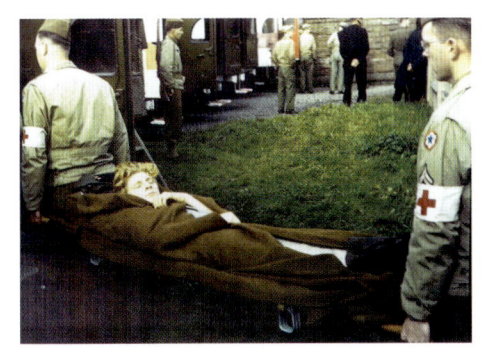

Litter patient (Q. Nicola)

Prisoner patients boarding bus to take them to Iscoyd Park (Q. Nicola)

Above & below: Prisoner patients boarding bus to take them to Iscoyd Park (Q. Nicola)

German prisoner patients being unloaded at Malpas Railway Station (Q. Nicola)

Right & below: Prisoner patients arriving at Iscoyd Park (Q. Nicola)

Stars and Stripes flying at half-mast at Iscoyd Park for the death of President Roosevelt (Q. Nicola)

St George's Catholic Church, Whitchurch

The Victoria Hotel, Whitchurch

Huts in use on Penley Industrial Estate (M. Collins)

Hut at Halston Hall (M. Collins)

Hut at Halston Hall (M. Collins)

Hut at Oteley Deer Park (M. Collins)

RETURN TO DUTY

Wiedorfer was unaware that he had been nominated for a Medal of Honor for his Christmas bravery until a fellow patient at the 137th saw it mentioned in the Stars and Stripes Newspaper and informed him. On 29 May he was presented with the medal by Brigadier General Egmont F. Koenig, while still in his hospital bed. A military band played in the ward to mark the occasion. He also received two Purple Heart Medals. Afterwards he complained that he was embarrassed by all the fuss.

On 11 June Wiedorfer returned to his hometown of Baltimore where a ticker tape parade was given in his honour. His injuries caused him to spend three more years undergoing hospital treatment. In the 1990s a man came to his home and offered to polish his medal. While pretending to clean it he replaced it with an imitation. Eventually the medal was returned to him; the thief served eighteen months in prison.

Paul J. Wiedorfer

The Medical Service of the 137th treated a large number of trench foot patients. The cases admitted during the latter part of 1944 were more acute, possibly due to the fact that they had not received treatment prior to arriving at the hospital. It was necessary to return a number of the more severe cases of trench foot to the Zone of the Interior.

The Medical Service also dealt with cases of dermatology and Venereal Disease. On the 29th of each month all enlisted personnel of the Medical Detachment were examined for Venereal Disease; the hospital was pleased to find that the V.D. rate was low.

Patients with venereal and skin diseases were kept in wards solely for this purpose, so that any infectious diseases could be isolated and the staff on these wards could become more specialised in the treatment of the diseases. The hospital found a camaraderie between the patients in these wards that they might not have had in the general wards, particularly as some skin complaints were disfiguring. The most common disease on the dermatological ward was scabies. It was estimated that since the hospital began functioning at Oteley Deer Park twelve percent of the enlisted men of the medical department caught it, consequently it was necessary to provide precautionary advice to prevent the disease spreading further.

The Detachment Commander of the Medical Detachment was also the Provost Marshall for the area. His duties included: providing for post security; policing of Ellesmere; and guarding and supervising garrison prisoners. Other services also performed by the Military Police in the area were: bicycle registration and color guard.

The post guard house was comprised of a cell with capacity for eight prisoners plus living quarters for the men detailed as military policemen. Because of the shortage of man-power towards the end of the war the force was reduced from twelve men to five. To supplement the unit a duty roster was drawn up from the 137th to provide three men for gate guard duty each night and four men to patrol Ellesmere. The auxiliary military policemen also acted as auxiliary firemen on call for the 24 hours of the day that they were on duty.

There was also a Neuro-Psychiatric section at the 137th. For the period of July to December 1944 the N.P. section occupied seven wards of forty-five beds (including adjoining tents). On 11 January 1945 this section was moved to the part of the hospital which had been designated for infectious diseases. This meant that the whole section was consolidated into one relatively compact area, with one supply room, one patients' clothing storage room, a central nurses' office and central messing facilities. Because of the increased number of psychotic and suicidal patients admitted to the hospital it was necessary to establish a 'closed ward' since no locked ward facilities were available. The Red Cross took recreational crafts equipment into this ward and also showed movies twice a week.

N.P. patients would spend on average about two months at the 137th. The time period was divided into four sections:

- Admissions – New patients were evaluated and either sent to the treatment section, a specialised hospital or the Zone of the Interior if it was felt that treatment would not be successful in returning the patient to duty in the military. Combat exhaustion cases not treated successfully at the 137th, but with the potential to be rehabilitated were sent to the Neurosis Center. Psychotic patients and aggressive constitutional psychopathic cases were transferred to the 96th Neuro-Psychiatric Hospital at Brickbarns, Malvern. Disciplinary problems and patients falling under the classification of 'unwilling soldiers' were transferred to the SOS Recovery Center where, in the majority of cases, satisfactory results were obtained.

- Treatment – Patients received amytal insulin therapy, narco-analysis, abreaction and individual and group therapy.

- Convalescent – Patients were re-evaluated then either given additional treatment, transferred out of hospital or sent to the Rehabilitation Department. Individual and group therapy was continued within this section. Patients convalescing in the N.P. Section were also given tasks around the hospital such as folding dressings for the Surgical Section.

- Rehabilitation – Patients were assigned to tents and placed under more 'military' conditions. The schedule included calisthenics, regularly assigned hospital duties, road marches, athletics and reorientation discussions. At the end of this process each soldier was evaluated then sent to either full or limited duty, returned for continued rehabilitation or transferred to the Zone of the Interior.

A separate wing of the hospital was set up for the use of the Rehabilitation Section in January 1945. Due to the acute shortage of beds this section was reduced to just thirty patients. In February it was increased to 120 and in March more hospital space was freed up so that capacity could be increased to 150 beds.

RETURN TO DUTY

Orientations, lectures, training films, basketball and volley ball were included in the rehabilitation programme. Formal Retreat Parade with the entire company assembled alongside hospital personnel was held once a week. Decorations were awarded to rehabilitation patients during this ceremony. On 3 May 1945 this section officially closed as the emphasis shifted from 'return to duty' to 'return to the Zone of the Interior'.

Towards the end of the hostilities in Europe a contingent of American Prisoners of War arrived at the 137th. Tec. 5 McConkey wrote home:

> "Some of them were almost as bad as the walking skeletons you saw in the pictures. They are here now getting back some of their normal weight. Naturally they are very bitter."

From January 1945 the hospital authorities began to look forward to the end of the hostilities in Europe. McConkey wrote home on 24 January:

> "For the first time in several months there is an exhilarating, lively spirit of victory in the air. Everywhere on the wards, in the clinics, among patients and members of the detachment alike you hear the word 'Russians' spoken in tones ranging from terrific enthusiasm to prayerful hopefulness. Bets are being laid that Berlin will fall by mid-next month or before."

Planning for the post-hostilities Army Education Programme commenced in January 1945 with a talk given by Captain Arthur Cohane, explaining the post V.E. Day educational programme. Captain Cohane had previously attended the I.E. School in London. Following the talk, questionnaires were distributed to all permanent personnel so that a file of data about pre-war education and experience and expectations of post-war jobs could be collated and a suitable post-war programme prepared.

In March McConkey mentions in letters home that he has been given 'full-speed ahead' to plan the post-war training programme and as a result he had little time to read or write home. (Personnel from the 137th, including McConkey, attended the 6819th Army Information Staff School during the week of 7 May 1945.)

Educational programme at the 137th being planned (J. McConkey)

Both personnel and patients were given the opportunity to study various courses which would help them in the post-war world. A number of patients looked for programmes of study which would give them extra high school or college credits needed for diplomas or degrees. Arrangements were made with the Denbighshire Technical College in Wrexham for G.I.s to study various subjects such as chemistry, typing, economics and welding.

In March programmes of language instruction were commenced at the 137th with classes in French, Russian, Spanish and Italian scheduled along with a literacy course. Classes began with reasonable numbers in attendance:

> "… which rapidly fell off with the advent of pleasant weather, until, after four weeks all classes were cancelled due to lack of attendance." (A.R.C. 137 G.H. NARA)

The Information and Education Officer also sought to keep both patients and personnel informed on the progress of the war by producing a 'Know Your War' bulletin board on which maps, clippings and pictures were posted on a daily basis. In addition to this Captain Spencer chaired a weekly discussion forum where the men could discuss topics such as: 'Do you want your wife to work after the war' and 'Labor Unions in the Post-War World'.

Chapter 11

More than Medicine and Surgery – 137th General Hospital, Oteley Deer Park

COLONEL CALDWELL, Commanding Officer of the 137th General Hospital, felt that it was important that the men of the detachment should have recreational facilities available to them. At the beginning of 1945 he noted in the official records that the men were becoming increasingly susceptible to illness because of overwork and fatigue due to the excessive patient load.

There was a dayroom provided for the enlisted men on the base for use during off-duty time. It was equipped with a billiard table, ping-pong tables, writing tables and a radio. It had a bar in one wing and a dance floor and fireplace in the opposite wing.

A number of sports were played at the 137th. Corporal Henry Goerke built a tennis court on base, there were already two softball and one hard ball diamonds, three volley ball courts and one hard ball court. Two horseshoe courts were set up outside the Red Cross Recreation Hall. Golf and badminton were also played on the base.

Softball and baseball were the most popular sports organised by the Special Service Section. A unit softball team was established by Tec. 4 Earl Forbes and entered into the Hospital Center League. An Officers' Softball League was also composed with teams from the 804th Hospital Center. On average, games were played twice a week. Within the hospital Captain William Hoffman organised a unit league comprised of four teams: Medical, Surgical, Administrative and Officers. Each team played twice weekly. The unit also had a baseball team run by Tec. 4 Edward Sieber. Patients wearing wine coloured dressing gowns were often to be seen spectating at the various sporting events.

U.S. Servicemen in the Wrexham area took part in various sporting events that the public were invited to watch. On 27 May 1944 two American Baseball teams: 'The Linesmen' and 'The Red Legs' took part in a charity baseball match at Wrexham

BASEBALL

TO-MORROW'S MATCH AT WREXHAM RACECOURSE

THE LINESMEN v. RED LEGS.

Two American teams—the Linesmen and the Red Legs—will visit Wrexham Racecourse to-morrow (Saturday) at 3 p.m. to take part in a charity baseball match. Great interest is being taken in this event and to enable spectators who are not familiar with the game to follow the play we have pleasure in publishing the following notes kindly sent by a friend.

THE GAME OF SOFTBALL.

The game of baseball is called America's pastime. It requires gloves for all players and a large padded mitt because when the man at bat connects with the ball it sometimes travels as far as 450 feet. The game of softball was devised to be played on a smaller field with less equipment. The ball used in the game is larger than the regular baseball and the bat used is smaller. This does not allow the ball to travel as far or as fast and the ball can be caught with the bare hands, if no gloves are available.

Ten men are required for each side. The game is played on a field with part of it called the infield and part of it called the outfield. The infield is in the shape of a square and each corner has a name. The player when trying to run starts at homeplate and running counter-clockwise goes to first base, second base, third base and then back to home-plate. The catcher stands behind home-plate. The pitcher stands between home-plate and second base, facing home-plate. The players occupying the bases are designated first baseman, second baseman, third baseman. Between second base and third base is a fielder called shortstop. The outfield has four players called fielders. There is a right fielder, left fielder, centre fielder and short centre fielder. The outfielders are farther away from the baseman and field the balls that go outside of the infield.

The game is divided into innings and seven innings comprise a game unless the score is tied at the end of seven innings, at which times the teams play on until one team has more runs than the other at the end of an additional inning. Each inning is divided into a said inning. First one team is at bat until three men are out. During this time the other team is in the field. They then switch around and the team that was in the field comes to bat and the team that was at bat is in the field.

The batter stands alongside home-plate facing the pitcher. The pitcher throws the ball to the catcher, and the man at bat tries to hit it. If the ball passes over the home-plate between the knees and shoulders of the batter without the batter being able to hit the ball it is called a "strike." If the batter swings and misses the ball also is said called a strike. If the ball does not pass over the home-plate between the knees and shoulders of the batter it is called a "ball." There is an umpire who stands behind the pitcher and decides whether it is a ball or strike. Each batter is allowed three strikes before he is called out. If the batter hits the ball before he has three strikes and the ball is not caught by a player in the field or is not fielded and thrown to a base before the man is allowed to make a base and this is not called an out. The farther the man at bat hits the ball the more bases he can take. If four balls are thrown before three strikes the man is allowed to advance to first base. There are three out in each inning. When three outs occur the side at bat then goes into the field.

If a man gets to first base and another man gets to bat and hits the ball the man on first takes second base and then third base or on to home base if he can make it. When a man's bat goes all round the four bases it is called a run. If a batter has reached first base and the next batter gets four balls before three strikes are called on him this is called a "walk." The man at bat goes to first base and the man on first base automatically goes to second base.

A "hit" is when the batter hits the ball and gets on base. A "fly ball" is one that goes up in the air. A "grounder" is when the ball rolls along the ground. A "foul ball" is when the ball is hit but does not go inside the playing field. The field will be marked off to show its boundaries and each one will be marked.

An announcer will be at the game to-morrow to explain the play as it progresses.

Wrexham Leader 26/5/44

ENTERTAINMENTS AT U.S. HOSPITALS

During the Christmas season Mr. Llewelyn Davies of Wrexham, was busy organising the departure and return of Welsh choirs or drama companies to and from American hospitals in other counties.

Mr. Davies, secretary of Wrexham Entertainments Committee, has since the summer, with the help of the British Council and the Ministry of Information, arranged a regular programme for American hospitals by fifteen Welsh choral, instrumental and variety and drama parties.

A choir of eighteen girls, conducted by Mr. Moses Edwards, Gwersyllt, near Wrexham, spent most of Christmas Eve singing in every ward of one hospital. Bro Alyn Glee Singers, of Treuddyn, Flintshire, gave a choral service at another hospital. The Coedpoeth Girls' Choir, conducted by Miss Hilda Edwards, have a hospital all their own to entertain, while Mr. Lloyd Evans, Brymbo, took a company to give Dickensian character studies.

The most popular of all is the Cefn Mawr Male Voice Choir, near Wrexham. It consists of miners, factory workers, shopkeepers, brickworks employees, and joiners. Their conduction is Mr. Wilfrid Butler, building contractors' clerk and grocer, of Acrefair. Americans at one hospital have asked the choir for its photographed signed by the conductor, and for recordings of its songs. When the choir visited this hospital on Christmas Eve it took to the patients 300 printed photographs. It toured the wards pulling along a piano on wheels. One factory permits night-shift choir members to turn in to work after the shift has started. Miners at Llay Main Colliery, ten miles away, return home from a concert, perhaps at mid-night, and leave home again shortly after 4 p.m. to go to their work.

On Christmas Day two American hospitals entertained a party of Wrexham children whose fathers are in the war, and a party of children from an orphanage.

Wrexham Leader 11/5/44

Racecourse. There was a long article in the Wrexham Leader explaining the rules of baseball and softball finishing with the comment:

> "An announcer will be at the game tomorrow to explain the play as it progresses." (Wrexham Leader 27/5/44)

In August of that year the racecourse played host to an Inter-Allied athletic contest between the British and American armies. It was a close run contest, won by the British Army by 34 points against 26.

The Chaplain's Office at the 137th covered the spiritual welfare of the patients and personnel. The three main faiths represented by G.I.s and nurses from the 137th had the shared use of the chapel on base. The Protestant Chaplain used it for two Sunday services, one 'Round table' discussion and one mid-week devotion and prayer service. The Catholic Chaplain conducted daily Mass and Rosary with a Benediction and Novena to the Lady of the Miraculous Medal weekly. Jewish services were held on Friday evenings.

The chaplains also visited the patients on the wards and conducted private interviews with those who requested them. Often they were called on to write letters home; notify soldiers of sudden bereavements and losses sustained in the death of loved ones at home and on the front; and write letters of condolence to families whose relatives had died in the hospital. On occasions the chaplains received requests to work off base: preaching at local churches; addressing civic meetings; visiting schools and colleges; accompanying convoys of patients to ships; and participating in ordination services.

The main responsibility of the five girls attached to the Red Cross unit at the 137th was to cater for the recreational and social welfare of the patients. The girls stated that their main purpose was to:

> "… meet immediate needs. These needs are both material and emotional. The serviceman can expect a Red Cross House where he can play cards, games, ping-pong. There will be dances and parties. There will be reading material and writing paper. There will be a set-up where he can obtain a loan of a pound for a pass when his pay has been held up because of being transferred about. … The serviceman can expect to go to a Red Cross worker to help arrange accommodation for a guest in an over-crowded town. He can also expect that, through the Red Cross, he will be entertained by local show units while he is hospitalised." (A.R.C. 137 G.H. NARA)

In January 1945, when the patient quota was at its highest, Doris Chatfield, the Assistant Field Director, wrote:

> "If we didn't like our patients so well there are times when we'd be tempted to look upon them as a nightmare. Regardless of how many of them are at hand

at one moment there are always herds more looming up in the back ground. We haven't got enough chairs. We haven't got enough workers to meet the numerous requests for services on the wards: letter writing, craft work, locating brothers in other hospitals, showing movies and helping with more serious problems. We haven't got enough room in our workshop, and four ping-pong tables in constant use doesn't begin to meet the demand. We haven't got enough space in our office for the unending procession of patients who stream through, each one with perfectly reasonable, but hard-to-answer questions, and we haven't got enough time to find the answers." (A.R.C. 137 G.H. NARA)

Another pull on Red Cross time was outside telephone calls. Calls couldn't be received on the wards so it was necessary for the Red Cross to pass on messages, although they drew the line at passing the message to tell:

"… someone called Mac, who's tall and has a gold tooth in front to meet Joyce at the gate at seven." (A.R.C. 137 G.H. NARA)

To help with the workload the Red Cross enlisted volunteers from the local area. Around twelve local ladies visited the hospital once a week to spend three and a half hours rolling bandages. Another volunteer came to the base two afternoons a week to help out in the lounge-writing letters sewing badges and wrapping packages for the patients. Two ladies took over the book cart service, delivering books to patients on the wards. The hospital provided transport for the volunteers.

Local people also visited the hospital to entertain the patients. A Welsh choir came to sing on the wards and a children's scavenger orchestra came to play their home made instruments. The Ministry of Information in Wrexham sent in speakers who would speak on a couple of wards in the afternoon and in the theatre in the evening.

In September a programme of encouraging G.I.s to visit English homes was initiated. The W.V.S. prepared a list of families who offered to act as host to a G.I. Tec.

Mrs Ransome, outside the gatehouse (J. McConkey) *Rector Pye and his family (J. McConkey)*

5 Thomas McConkey found the local people to be very friendly. In his letters he mentions with fondness Mrs Ransome who lived in the gatehouse to the deer park and Rector Pye and his family.

Trips were also arranged to places of interest by the Red Cross and Special Service Section; arrangements were made with hotels in Llandudno and Llangollen to accommodate the men for two days at a time. Tec. 5 McConkey was one of the detachment personnel who had the opportunity to visit Llangollen once the patient load had decreased. He described it to his family in a letter:

> "A tiny little resort and farmer's market down by a swift running rapid in the Dee River."

He was impressed by the castle (possibly Castell Dinas Bran) about which he noted:

> "It stands on a lofty pinnacle of rock, two sides of which fall a full hundred feet on a straight cliff, the other two sides being protected with a moat."

While sitting on the grass by the castle McConkey writes that he and his colleague became a target for three small boys who began to pelt them with moss, but they were soon appeased with the offer of chewing gum.

McConkey was also in a group that had the opportunity to visit Liverpool. He described the cathedral there as a 'truly magnificent pile' in his letters back home. The visit included a

Michael Levich of the 137th on a bike (J. McConkey)

service in the cathedral with a sermon 'not more than six minutes', much to McConkey's relief, although he noted in his letter that he enjoyed the singing and pageantry of the service:

> "The young voices of the white robed boys, sharp against the black oak panels of the choir stalls and the deeper voices of the adult men, rose in anthems that at many points in the service almost carried me off to never-never land, or at least back into the middle ages."

While in Liverpool the men went to watch Tranmere Rovers play Everton at Goodison Park Football Ground. McConkey noted that they played 'with a skill rarely seen in America soccer'. After a goalless first half, Tranmere scored five minutes into the second half.

Thomas McConkey with Marion Finkle and Mari Graysman in New Brighton, on the Wirral, near Liverpool (J. McConkey)

> "…sinking a shot into the net which no goalie, no matter how good, could have stopped since it was above his head and moved at almost bullet-like speed."

However, before the end of the game Everton were able to 'put over two tricky ones' and the game finished 2-1 to Everton. Towards the end of the war when the patient load had dropped more it was possible for the personnel to go further afield and McConkey was able to visit relatives in Northern Ireland.

The Red Cross found the social case load heavy at the 137th, particularly when the hospital was full to capacity in the early part of 1945. They were involved in sorting out relationship problems such as unmarried fathers; destitute and pregnant wives; divorcees who didn't understand the paperwork they were given; fiancées who needed a priest's statement of freedom to marry and patients whose army authorisation to marry had been left behind on the Siegfried Line.

The Red Cross also worked to help the patients face the emotional problems caused by their injuries. Some had lost limbs; others had lost confidence in their recovery; there were patients with brothers killed in action; men who were too ashamed to tell their parents that they were receiving neuro-psychiatric treatment and patients that were facing returning to the combat zone. On this subject one of the patients told Miss Chatfield that the second trip to the front:

> "... was a little like a second honeymoon, the essential element – adventure into the unknown – was lacking." (A.R.C. 137 G.H. NARA)

A large number of the patients had emotional problems caused by their combat experience. One man, who had never owned a gun before the war and had been a pacifist in civilian life, had unexpectedly been made a platoon leader as he was the only N.C.O. left in his platoon after a battle. The very night that he was made sergeant he had received a back injury and was sent to the 137th. Although he was very quiet on arrival, eventually the Red Cross worker was able to encourage him to express some of the horror that he felt through painting and model making. This helped him to open up and talk about his experiences.

Another case study involved a fiancée of one of the patients who was trying to contact him because she was pregnant. The patient told the Red Cross that he 'wanted to do his duty' but was struggling to write to the girl. The Red Cross were able to arrange for the girl to visit the hospital so that they could talk and arrange the wedding. The patient stated that he:

> "... was glad that there was an organisation like the Red Cross that could help a fellow along." (A.R.C. 137 G.H. NARA)

In a further case the Red Cross received information that the father of a patient who was awaiting transportation back to the U.S. was terminally ill. The girls managed to get the patient's Z.I. date pushed forward through working with the military authorities. The Red Cross found that when they presented sound reasons for having a patient given priority on the Z.I. list or being transferred to another hospital in the U.K. the Registrar's Office would willingly make the necessary arrangements. They reported that:

> "From start to finish we've had a more than satisfactory degree of cooperation from the hospital unit and this is on the sound basis of their own conviction that patients need something more than medicine and surgery. ... Medical Officers are never too busy – and they're always busy – to give us a report on a patient's condition and a number of them call our attention to particular patients who might use our services.
>
> In general there seems to be a higher than average awareness of individual needs. ... It's no wonder that the patients trail back to spend at the hospital their last 48 hour pass from the Replacement Depot before they return to combat." (A.R.C. 137 G.H. NARA)

Some of the social work carried out by the Red Cross involved replying to health and welfare inquiries from family members who had not heard from their relatives and were concerned about their injuries. Miss Chatfield was surprised at:

"... the percentage of patients who don't know how serious their injuries are."
(A.R.C. 137 G.H. NARA)

This was often because the patients were too afraid to ask the doctors. In these circumstances the Red Cross was able to direct the appropriate medical officers to talk to and reassure the patients.

A number of the patients with emotional problems found craftwork therapeutic. The most popular activity at the 137th was jewellery making, with leather work a close second. The patients also enjoyed card weaving with looms made by the utilities department from scrap lumber and card that had been used as packing in the Special Service kits of books. On the wards the patients made model aeroplanes, aircraft carriers and ships. Semi-bed patients also enjoyed creating Egyptian card woven belts.

The girls were able to adapt one of their store rooms for use as a workshop. A small tool bar with electric plug sockets was built in, so that soldering irons could be used. The room was open from 1.30 to 4.30 p.m. each day and one of the patients took responsibility for the signing in and out of tools as previous to this a number of tools had gone missing.

Towards the end of 1944 a new craft was created, a patient in traction had asked the Red Cross to design a bootie for his foot that was in traction, because his toes were cold. The girls designed a three piece shoe from pieces of felt that fitted above the ankle and were held in place with shoe laces. The patients made them with two and three toned effect with their initials embroidered on the toes.

The Red Cross also organised social events on the base. In August 1944 the girls held two dances. The first had a Hawai'ian theme and WAAFs from a nearby camp were invited as guests. As each girl entered the room she was presented with crepe paper lei and flowers for her hair. The second dance was an August birthday party with a Zodiac theme. This time a group of A.T.S. girls were invited.

V-mail sent home by Tec. 5 McConkey in November (J. McConkey)

Copies of 'Hit Kit' (Author's collection)

Other parties organised by the Red Cross had themes of: Carnival, School Days, The Club Moderne and American Football.

Thanksgiving was an 'At Home' evening. Cider and doughnuts were served in the lounge and the activity was singing. Once all the songs from 'Hit Kit' had been sung the men sang all their old favourites and finished up with the National Anthem.

> "Everyone went home hoarse, full of cider and doughnuts, and as contented as men away from home can be." (A.R.C. 137 G.H. NARA)

As Christmas 1944 approached packages for the men and women of the 137th started arriving. McConkey wrote home to describe the ritual of opening a parcel on base.

> "Here they are opened under the envious eyes of the fellows with many an Oh! and Ah! And finally passed around the gang leaving you in many cases the recipient of only the wrapping and a few sprigs of decorative holly. However no-one moans the rapid passing of his Christmas box in this manner for there will be many boxes and much sharing, so that over a period of days he will probably eat more from other sources than he ever received alone!"

Three days before Christmas the Red Cross finished installing a public address system with outlets on all wards and messes. McConkey and a colleague were given the responsibility of broadcasting to the hospital over the Christmas Season. Their studio was the utility room in the Headquarters building and they shared it with mops, brooms and buckets. In his letters home McConkey writes:

> "So mostly we've played and replayed every Christmas carol record we could conveniently lay our hands on, plus working into special programmes everyone who 'claimed' he or she could sing carols. It has been pretty successful though, with a good response from the wards for specific requests. Lots of the requests have been for 'hot' and 'jive' and since we now have an adequate supply we spend at least two hours nightly playing discs interspersed with wise cracks, remarks about the staff, trick effects and generally horsing around in the studio."

Just before Christmas the Red Cross went to collect a number of tops of larch trees for the hospital. (The trees were being cut down to use as pit props in a coal mine.) The girls recorded:

> "We went after fifty small ones and came back with sixty large ones." (A.R.C. 137 G.H. NARA)

Each tree was large enough to fit floor to ceiling. This made the job of decorating them more challenging. Each ward decorated their own tree, the Red Cross supplied coloured paper but the men had to find the other materials themselves. They used everything they could find from corn-cob pipes to medicine bottles filled with coloured liquid. McConkey wrote home:

> "Although there were no ornaments available, paper cut outs, strings of popcorn, make-shift dolls, holly and fir tree branches in the form of crosses, stars etc., ornamented each ward and tree. Liberal quantities of water colours were used to place artificial snow on trees, windows, floors and on the patients themselves, which will take much scrubbing to remove."

The best decorated ward had the prize of a party with the A.T.S. as guests. The prize was won by the Contagion Ward, unfortunately it was necessary to remove the most highly contagious patients before the party could go ahead.

On Christmas Eve the 137th held a children's Christmas party, the high spot of which was the distribution of candy collected from patients and staff. Some of the children had not tasted chocolate since the beginning of the war; others refused the ice cream as it was 'too cold'.

ENTERTAINMENTS AT U.S. HOSPITALS

During the Christmas season Mr. Llewelyn Davies of Wrexham, was busy organising the departure and return of Welsh choirs or drama companies to and from American hospitals in other counties.

Mr. Davies, secretary of Wrexham Entertainments Committee, has since the summer, with the help of the British Council and the Ministry of Information, arranged a regular programme for American hospitals by fifteen Welsh choral, instrumental and variety and drama parties.

A choir of eighteen girls, conducted by Mr. Moses Edwards, Gwersyllt, near Wrexham, spent most of Christmas Eve singing in every ward of one hospital. Bro Alyn Glee Singers, of Treuddyn, Flintshire, gave a choral service at another hospital. The Coedpoeth Girls' Choir, conducted by Miss Hilda Edwards, have a hospital all their own to entertain, while Mr. Lloyd Evans, Brymbo, took a company to give Dickensian character studies.

The most popular of all is the Cefn Mawr Male Voice Choir, near Wrexham. It consists of miners, factory workers, shopkeepers, brickworks employees, and joiners. Their conduction is Mr. Wilfrid Butler, building contractors' clerk and grocer, of Acrefair. Americans at one hospital have asked the choir for its photograph signed by the conductor, and for recordings of its songs. When the choir visited this hospital on Christmas Eve it took to the patients 300 printed photographs. It toured the wards pulling along a piano on wheels. One factory permits night-shift choir members to turn in to work after the shift has started. Miners at Llay Main Colliery, ten miles away, return home from a concert, perhaps at mid-night, and leave home again shortly after 4 p.m. to go to their work.

On Christmas Day two American hospitals entertained a party of Wrexham children whose fathers are in the war, and a party of children from an orphanage.

Wrexham Leader 29/12/1944

Christmas 1944 at the 137th (J. McConkey)

On the evening of Christmas Eve there was a concert in the chapel. After the service everyone went carolling along the ramps of the hospital, finishing off at the Red Cross Hall for refreshments. For the first time the girls had a mixed group in the building – patients, detachment men, officers, local villagers and a group of Welsh carollers. The singing continued in the Red Cross Hall. Finally, long after the usual closing time, the British and American national anthems were sung and the group returned to their wards, billets and homes. At the end the Red Cross Staff:

> "… was tired physically, but warm and content with the knowledge that Christmas Eve 1944 in the E.T.O. would be remembered by many as one of song and fellowship and not as a lonely night." (A.R.C. 137 G.H. NARA)

Tec. 5 McConkey listened to the singing from the outskirts of the camp. He noted that the area:

> "… rocked with the two different types of noise. The sweet, thin carolling in the distance of a mixed choir of over 100 voices of hospital personnel and patients who sang on all the wards and carolled outside the chapel. In a contrast, the shouts and muffled, garbled and bawled singing of the drunks returning from town or just celebrating in their billets. But no matter which way the men and women of the army chose to celebrate the coming of the Christmas Season, everyone seemed to be having a wonderful time, making allowance of course for painful wounds and less obvious, but equally intense pain of separation from loved ones."

McConkey decided to celebrate Christmas Day with a seven mile bike ride. After his morning duties had finished he cycled into the countryside to see sights similar to traditional Christmas card scenes. He describes:

> "… the hanging branches of the willows clothed in festoons of glittery silver silhouetted against the dark of the thick matted woods of the hunting preserves or standing clothed in the pastel reds and blues of the winter twilight. The bright red berries of the holly peering unblinking through the covering of frost that clung to the green leaves making them tints lighter. The orange-red in the light of the windows of the farm cottages stood in diffused contrast to the pale white slice of a moon that was high in the sky even at four o'clock in the afternoon. I looked down on a tiny lake to see it, the moon competing with the rusty gold of the sun for reflection space in the lake's limited waves."

On Christmas Day the wards threw their own spontaneous parties with kegs of beer supplied by the ward officers. McConkey wrote home that:

> "As usual the Army did itself proud with the Christmas meal with tremendous quantities of fine turkey, pumpkin pie, cranberry sauce, brussels sprouts, asparagus tips, coffee … and of course, stuffing and gravy."

Another cause for celebration in the New Year for the 137th was the number of weddings involving patients or personnel. The Red Cross was given the responsibility of staging a wedding reception for a patient on the orthopaedic ward and a British girl. She wore a suit of royal blue with a matching hat and accessories. He wore a blue dressing gown and plaster of paris. The Red Cross recorded:

Oteley Park in the snow (J. McConkey)

Oteley Park in the snow (J. McConkey)

View of lake looking from camp, photo taken from billets (J. McConkey)

Looking towards rear of Oteley Park (J. McConkey)

Upper gatehouse (J. McConkey)

Lower gatehouse – used as main entrance (J. McConkey)

"When the Bridal party returned after the ceremony the best man pushed the groom in his wheelchair the length of the ward. The bride bravely stood by his side as they were pelted with rice from each bed."(A.R.C. 137 G.H. NARA)

The Patients' Mess managed to create a four tier wedding cake which the groom cut with a mess gear knife decorated with ribbon.

Thirty-four year old Jack Harris, a member of the detachment met his future bride in Liverpool in November 1944. Twenty-six year old Sylvia Smith was leaving a restaurant with a friend when Jack arrived. As the restaurant was just closing, the two

MORE THAN MEDICINE AND SURGERY

Captain Spencer, Lieutenant 'Sunshine' McCarthy and McConkey outside the ward (J. McConkey)

women agreed to take him somewhere else where he could eat.

Sylvia and Jack struck up a friendship straight away. They had much in common, including the fact that they were both Jewish. Jack regularly visited Sylvia's home and they became engaged in February 1945. The wedding date was set for 1 May 1945 and Sylvia's parents organised the wedding reception with a kosher menu of smoked salmon. To Sylvia's parents' surprise Jack declared that he didn't eat fish so it was necessary for the chef to find him two eggs to eat for his wedding breakfast.

Jack returned to the U.S. after the war shortly before Sylvia discovered that she was expecting their baby. In 1946 she was able to travel to the U.S. aboard the Queen Mary with her twelve week old son, Louis, to be happily reunited with her husband.

Patients at the 137th January 1945 (J. McConkey)

Chapter 12

Filled to Capacity – 129th General Hospital, Penley

THE 129th General Hospital commanded by Robert Estes Blount, a medical officer with eleven years' experience, arrived at Penley in July 1944 to relieve the 16th General Hospital.

The 129th had left Boston on the U.S.S. West Point on 26 June 1944 and arrived in Glasgow on 4 July. From Glasgow it entrained to Colwyn Bay, a staging area, where the unit remained until 9 July. The quota of nurses from the 129th was made up from groups of nurses from other hospitals already in the U.K. At first this caused some problems as a number of nurses were reluctant to leave the units they were already serving with.

On 9 July half of the 129th were sent to Plant 4191 at Penley. There was an orientation with members of the 16th General Hospital and the 994 patients were turned over to the new hospital. The 16th then left before the second half of the unit, consisting of 252 enlisted men, arrived the following day.

Colonel Robert Estes Blount (U.S. Archives, NARA)

Colonel Blount was impressed with his first view of Penley. He wrote that the site was:

> "… beautiful with many large oak trees and a fine expanse of grass." (A.R.C. 129 G.H. NARA)

He was soon to find out that the 'fine expanse of grass' was a problem to maintain. The problem was solved by borrowing a hay mower from a neighbouring farmer and pulling it around the field behind a jeep. This method, supplemented by hand sickle and scythes, kept the area presentable. A further problem concerning the grounds was the amount of mud around the narrow paved paths. A supply of slag was made

Buildings and ward tents at Penley (M. Engelman)

available to the 129th and used either side of the paths to make the tracks wide enough for trucks to drive on. Another difficulty caused by the hospital being in such a rural area was the flies. Fly breeding was occurring in droppings in the dairy farms surrounding the hospital. It became necessary to procure liquid insecticide to spray them with. An additional insect problem was the outbreak of straw mattress dermatitis caused by rodent mites in the straw. Disinfecting the mattresses with steam eliminated these pests.

Some of the problems encountered by the 129th in the first couple of months at Penley were settled with support from the other hospitals in the 804th Hospital Center. The staff at the 83rd and 99th General Hospitals supported the 129th with administrative procedures and other hospitals in the Center coordinated the use of their vehicles to cover shortages at Penley. The British Ordnance Depot at Overton-on-Dee was also able to support the 129th on several occasions by cutting through channels to supply the hospital with critically needed items.

The 129th employed 45 British civilian workers as telephone operators, carpenters, plumbers, electricians, foremen, kitchen workers, stokers and a gardener. Percy Richards worked at the 129th as a stoker. His son, Gordon, remembers his father telling him that after D-Day limbs were routinely amputated at the hospital and he had the unpleasant task of incinerating them.

Although his father did not enjoy this part of his job, Gordon remembers that there were compensations for working at the American hospital in the form of extra food and clothing. Gordon recalls:

British employees at Penley (G. Richards)   *Percy Richards with son, Gordon (G. Richards)*

> "We had our first taste of tropical fruit in the war years from supplies shipped over for the Americans. We were given cigarettes, chewing gum and tinned food that we had never seen before. Some surgical enamelware, like kidney dishes and larger bowls also found their way to our house, as did hospital dressing gowns in maroon and blue corduroy."

As a youngster Gordon earned his pocket money by collecting ashes and rubbish from people's houses and wheeling them about ¾ of a mile to the tip. (There was no weekly rubbish collection in those days). Once Gordon arrived at the tip he would have the opportunity to scavenge for waste from the American camps in the area. If he was lucky he would find unopened ration boxes, packets of cigarettes and surgical tools.

On one visit Gordon found a box of matches. He struck one but was unprepared for the speed with which it burnt down so he dropped it – unfortunately it landed on a pile of wood shavings and in seconds the whole tip was on fire. He fled home in a panic and later learnt that the fire engines had completely emptied a nearby pond of water before they decided to let the fire burn itself out. Gordon's parents were visited by the local policeman and needless to say he was banned from the tip and lost his source of pocket money. One positive outcome of the fire was that it destroyed the nests of countless rats that inhabited the site.

Gordon, along with the other local youngsters, supplemented his pocket money by running errands for the American troops at Bryn Y Pys, who were confined to camp in the run up to D-Day. In return for fetching fish and chips and beer the soldiers would give the boys cigarettes and gum as well as money. Many of the G.I.s didn't understand British currency and the boys didn't seek to enlighten them when they were told to keep the change.

By the time the 129th had arrived at Penley, the bed capacity of the hospital had already been expanded to 1515 by setting up 30 ward tents with concrete floors and electric lights. At first the ward tents were only used occasionally, but in November two platoons of black engineers arrived to winterize the tents so that they could be used through the winter months. By the end of December the tents were full to capacity.

The first hospital train with patients for the 129th arrived at Ellesmere Station on 13 July 1944. The 232 litter cases and 60 ambulatory casualties came from the Battle of St. Lo and Avranches break through. It took 70 minutes for detachment personnel to unload the train. Six days later a second hospital train arrived at Ellesmere with 304 patients for the 129th. This time the procedure took only 55 minutes.

Form for admission of patients to 129th (129 G.H. NARA)

The Receiving and Evacuation Officer devised an efficient plan for receiving new patients. When a hospital train was expected an advance party, consisting of the Receiving and Evacuation Officer, Assistant Chiefs of Medical and Surgical Services as well as several clerks, would board the train when it stopped for refuelling at Shrewsbury Station. All patients, whether ambulatory or litter, would be tagged with the ward assignments in accordance with their injury or illness.

Form for Evacuation of Patients from the 129th (129 G.H. NARA)

From Overton or Ellesmere Stations the patients could then be loaded on ambulances. Litter patients were transported directly to the appropriate ward at Penley while ambulatory patients were transported to the theatre building for guidance to the wards or to the Mess Hall if a meal was needed.

From July to September practically all of the patients received came from the conflict on the Continent, 90 percent of them were surgical patients. Amongst the 185 casualties evacuated from the continent on 10 August were 45 seriously injured German prisoners. They were kept in the N.P. ward (as this could be locked) until they were evacuated to the Prisoner of War hospital at Iscoyd Park on 30 September. The guard for the prisoners was furnished by the Rehabilitation Detachment at first but this proved inadequate so the 129th requested extra guards. Four M.P.s from the 556th Military Police Escort Guard arrived on 16 August and were attached for duty.

Tec. 5 Edgar Seely, Medical Technician at the 129th (D. Ulloa)

Simeon Cummings, Medical Technician at the 129th

A larger than normal train load of patients arrived at Penley on 15 August. Fortunately, just prior to this, ten additional nurses from 79th General Hospital and six from a hospital train had been attached for duty to Plant 4191.

On 27 August the 129th was designated as the hospital for nurse patients from the Center, 80 beds were allotted to this section. One of the difficulties encountered by this department was the transfer of nurses with more serious health issues to the Z.I. Female patients could only be evacuated to the Zone of the Interior on hospital ships (rather than troop ships) so there were some prolonged delays while patients awaited a space on a hospital ship.

The 129th was also designated as a Center for the treatment of severe maxillofacial injuries and burn cases. The skilled plastic surgeon at the 129th treated the majority of the patients in the Center who needed plastic surgery; he also acted as a consultant for cases in the other hospitals of the Center. Particular attention was devoted to early skin grafts and the motion of fingers.

In September 1944 the hospital commenced evacuating patients either to Z.I or replacement depots. On 24 September 78 men were transported to Overton Railway Station for evacuation. This eased the bed situation a little. In October there was a change in the type of casualties arriving at Penley, less were sent directly from the combat zone and most had already received some hospitalisation.

FILLED TO CAPACITY

On 10 October the Outpatient Department experienced a considerable increase in activity due to the fact that the 129th was instructed to act as a station hospital for several battalions of combat engineers stationed at Doddington Park.

When the 129th took over from the 16th at Penley the Rehabilitation Section was reorganised to be more effective. The department had been under the command of a nurse and N.C.O. and was operating under an individual ward system. Two officers, Captain John Portman and 1st Lieutenant Lawrence Lee Junior, were given the task of converting the department to a Convalescent Section. When the above two officers were transferred to other duties Major Robert Nelson was appointed Officer in Charge of Rehabilitation and Captain John Pacifici was assigned as Rehabilitation Surgeon. A patient officer, Captain Frank Bowen, was appointed Rehabilitation Troop Officer. This section had its own schedule of activities consisting mainly of Physical or Military Training. A sports programme was also organised as part of the reconditioning efforts and space was acquired for a gymnasium.

On 14 December the patient census rose to 1800. It was necessary to move all rehabilitation trainees out of their wards to make more bed space available. The Convalescent Section was moved into tents adjacent to the wards. British double decked beds were used. Latrine and bath facilities were shared with patients on the wards.

On 16 December the Convalescent Section was disbanded and the patients were organised into a grade system. Those graded A or B were the patients previously labelled as 'rehabilitation'. They continued to occupy the tents and were under the command of patient officers.

Near the end of December it was necessary to raise the bed capacity to 2100. This was achieved by increasing the 33 bed wards to 46 bed capacity. Beds were doubled in the private rooms and placed in doctors' offices and in the aisles. Two large trailer trucks were furnished by a nearby engineering battalion for the transportation of 200 folding beds. Fortunately at this time the staff of seven general hospitals and an evacuation hospital were staging in the area and were able to help staff the 129th. The hospital was grateful for the extra man-power but found housing them all difficult.

One of the patients arriving around this time was Leroy P. Cutsail – he had been hit in the arm by a shell fragment during the battle for Aachen but he was lucky to be alive, as another fragment heading towards his heart was stopped by the New Testament he was carrying in his left shirt pocket.

Because of the staffing shortages Grade A and B rehabilitation patients were used to carry out

> of grievous injury tended on by a soldier's equipment or by some personal possession.
>
> Pfc Lercy B. Cutsail, of Frederick, Md., now at 129th General Hospital, was hit in the arm by a shell fragment during the battle for Aachen, but another fragment lodged in the New Testament he was carrying in his left shirt pocket, just over his heart.
>
> *Excerpt from Stars and Stripes 28/12/44*

some of the tasks around the base such as painting and cleaning up. They also helped with administration and driving. The policy of using convalescent patients in this way had the joint purpose of boosting the hospital's manpower and aiding the patients' convalescence.

Transportation was used to full capacity between October and December 1944. At times it was necessary for some of the drivers to work 24 and 30 hour shifts without sleep. During the final three months of 1944 ambulances transported 6,000 patients; and heavy trucks carried 5,000 tons of supplies and covered 250,000 miles. All service and repair work of vehicles was carried out by the Transportation Section of the 129th.

A large percentage of the litter patients arrived with no outer clothing or shoes, so as soon as possible after arrival new clothing was drawn and issued. In a number of cases trucks were required to travel a number of miles to collect the clothing. Patients on wards were kept in pyjamas or fatigues and dress uniforms were issued alongside passes. Until this point they were kept locked away to prevent patients from going AWOL. The hospital adopted a liberal pass policy with the rehabilitation patients to off-set the tendency to go AWOL; summary courts were held at the hospital for those who did offend as an example to others.

The 129th handled a large number of trench foot cases. The first 100 cases arrived on 3 December and were treated by the Surgical Service.

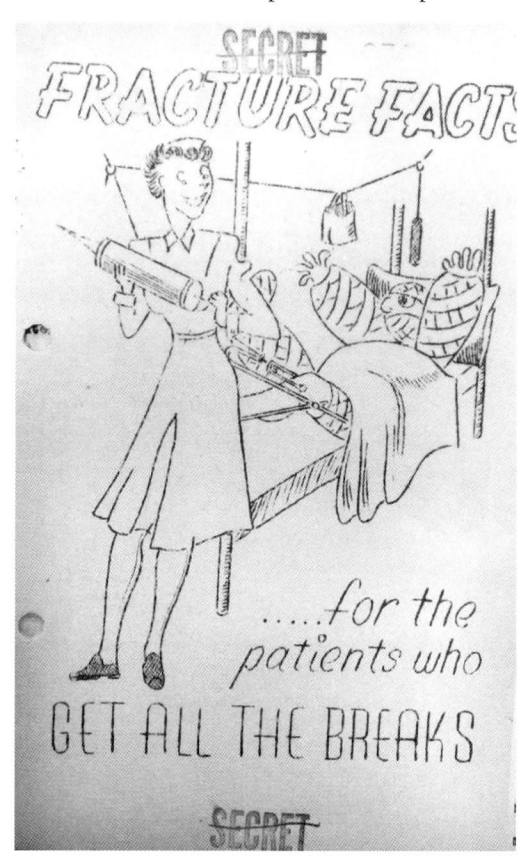

Booklet produced for patients with fractures (129 G.H. NARA)

Subsequent cases were handled by the Medical Service, unless there were surgical lesions. By the end of December 1944 the hospital had received 359 trench foot cases. A large number of these were transferred to the Z.I. as their treatment would take longer than the 90 days allowed by policy at that time.

Towards the end of 1944 there was a concern at the hospital regarding the increased incidence of what seemed to be self-inflicted foot wounds. The usual story from the patient was that he had accidentally discharged his rifle while cleaning it. It was almost impossible to get an accurate report from the unit (which would be in action at the time) to find the truth of the situation. It was sometimes necessary to retain these patients for longer than usual at the hospital while awaiting a report as they could not be returned to the Zone of the Interior without one.

FILLED TO CAPACITY

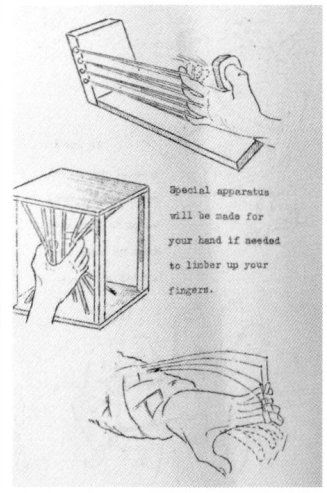

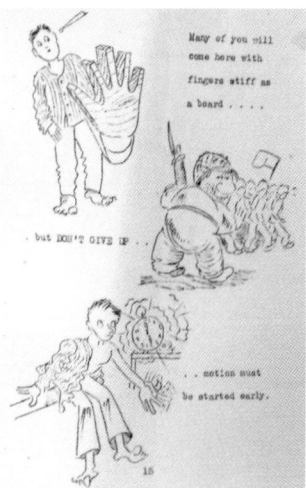

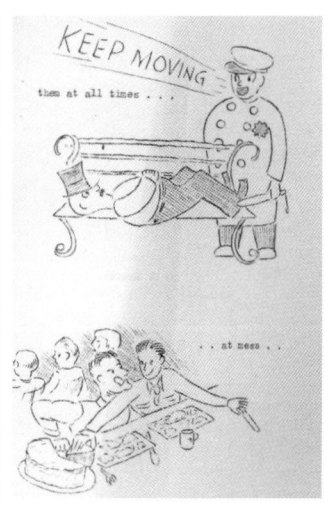

Pages from booklet: The Hand Book (129 G.H.)

Group of patients including Paul J. Curtis (front right) at Penley (P. Curtis)

During November to December various items of field equipment such as mess gear, arctic clothing, M1 stoves and olive drab blankets were recalled from the 129th and turned in to the supply services for re-issue on the continent. Once the olive drab blankets had been given in, the hospital used white blankets which tended to look grubbier quicker, particularly in the winter when the stoves in tents and wards were being used.

During the summer of 1944 the British Barracks Officer had supplied 3686 tons of coal and 450 tons of coke to the hospital. The Transportation Section's first job had been to unload the coke from railway cars five miles away. Two ½ ton dump trucks were borrowed from the Area Engineers to transport it to the hospital. The last load of coal had been moved by a civilian truck loaned to the hospital by the British Barracks Officer in September. Unfortunately the fuel was stored in the open on a hard standing at the hospital and by the time it was needed very little was left.

By Christmas 1944 the coke supply had been used up and at the same time the British authorities announced a general shortage of coal. The hospital had no choice but to use the soft coal already issued, which caused blockages in the chimneys and more dirt in the huts, wards, tents and kitchens. The crew of utilities men were kept constantly occupied clearing out stove pipes.

In the New Year patient numbers decreased a little and the hospital personnel had more time to improve facilities and procedures. In January a cartoon-based booklet called 'Fracture Facts' prepared by Major Philip Foisie and illustrated by Sergeant William Pitney, was written and printed. It showed patients what they could do themselves to help the healing process. Subsequently the booklet was adopted by Chief Surgeon, European Theatre of Operation and distributed to the various hospitals in the E.T.O.

The Red Cross commented about it:

> "Cartoons give a comic touch and the surgeon's explanation helps to make each patient understand the importance of his constant cooperation during convalescence."(A.R.C. 129 G.H. NARA)

In March 1945 the 129th was designated a 'Hand Center' for the 804th Hospital Group. The Hand Section was led by ward surgeon, Captain Johnson. Approximately 150 cases were immediately transferred from other hospitals to the 129th and two wards and one tent were set aside for this section. Sergeant Pitney was also responsible for the illustrations in a booklet written and printed by the department called 'The Hand Book'. This booklet set out exercises in cartoon form that could be carried out to improve hand use after surgery. The Red Cross also managed the recreation time of 'hand patients' by encouraging them to use their hands to play ping-pong or billiards or to take part in handicraft sessions.

Also in March 1945 the hospital admitted a number of freed American Prisoners of War or 'RAMPs' (Released American Military Prisoners). On 2 March the train of patients that arrived included those that had been on the Remagen Bridge in Holland

Paul Dunn at Penley (D. Moore) *Paul Dunn at Penley (D. Moore)*

when it fell. On 23 April another train arrived, carrying 39 RAMPs along with other patients.

PFC Paul Dunn of the 83rd Infantry Division was one of the patients that arrived at Penley around this time for the treatment of a third combat injury. He had suffered a wound to the shoulder and upper body from an artillery shell explosion which occurred on 10 April during the push from the Rhine to the Elbe. The 83rd had landed on Omaha Beach on D+14 and then participated in the thrust across Europe from the break out in Western Normandy and the Battle of the Bulge, through the Siegfried Line, across the Rhine and on to the Elbe where the 83rd established and held the only bridgehead across the river. Dunn had previously been hospitalised at the 107th General Hospital in Le Mans in late January to early February 1945 for a previous wound.

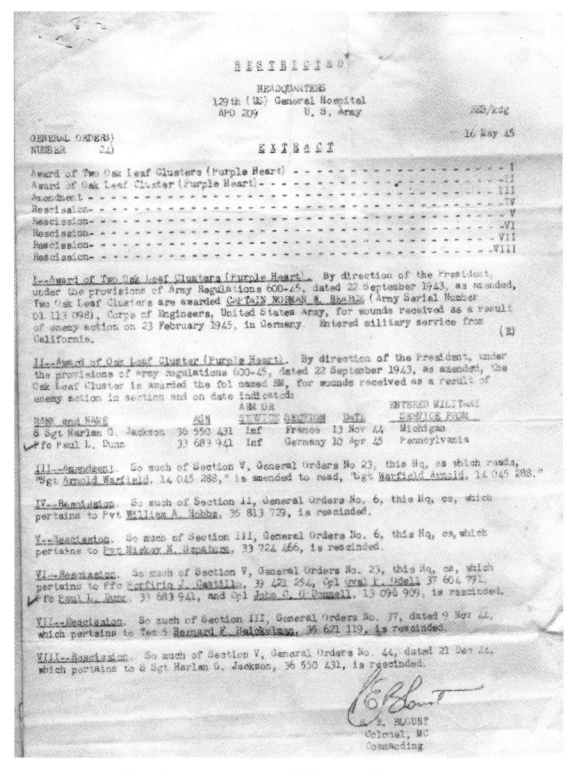

Paperwork relating to awards for Paul Dunn (D. Moore)

In March the hospital was notified to prepare for a different type of prisoner of war, this time of German nationality. They were assigned to carry out work in the hospital. On 12 March forty-five black engineers arrived at the post to help to build a Prisoner of War enclosure, and the following day the area Provost Marshall arrived. Because the building work was behind schedule another platoon of black troops arrived on 20 March, thus bringing the total man-power to 90 enlisted men and two officers. The enclosure was completed on time and two infantry officers were assigned to the P.O.W. enclosure to handle the administration.

On 26 March one hundred German prisoners arrived on the post, they were each given a complete physical and then billeted in the P.O.W. enclosure. (One of the men had to be admitted as a patient to the hospital because he had pneumonia.) On the 27th the men were ready to take on duties around the hospital such as: cutting the grass, painting, cleaning and building their own camp within the enclosure. The Germans were allowed to attend Sunday services in the chapel on the base.

Chapter 13

Everything is fine in the 129 – 129th General Hospital, Penley

AT THE 129th the spiritual welfare of both patients and staff came under the jurisdiction of the three chaplains on the post. The Protestant Chaplain, Captain Ralph Crosby, held three services on Sundays and a singing session on Thursdays in the chapel on the base. The Catholic Chaplain, 1st Lieutenant Edwin McManus, held a daily mass and also heard confessions in the chapel. The Jewish Chaplain, Captain Edward Friedman, used the chapel for Friday services. Around twelve to fifteen people attended the Jewish services, about half of these were patients and the other half were the enlisted men and officers of the detachment. There were opportunities for some of the Jews to be bussed to Liverpool to celebrate some of the Jewish festivals, such as Jewish New Year and Passover, with Jewish families living there.

In the week the chaplains visited the wards. Captain Crosby gave communion and bedside devotions to those unable to attend the services in the chapel while Lt. McManus administered the last sacraments when required. Coincidentally both Christian chaplains had had hernia operations a few weeks prior to embarkation from the U.S.A. but:

> "They were both so popular and both strongly desired to accompany the unit, so they were retained and brought over in 'cotton batting' as it were." (A.R.C. 129 G.H. NARA)

The Special Service, under the leadership of Captain John Bradford, was responsible for sporting, social and educational activities for the personnel of the detachment. He established foreign language classes at the base and regular orientation lectures and forums, where international and national issues were discussed.

The 129th had a softball team put together by the Special Service which:

> "… consistently beat every team it encountered in the E.T.O." (A.R.C. 129 G.H. NARA)

Altogether it won 26 out of the 28 games played, including the Championship of the VI Hospital Group. The team's only loss was to the 82nd General Hospital. Transportation was furnished for all patients and detachment personnel who were interested in supporting the team when playing at other bases. Because the team did so well it was given the reward of watching a professional English football match at Goodison Park (Everton's home ground).

The Special Service also helped to equip and run the dayrooms and clubs on the base. Two dayrooms were established for the enlisted personnel, one for games and the other for reading and letter writing. There was an Officers' Club at the 129th which catered for both the male officers and the nurses. Personnel were encouraged to join in the programme of events held in the Officers club as it helped to:

> "… cement the officer-nurse personnel into a functioning unit." (A.R.C. 129 G.H. NARA)

Bearing in mind the fact that the nurses had been brought together from a number of different units. Occasionally the Officers' Club was loaned to the enlisted men or N.C.O.s for particular functions.

British shipping firms in Liverpool loaned furniture and fittings taken from converted passenger ships as furniture for the Officers' Club. A fireplace, which was paid for by the nurses themselves, was fitted in the Nurses' Lounge. At the beginning a number of slot machines were installed in the Officers' Club but it was necessary to remove them as War Department and European Theatre of Operations rulings forbade them on military bases.

The detachment had an orchestra which played alternatively for officer and detachment dances. It was also in demand from other organisations. In addition to this there was a Patients' Orchestra which began with a drummer who set up in the latrine of the Red Cross building to practise in solitude. A friend who played saxophone started joining in and gradually the orchestra grew so that eventually it was able to entertain the patients and detachment personnel at the Red Cross, Enlisted and N.C.O. Clubs and later on the wards.

The Red Cross also established a drama group at the 129th which presented shows most weeks in as many wards as possible. In September 1944 the group performed in the Officers' Club, a neighbouring hospital's theatre and a children's hospital. In October the group performed a show at a theatre in the nearby town.

The theatre on base was mainly in use for showing movies. The 129th had a movie projector but unfortunately early in its use, the exitor bulbs blew and no replacements could be secured. Two enlisted men: Tec. 5 Blake and Pfc Durbin, managed to improvise with a bicycle lamp and a dentist's mirror. They also built a projector booth in the theatre. The theatre was occasionally used for dances although the concrete floor was poor and not good for dancing on. The Special Service organised a number of dances each month, arranging for local girls to be invited and providing transport and refreshments for them.

In September the Patients' Recreation Hall, which had formerly been the Officer Patients' Mess, was assigned to the supervision of the Red Cross. This meant that recreational and social activities no longer had to be separated into two different buildings. The Recreation Hall was structured so that there were two large rooms, one of which was used for crafts and games, and the other was furnished as a day room with upholstered chairs, reading and writing tables, bookcases and a piano. It was noted that as the weather got colder, the furniture moved closer to the fire and away from the walls. Two smaller rooms at the rear of the building provided offices for the Red Cross Field Director and Secretary.

A member of the detachment, Private Hayes, was assigned to the Red Cross to keep the building clean and heated. He was assisted by two patients from the Rehabilitation Group. Two patients from the Neuro-Psychiatric Ward were also directed to the Red Cross by their ward officer as he felt that clerical work would be of therapeutic value to them. One of the men, who had been a tank driver, had seen some horrific sights which had affected him badly. He was gradually able to take over most of the administration for Red Cross supplies. As time went on the girls could see that this type of work was improving the men's outlook. Frances Gray, Assistant Field Director, noted about the tank driver:

> "He was quite confused during the early days of his apprenticeship but his depression seems to have lifted and now he whistles or sings cheerfully as he works." (A.R.C. 129 G.H. NARA)

Another man assigned to help the Red Cross was Sergeant Bill Pitney, who had carried out the art work for the 'Fracture Facts' and 'Hand Book' booklets. He also did the artwork on Red Cross programmes and painted signs for the buildings on the post.

One side of the Red Cross craft shop was devoted to ping-pong and the other side had work tables and a toolbar. Here the men could work with metal, plexiglas, wood, leather and plastic. The Recuperative Neuro-Psychiatric ward had a similar craft shop where the Red Cross could give craft work instruction. The Red Cross Recreation worker, Mary Flock, noted:

> "We don't urge the men to do stipulated things but much has been accomplished by hinting that we are in dire need of ... whatever it is that men can do or make." (A.R.C. 129 G.H. NARA)

The Special Service managed to obtain a wood-carving kit for the Red Cross. Some of the men used it to make plaques of their unit insignia and one man carved the Lord's Prayer on a block of Poplar. Leather craft was also one of the popular activities at the 129th; one patient requested a pattern for a leather guard to be made for the sensitive part of his hand since having an amputation. Another patient asked for enough leather to make a jacket, but stocks of leather were limited so most patients made small items such as match holders, glasses cases, belts and watch bands. Miss Flock recorded:

> "Scrap leather has surrounded many a sweetheart picture … and leather wallets are pocketing the pound." (A.R.C. 129 G.H. NARA)

Because the 129th was a Female Patient Center, additional craft work was carried out at their request. Miss Flock commented:

> "Naturally wool is their favourite material and stock is always low. Wool mats, pot holders and dog tag cases keep the skein department at low stock. The chapel has a beautiful cover woven by one patient. I'm sure that many a table at home will be warmer with mats woven in the E.T.O."(A.R.C. 129 G.H. NARA)

Working with gimp braid was also popular. It was used to replace:

> "… dog tag chains and also to link British currency to American wrists."(A.R.C. 129 G.H. NARA)

There were a number of blind and partially sighted patients at the 129th and the girls managed to teach some of them to braid using flat and round strands of gimp. They also managed to convert some games for the blind patients. A game of chequers was adapted:

> "We outlined the squares with a stylus – making the outline ridged and rough. Using the same instrument we marked (with a cross) the yellow squares. With a needle we marked a set of playing cards and we're going shopping to see if the cards of the Braille type are available because it takes more time than we have to mark fifty-two cards." (A.R.C. 129 G.H. NARA)

The Blind Institute supported Special Service and the Red Cross when coordinating activities off base for those with eye injuries.

In October a felt toy project was commenced to make Christmas gifts for children in the local orthopaedic hospital. Forty horses, elephants, dogs and deer were turned in for the children as well as at least three hundred toys that were posted home for relatives of the patients. Miss Flock remarked:

> "Practically every doctor, nurse, enlisted man and patient has made a toy. There can't be much floss or stuffing left in Wales." (A.R.C. 129 G.H. NARA)

The patients on the wards spent the ten days before Christmas making decorations for the large trees that had been procured by the Red Cross for every building. The men cut out stars, chains, angels and reindeers and painted ping-pong balls and candy canes while the female patients wrapped all the detachment's, officers' and nurses' gifts.

Both Catholic and Protestant Chaplains held Christmas services. On Christmas Eve a combined Protestant and Catholic choir sang carols throughout the wards. On Christmas Day thirty children from an orphanage came to spend the day at Penley. Two of the officers dressed as Santa, distributed gifts to the children and each patient in the hospital.

Also on Christmas Day a public address system was presented to the hospital. 63 loud speakers were distributed among the 38 wards and ward tents, the Red Cross building and detachment and patient mess halls. Unfortunately insufficient switches and volume controls were supplied so the unit electricians subsequently installed a separate switch for each ward. The system was run like a radio station and the by line was: 'Patients Broadcasting system on the Road to Recovery.' Selected individuals from among the convalescent patients were given responsibility for the selection and presentation of the daily programme. The Patients' Orchestra was also able to broadcast over the system. One of the patients remarked to the Red Cross that they:

> "… could hardly realise what it meant to be able to listen to music again, and that it certainly was one of the things he had missed most in his days on the front line." (A.R.C. 129 G.H. NARA)

In the early days of the 129th being at Penley the Red Cross unit was limited in its activities due to staff shortages and turn over. In August two of the members of the unit were transferred to other units and one girl who was suffering with health problems, was returned to the U.S. Fortunately the Staff Aide of the Red Cross unit with the 16th General Hospital, Miss Doris Buck, had remained at Penley to support the 129th when the 16th left. By the end of September 1944 extra staff had been drafted in from other hospitals so that the unit at the 129th was brought up to the full strength of five.

It wasn't until March 1945 that the Red Cross were able to establish a complete volunteer rota of 40 local British women from Wrexham and Bangor. The Red Cross reported that:

> "Most of the Bangor ladies are farm folk – simple, clear, generous women with an overflow of kindness for the 'Yanks' that has quickened a warm response from the patients, many of whom are farm lads themselves." (A.R.C. 129 G.H. NARA)

The Wrexham ladies were selected from the Hospital Service Committee of the Wrexham W.V.S. after the Red Cross had given a presentation to them. The girls noted:

"We were impressed with the enthusiastic response given by the group to this new appeal in spite of the many years of war service and sacrifice which all had rendered."(A.R.C. 129 G.H. NARA)

The volunteers took on various duties at the hospital which freed the Red Cross up for other tasks. They took the book cart, magazines and games around the ward, assisted with the craft programme, sewed and mended the patient's uniforms, made new blackout curtains and brought flowers for the Recreation Hall. At Easter they made baskets of vari-coloured construction paper and filled them with flowers to give each ward 'a taste of springtime.'

Detachment officers, enlisted personnel and rehabilitation patients were given regular passes into the local town of Wrexham and arrangements were made between the Special Service and the British authorities for free bus transportation to and from Wrexham, leaving the camp at 1715 and 1915 and departing from Wrexham at 2215 although it was noted in the 129th archives that:

"Recreation facilities in the nearby cities and towns for officers and nurses are very meagre." (A.R.C. 129 G.H. NARA)

In October 1944 Colonel Blount noted in the log book that there had been:

"… various misdemeanours in Wrexham."

but added:

"this is not believed due to the personnel of the 129th General Hospital. All patients are instructed to depart Wrexham on the 2215 bus each night." (A.R.C. 129 G.H. NARA)

Excerpts from logbook (129 G.H. NARA)

However, in January 1945 it was reported that:

> "Charges have been made against Lieutenant Gidney D.O.P. [Detachment of Patients] for assaulting an M.P. Officer, general court has been recommended." (A.R.C. 129 G.H. NARA)

In February 1945 the 'offence' noted in the log book was that of 'an association between a nurse (officer) and an enlisted man'. Due to this transgression it was necessary to make 'special arrangements' so that the couple were seated separately when travelling on buses and visiting the theatre. A request was made to the M.P.s on duty at the time to check if the nurse was seen in the local town with the man.

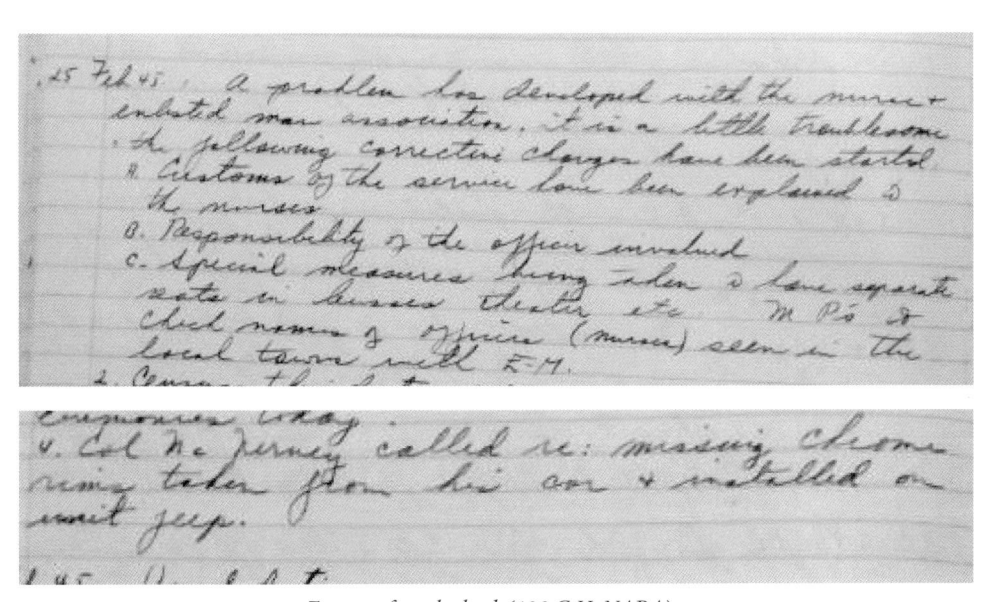

Excerpts from logbook (129 G.H. NARA)

Also in February there was a complaint recorded in the log book from Colonel McNerney, the C.O. for the 804th Hospital Center. He stated that the chrome rims from his staff car had been taken and installed on the 129th General Hospital jeep.

As well as organising trips into Wrexham, Special Service arranged weekly tours for the patients and detachment personnel to Chester, Liverpool and Stratford Upon Avon. The British Council also took responsibility for arranging tours and lectures for the unit personnel as well as for patients and rehabilitation trainees.

The British Ministry of Information also organised visits to British homes in the locality and secured weekend visits for patient and detachment personnel. They furnished guides for the tours and concluded visits with an afternoon tea for the men. A small local organisation known as 'The Fund for Wounded Soldiers' arranged a series of Saturday afternoon football game excursions for patients serving tea afterwards with the aid of a women's volunteer group. Special Services noted that:

"These contacts have helped to improve Anglo-American relations and consequently have improved the morale of our own personnel." (A.R.C. 129 G.H. NARA)

The 129th General Hospital Red Cross unit concluded their report for their time at Penley:

"We believe a more definite, if less tangible service, is being rendered by us in our attempts to help servicemen in this hospital work out various problems of adjustment that they face at this time, which includes facing the reality of and adjusting their attitude towards physical handicap, towards the army, towards going back to combat, or, in some instances, the Zone of the Interior or another hospital. ... We may quote from our hospital slogan: 'Everything is fine in the 129th.'" (A.R.C. 129 G.H. NARA)

Chapter 14

Detention of Prisoner Patients – 82nd General Hospital, Iscoyd Park

ON 21 March 1944 official approval was given for:

> "the provision of fencing around a ward at each of the following hospitals for the detention of Prisoner Patients:
> a). Acton, Suffolk
> b). Musgrove Park, Belfast
> c). Longleat, Warminster
> d). Sudbury, Western Command
> e). Iscoyd Park, Western Command" (U.S. Archives NARA)

In due course the 82nd General Hospital was notified that on 28 September 1944 it was to be charged with the care of German Prisoners of War. On 1 October the Red Cross unit was withdrawn from the 82nd and 42 German female civilians were transferred to the hospital. The majority of them were assigned to ward details assisting in the care of Prisoner of War Patients. Colonel Rich asked for nurses from the 82nd to volunteer to work in the P.O.W. wards but this was not a popular assignment as most of the nurses had husbands, sweethearts, brothers or fathers fighting the Germans and some of their loved ones had been killed or taken prisoner. Finally the Colonel decided to appoint Nurse Angela DeGioia as Head Nurse in the P.O.W. wards as she was several years older than most of the other nurses and very level headed. Miss DeGioia took on the task but her daughter recalls that she was not happy with it. After carrying out the role for a couple of months DeGioia requested a transfer to a frontline hospital in France but her request was denied. She appealed and was interviewed by Colonel Rich. She told him that she would rather risk enemy fire working in a hospital in the combat zone than continue to nurse the German P.O.W.s but she was still not allowed to transfer. Thirty enlisted men were also selected for a thorough course of training to qualify as nurse replacements. The men were chosen on the basis of aptitude and an ability to assume all ward responsibilities normally fulfilled by A.N.C. personnel.

The patients were guarded by the 415th Military Police Escort Guard Company consisting of 55 enlisted men and commanded by 2nd Lieutenant Sidney E. Jacobson. In view of the relatively small Military Police detachment detailed to guard the prisoners there was initially some concern over potential outbreaks. To complement the M.P. Detachment some of the personnel of the 82nd took on guard duty. The September monthly report notes:

Nurse Angela DeGioia (A. Weiss)

> "Rendering aid to the sick and wounded was not the only function performed by the detachment. Many of the men were called upon to guard the post for 72 hours following the admission of over 500 prisoners of war with nothing but their clubs and courage for protection." (82 G.H. NARA)

Extra security measures were put into place such as meticulous searching of all prisoners for concealed weapons or stolen items and prompt transfer to Prisoner of War camps as soon as the men were healthy enough.

German nurses (Q. Nicola)

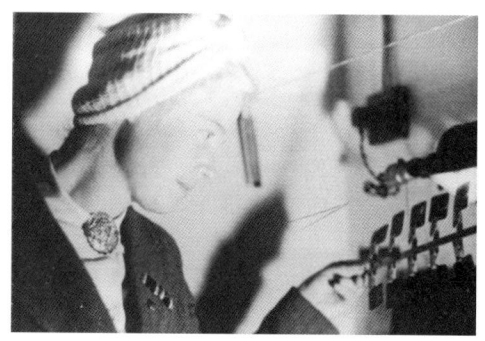

German female worker with dental radiographs (82 G.H. NARA)

The first group of Germans to arrive at Iscoyd Park had been seized at the fall of the French Port of Brest to the Allied Forces. One of the patients was Matrosen Obergefreiter (Leading Seaman) Karl Bauman. Bauman, a U-boat Kriegsmarine, had been wounded by shrapnel from an exploding gun barrel while at Brest. He had spent a number of weeks at a field hospital as his condition prevented him from being moved.

After the surrender of forty thousand German military personnel at Brest, able bodied soldiers and sailors were transported by boat to P.O.W. camps in the U.S.A., while wounded prisoners from the underground hospital were assigned to Prisoner

Patient hospitals in the U.K. The German patients were accompanied by French civilians wearing white armbands. Bauman was concerned that some of them may be part of the French Resistance group which had been terrorising the German troops through guerrilla warfare. Whether they were or not, this group of Free French had been placed under the jurisdiction of the American Army and so were prevented from exacting any revenge that they may have liked to have on the German prisoners.

From the underground hospital at Brest, Bauman was transported by ambulance to the port. Stretcher cases were placed aboard a landing craft which shuttled the patients to a hospital ship painted white with a red cross. Once the patients were all on board, the ship set sail for Southampton. Bauman sailed without any belongings as his kit bag had been stolen shortly before he left Brest; he only had the pyjamas he was wearing and a toiletry bag. From Southampton he was carried on a stretcher to a hospital train which would transport him to Iscoyd Park.

Detraining Prisoners of War (82 G.H. NARA)

Detraining Prisoners of War (82 G.H. NARA)

Ambulatory Prisoners of War (82 G.H. NARA)

Upon arrival at the 82nd Bauman was given a thorough examination as he had no medical records. After the examination a German speaking officer explained that a minor operation would be necessary to repair an internal wound.

Many of the German patients arrived at Iscoyd Park in poor condition and a number had infected wounds due to lack of early treatment and a shortage of drugs. There were nine deaths of German patients at Iscoyd Park. One man was only 18, another was a Slav who had been made to carry out forced labour which led to an early death from tuberculosis. The medical cases amongst the prisoner patients included a high incidence of Pulmonary Tuberculosis, particularly among the conscripted Georgian and Polish captives who had previously been subjected to hard labour under adverse shelter and dietary conditions. The Medical Service was charged with the general care of chest injuries for which a specialist ward was established. The scientific conduct of this section earned a written commendation from the Senior Consultant in Medicine, E.T.O.U.S.A. for the Chief of the Chest Ward, Captain William Cohen and the Chief of the Medical Service, Lieutenant Colonel Frederick Kellog. A number of the prisoners required blood transfusions but Nurse Angela DeGioia recalled that some refused them as they did not want 'mongrel American' blood. A small number died as a result of this decision.

No amputations of limbs were necessary for the prisoners and there was conservative treatment in the cases of severe fractures of long bones, even though several men had been informed by German medics that amputation was inevitable. The Surgical Section performed 90 major operations and 627 minor procedures on the prisoner patients. In addition 815 plaster casts were applied.

German P.O.W. patient (Q. Nicola) *German officer patient (Q. Nicola)*

Once prisoner patients started responding to treatment, they commenced rehabilitation. Part of their rehabilitation included work details in the hospital. The monthly report of the Rehabilitation Section notes:

> "In this installation of necessity our efforts have been directed towards German Prisoners of War. Advantage has been taken of their extreme susceptibility to regimentation and their love of group singing. ... For one-half hour twice daily the patients gathered together for group singing. Germans require no coercion for this form of exercise which promotes diaphragmatic control, aids lung expansion and, what is more important, firmly establishes in the patients' mind the idea that the entire regime has been formulated to return him to a full and complete life as a normal individual." (82 G.H. NARA)

DETENTION OF PRISONER PATIENTS

Another form of rehabilitation was Physical Training, but it was necessary to modify the work of the P.T. Department when the unit began to function as a P.O.W. hospital:

> "Language difficulty and the necessity of scheduling 'by wards' curtailed the number of treatments given over a period of time." (82 G.H. NARA)

Chaplains allowed the German patients to attend services at the chapel and a special mass was held for them. The chaplains' monthly report notes:

> "The response of those who attended service was apparently the same as those of our own people. However, there was definitely a greater number among prisoner personnel who professed to have no religious denomination, than among our own." (82 G.H. NARA)

While at the 82nd the Germans were clothed in Class X fatigues. They were confined to the guarded section of the hospital but were given adequate food rations (including candy and 200 cigarettes a month). A black American orderly played chequers with Bauman; neither could speak the other's language but they communicated through hand signals and gestures.

After he had recovered from the successful surgery Bauman was able to walk to the prisoners' mess hall for meals. On one occasion another prisoner attempted to push his way to the front of the line. When he was challenged by the guard his defence was that 'he was Austrian'. This did not impress the American soldier who sent him to the back of the queue.

By January 1945, seven months after his injury, Bauman was fully recovered from his wounds. He was released to a Prisoner of War Camp in England and from there he was transported to America in the hold of a troopship. Ironically half-way through the crossing there was a German submarine alert and the prisoners were fearful that their own sailors would send them to the bottom of the ocean.

Iscoyd Park ceased being a Prisoner Patient hospital on 27 January 1945. According to the official records during the months that the Germans were at Iscoyd Park there were no instances of attempted escape or significant breaches of discipline by any of the P.O.W.s. Nurse Angela DeGioia told her daughter otherwise: she was one of a group of nurses who was attacked by one of the prisoners. She was hit on the forehead with a blunt instrument; an abscess developed just above her eyebrow and it was feared that she may lose the sight in her eye. Fortunately that did not happen, although she did bear a small scar on her forehead for the rest of her life. (This was not Nurse DeGioia's only health problem encountered while at the 82nd. She was also one of a small number of staff who caught rheumatic fever in the winter of 1944/45. She was told later that she would have died had penicillin not been available at the hospital.)

When Nurse DeGioia was injured and thought to be in danger of losing her sight Colonel Rich the Commanding Officer, contacted her fiancé, Lieutenant Gilbert Weiss, who was in France with the 415th Dump Truck Engineer Company, a division of the 37th Engineer Combat Battalion. This unit was made up of black enlisted men who repaired and maintained dump trucks, tanks and jeeps and delivered them to various military units. They were then used to build roads, bridges and clear debris for the safe passage of troops and the building of camps and air fields.

Lieutenant Weiss was given two weeks leave to visit his fiancée so he hitch hiked to Cherbourg where he intended to catch a plane to England. Unfortunately bad weather had caused the grounding of all planes in the vicinity so he decided to travel across the English Channel by L.S.T. The poor weather conditions had also affected the sea traffic so it was necessary for him to wait until the next day to make the crossing. Unfortunately, although he was able to sail across the Channel on the L.S.T., the continuing adverse weather meant that it was not able to land in the harbour and it was necessary to transfer all the passengers onto a Victory ship which could dock safely. From Southampton Weiss travelled to Shropshire. The complete journey from his base in France took him six days.

The two lieutenants had first met at Camp Beale, California where Weiss was attending an Advanced Officers' Training Class. DeGioia's best friend, Eleanor Savatius had had one date with Weiss and he had asked her to bring a friend along next time as company for his friend. She invited Angela. The two couples travelled into town to watch a movie in the only transport available, an ambulance.

Angela was very fond of Hershey chocolates and she had a few Hershey Kisses in her pocket. As she sat in the ambulance on the way to Sacramento she turned to Gilbert with a handful of Kisses in her hand and said, 'Lieutenant, would you like a kiss?' He replied, 'Yes, Lieutenant, I would' and then he kissed her. As their daughter comments, 'The rest is history'. Angela's friend, Eleanor, ended up dating Gilbert's friend and there were no hard feelings.

Lieutenant Weiss was shipped to the U.K. in September 1943 and Lieutenant DeGioia arrived at Iscoyd Park with the 82nd in March 1944. Before she travelled to England she was allowed leave to visit her sick mother in New York. (Sadly this was the last

Lieutenant Gilbert Weiss 1943 (A. Weiss)

time that she saw her as she died one month later while Angela was at Iscoyd Park.) Once the couple were in the same country they thought they would have plenty of opportunities to get together but this was not so. They only managed to meet up on one occasion. They spent the time in London and were sitting hand in hand on a park bench in Hyde Park when the air raid sirens went off. Everyone ran towards the nearest shelter but they decided to remain sitting there for the duration of the air raid. They heard the English people muttering 'Crazy Americans' as they ran past; fortunately the bombs did not land near the park.

DETENTION OF PRISONER PATIENTS

After this the couple applied for permission to get married, which they received. The date of the wedding should have been 18 August 1944, but on 14 August Weiss was sent with his unit to France so the couple's plans had to be shelved. In preparation for her wedding Nurse DeGioia started looking for a wedding cake in July 1944. She bought a large fruit cake from a baker's shop in Whitchurch and kept it in a tin. At the 82nd each nurse was given a ration of rum each week. As Angela did not like rum she poured her ration over her cake as she had been instructed by various 'fruit cake experts'.

When Lieutenant Weiss arrived at the 82nd in November 1944 he found that the operation on his fiancée had been a success and she was well on the way to recovery. The couple decided that as they were finally both in the same place they should get married as soon as possible. Unfortunately Weiss discovered that the marriage licence issued to him in August had expired so it was necessary to apply for a new one. The couple managed to secure a short pass for the hospital chaplain who was to be the best man but Nurse DeGioia was unable to get 'official leave'. However she had Colonel Rich's blessing; he advised her to take two days AWOL but to do her best not to be caught.

As Angela was a Catholic and Gilbert was a Protestant they were unable to have a wedding service at the altar of St George's Catholic Church in Whitchurch so the priest agreed to marry them in the porch. They were both married in uniform on 27 November and afterwards went to a photography shop in Whitchurch to have their photo taken.

The wedding party started at one of the nurses' huts and then moved to the mess hall where they were greeted by a broadside of rice thrown by the enlisted men. The couple had not informed the Mess Sergeant of their plans to marry that day so their wedding breakfast consisted of C-rations and cabbage. Mrs Weiss had her fruit cake which was so rich with alcohol that she told her daughter that simply opening the tin and breathing in the fumes made some people 'tipsy'.

Angela and Gilbert Weiss after their wedding in November 1944 (A. Weiss)

Marriage licence (A. Weiss)

The couple spent their honeymoon at the Victoria Hotel on Whitchurch High Street. Not long after the Weiss wedding, on 8th January, another nurse from the 82nd General Hospital, Agnes Doyle, married her sweetheart, Captain James Mulville who was also stationed at Iscoyd Park.

Once the 82nd ceased being a P.O.W. hospital plans were made for a Red Cross unit to be attached again. The new unit arrived in February 1945. One of the American patients to be received by the hospital in March 1945 was Private John Price, who had been wounded at Aachen on 26 February. He had been injured through the left shoulder with a machine gun. The bullet had gone through the top of his shoulder and come out of his back.

With his unit, the 117th Infantry Regiment, Price had been awaiting the support of tanks of the 793rd Tank Battalion. When the men saw a group of tanks coming towards them they moved out of cover; it wasn't until they got up close to the tanks that they realised that they were German. In the same way the German tank crews did not realise that the infantrymen were American until they were in the midst of them.

The tanks opened fire at short range and several injuries resulted, including to Price. Fortunately he managed to crawl to the safety of a ditch, losing his helmet and glasses in the process. When the tanks had gone he started making his way towards the first aid station where he was instructed to walk to the 117th Regiment Collecting Station. Eventually after three hours of walking, losing blood all the time, he arrived. He was given a cup of coffee, but promptly passed out due to loss of blood.

An ambulance took Price to Maastricht, Holland, where he was operated on for the bullet wound in his shoulder. He was fortunate as the bullet had only 'creased' his lung, if it had gone any closer to his spine he would have been paralysed. From Maastricht he was transferred to an evacuation hospital in Liege, Belgium, and then flown to England, where he travelled by hospital train to Iscoyd Park, arriving on 1 March.

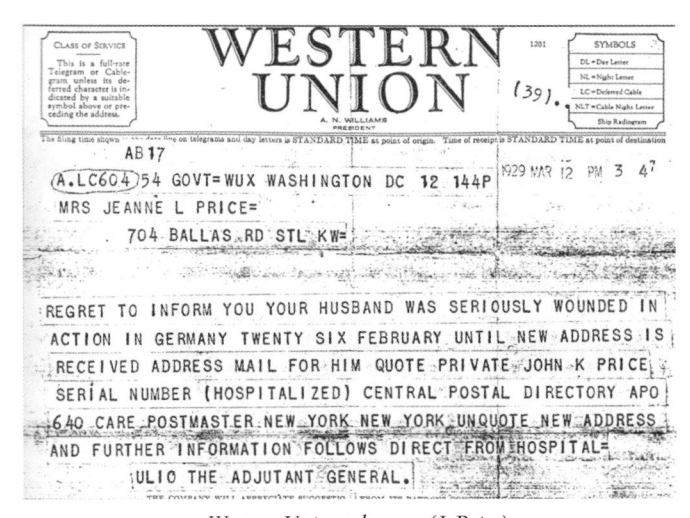

Western Union telegram (J. Price)

On 10 March the incision where the bullet had come out of his back was sewn up and it was discovered that the bullet had chipped the shoulder bone. The stitches began

Letter to inform next of kin of progress of patient (J. Price)

to fester so it was necessary to remove them and tape the wound closed. Price also needed treatment from the dentist at the 82nd as the vibrations caused by the artillery barrages on the Continent had loosened the fillings in his teeth.

Medical Report from 82nd General Hospital

To his relief, on 18 March Price received a pair of glasses to replace the ones he had lost when he got hit. He was so glad to be able to see clearly that he celebrated by going to watch a movie on the base. On 19 March he received his Purple Heart Medal.

Patients receiving medals at Iscoyd Park (Q. Nicola)

U.S. ARMY HOSPITAL CENTER 804

While at the 82nd Jack underwent Physical Therapy and helped out in the ward kitchen as part of his rehabilitation treatment but he was still struggling to use his arm. On 14 April he was evacuated to the Zone of the Interior.

Letter to inform next of kin of Private Price's evacuation to the U.S.

Chapter 15

Haec Olim Meminisse Juvabit – One Day this will be Pleasing to Remember

THERE WERE a number of other American military camps in the Wrexham area as well as the hospitals. Some were temporary camps for soldiers awaiting the invasion of France such as the 11th Replacement Depot at Bryn Y Pys. Others were more permanent stations such as the U.S. Supply Depot at Wem. From mid-1943 until the end of the war, Wrexham, as one of the largest towns in the area, gave hospitality to American troops in their off-duty time and in the evenings. Some American units like the 400th Field Artillery Battalion, whose Piper Cubs used the airstrip at RAF Wrexham, were billeted in houses in the town. G.I.s were compulsorily billeted by the British police on those that had spare bedrooms. It appears that most families welcomed the American servicemen and the extra rations they brought. Frank Mackreth, who lived at Beechley House with his mother, sister, wife and baby, remembers that the twelve American soldiers living with them became close friends of the family.

American soldiers billeted at Beechley House in Kingmills Road Wrexham (S. Mackreth)

G.I.s billeted with Keith Nurse's family (Wrexham Archives)

Keith Nurse remembers the four G.I.s who were billeted with his family in their terraced house close to the town's gas works. Seven year old Keith was thrilled to have the Americans living with them, as he felt that they were "just like those we'd become accustomed to in the pictures at the Odeon in Brook Street. I was thrilled and overawed by their whirlwind presence." Keith remembers that metal bunks were set on each side of their bedroom and that he was encouraged by the G.Is to march up and down their room, buckling under the weight of a kitbag and helmet, giving a U.S. style salute. When they left Wrexham, shortly before D-Day he remembers going into their room and feeling quite lost.

As early as March 1943 the Mayor of Wrexham, Councillor Mrs E.G. Breese, presided over a meeting in Wrexham to formulate plans to give hospitality and provide social amenities for the American troops in the North Wales area when they visited the town. Representatives of the Wrexham Town Council, Rotary Club, Royal British Legion (Men's and Women's section), W.V.S. and a number of churches unanimously decided to take steps to organise hospitality and entertainments. Major Thompson, on behalf of the U.S. forces in the area at the time, expressed his gratitude for their hospitality. At their next meeting in April the committee reported that the American Red Cross had obtained the use of the old Conservative Club as a Welfare Club. Mr Chapin, Field Director of the American Red Cross in the area, attended the meeting to answer questions.

> **HOSPITALITY FOR AMERICAN TROOPS**
>
> The Mayor of Wrexham, Councillor Mrs. E. C. Breese, J.P., presided over a representative meeting at Wrexham, on Friday evening, called for the purpose of formulating arrangements to give hospitality and to provide social amenities for American troops in the North Wales area, when they visit the town. Representatives of the Wrexham Town Council, the Wrexham Rotary Club, Toc H., British Legion (Men's Section), British Legion (Women's Section), the Church in Wales, the Free Churches, the Catholic Church, W.V.S., and the various social and sporting organisations of the town and district were present. It was unanimously decided to take steps to establish a Welfare Club and a committee was appointed to organise hospitality and entertainments. Major Thompson, of the U.S. Forces, addressed the meeting by request, and expressed, on behalf of the American Troops, his gratitude for the spontaneous hospitality already extended to them.
>
> *Wrexham Leader, March 1943*

Although the Red Cross units of the various hospitals in the vicinity of Wrexham organised sight-seeing trips for further afield, both patients and personnel were able to use either military transport or daily bus services to travel into the town by themselves or in groups. Each evening would see an influx of soldiers into the Welsh town.

There were a number of reported incidents of American servicemen causing trouble in the town; some of these were due to racial tension between black and white American soldiers. The worst scene of racial tension was known as 'the Battle of Mount Street'. At the time Mount Street was a street of 'ill repute' and there were a number of pubs in the vicinity. On this occasion a fight between black and white soldiers spilled out onto the street from one of the pubs. A group of Royal Commandoes based at the Hermitage, joined in on the side of the black soldiers, withdrawing only when the American M.P.s from the 82nd General Hospital at Iscoyd Park, arrived. The M.P.s were commended in the 82nd's archives for:

> "... performing commendably while doing military police duty in a neighbouring city during tension between Negro and white soldiers." (82 G.H. NARA)

Previous to this incident, in January 1943 a war reservist policemen had been hurt while trying to prevent the admittance of two black soldiers to a dance at the Plough Hotel. The two soldiers were court-martialled for their part in the affair.

In Wrexham there was a Red Cross 'Donut Dugout', a W.V.S. canteen, four cinemas and a number of pubs for the G.I.s to spend their off-duty time visiting, but the Red Cross unit from the 83rd General Hospital at Llanerch Panna was concerned that the pubs were the only places that the soldiers could take civilian girls after the cinema. Thelma Menzer, Assistant Field Director reported:

> "As the situation is now the soldier has little opportunity of meeting the more desirable people in the community. ... A few civic groups in the city are aware of the problem and are trying to meet it. The W.V.S. is starting a series of parties and the Y.W.C.A. hopes to open a café." (A.R.C. 83 G.H. NARA)

Unfortunately in February 1945 the plans to open the café were cancelled because of the lack of available buildings.

Whether there were enough 'suitable' places for the G.I.s to meet the 'right kind' of girl or not it was inevitable that there would be romantic liaisons between the G.I.s and the local girls. In the annual report for the 82nd General Hospital the Commanding Officer notes:

> "The conduct of the men amongst the British population has been creditable to themselves and the unit. The only noteworthy incidents were the marriages of three members of the detachment to English girls, and in each case the tying of the blessed knot was strictly in accordance with prescribed military regulations and procedures." (82 G.H. NARA)

Marriage of Corporal John Vogel and Miss Enid Williams (Wrexham Advertiser 23/8/43)

Cpl. John R. Vogel, eldest son of Mr. and Mrs. Vogel, Pittsburg, U.S.A., and Miss Enid Williams, youngest daughter of the late Mr. and Mrs. David Owen Williams, of Vroncysyllte, who were married at Poyser Street Methodist Church, Wrexham, by the Rev. J. A. Tingle, on June 24th.

There were a number of weddings between local British girls and American servicemen from other units in the area as well as the U.S. military hospitals. Corporal John Vogel and Miss Enid Williams were married on 24 June 1943 at Poyser Street Methodist church in Wrexham. Pfc Ivan Crary and Miss Joan Griffiths were married at St Mary's Cathedral in Wrexham on 28 June of the same year. Pfc Ullyses Hatfield and Miss Joan Delaney were also married at St Mary's Cathedral on 6 November 1943. Corporal Dennis Templeton married Miss Denise Allen at Wrexham Parish church on 26 February 1945.

Weddings involving nurses from the hospitals and U.S. servicemen also took place in the local area. On 1 October 1944 Nurse, 2nd Lieutenant Kathleen Gaines married 1st Lieutenant Richard Kubeck of the 459th Fighter Group, which was based at Honington, Suffolk. The marriage took place at St Oswald's Church in Oswestry. On 21 October Kathleen was transferred from the 129th General Hospital at Penley and subsequently was sent to the U.S.

There were also some 'less savoury' liaisons between American servicemen and the girls of Wrexham. A married woman, who was labelled as an 'Unworthy Wife of a Hero' in the Wrexham Leader, was brought before the court in June 1944. Twenty-six year old Kathleen Davies of Wrexham was charged with the wilful neglect of her four children. Mrs Davies, whose husband had been a prisoner of war since Dunkirk, had been warned by the police nine months before not to leave her children home alone at night. On that particular occasion Mrs Davies had gone out with her female lodger and paid a teenager a 'few coppers' to look after the children. When the teenager's mother had realised what was happening she had fetched her home.

On the occasion on 1 June she had left the children (aged six, four, one and seven months) with a fourteen year old. At 1.45 am the teenager had become frightened and a neighbour had called the police who waited with the children until 3.30 a.m. for their mother to return home. When she returned she told them she had been out with an American soldier but she had got drunk and fallen asleep; she had returned home as soon as she woke up. She stated that she would 'do away with herself' if she was summoned.

The policeman stated that he considered the house to be in a 'very dirty condition' and although the children were in 'a fair state of health' they were 'not very clean'. In her defence Mrs Davies explained that she had financial difficulties as her husband had stopped her allowance since the younger two children, who were not his, had been born.

Margery Jones remembers that a number of young women from Wrexham were to be seen loitering outside the camps at Penley and Llanerch Panna. She recalls that the local people from Penley were unhappy with the situation. In January 1945 both the Wrexham Leader and the Wrexham Advertiser and Star reported on:

> "Young girls who need control."

Apparently the Overton Bench had expressed their concern over the number of cases being brought before them of young girls who were choosing:

> "... a course of life which is in the highest degree undesirable and reprehensible."
> (Wrexham Leader 12/1/45)

Two girls had been brought before the bench at the end of 1944 for similar cases. A twenty-two year old girl from Pwhelli was charged with:

> "... associating with soldiers in Chester."

as well as several cases of theft. (She had already spent some time in Strangeways Prison in Manchester for similar offences.) She was given a three years' probation and it was stipulated that she must remain at such establishment as was selected for her by the Probation Officer. She was told:

> "We are giving you a chance to pull yourself together and become a respectable member of society." (Wrexham Leader 12/1/45)

The sixteen year old was charged with 'trespassing on an army camp' on 29 December 1944 after she had absconded from a home in Wrexham where she had been placed after being charged with theft at Overton. She said that she had run away to meet her American army boyfriend who had failed to keep the appointment. Police Sergeant Smith stated that young girls were invited to the American camps by soldiers who had no problem in procuring passes for them. After the dance or social event the girls would remain on the base, hiding during the day. (In October 1944 Colonel Blount from the 129th General Hospital at Penley notes in his log book:

> "An occasional unattached female has been found on the post after hours." (A.R.C. 129 G.H. NARA)

The sixteen year old girl had been found several times before in or near billets occupied by U.S. soldiers and P.S. Smith stated that he would describe her as an 'inveterate liar' as she had told the other girls in the home that she had swum the Channel. She was bound over for three years and placed under a probation officer.

Major Peel, presiding at Overton's Justices Court remarked that he hoped that the U.S. authorities would:

> "… cooperate in an effort to stamp out an evil which was becoming all too common in the area." (Wrexham Leader)

Miss Hitchcock, the Welfare Officer, stated that she had received excellent assistance from the Red Cross Field Director at one of the camps where those problems were not experienced now.

Some of the local girls befriended American servicemen in order to steal from them. A Mrs Gladys Pugh of Wrexham, who already had a criminal record, was convicted of stealing a gold watch from U.S. Serviceman Luther Boyer in February 1944. Boyer had met Mrs Pugh outside the Wynnstay Arms Hotel and had walked her home. When he looked at his watch he realised that it had stopped working so Mrs Pugh offered to fetch Boyer a cigarette from the house and reset the watch for him.

Wrexham Leader 23/6/44

The soldier waited but the woman did not reappear and when he knocked the door there was no response.

Boyer reported the matter both to the civilian police and the American Military Police who visited the house. At first Mrs Pugh insisted that she didn't have the watch and nothing was found during a search of her bedroom or the outside of the house. Eventually she admitted that she did have the watch but then ran away. When the police caught her she told them she had put it on a table but now it was gone. Fortunately the sharp-sighted police constable saw that one of the floorboards was broken and when he shone his torch in the hole he found the watch and recovered it. Mrs Pugh attempted to run away again but she was caught and charged.

STOLE WATCH FROM AMERICAN

WREXHAM WOMAN FINED £10

At the Wrexham Borough Magistrates' Court on Monday, before Mr John Hughes (presiding) and other magistrates, Mrs. Gladys Pugh (26), of 3, Chapel Buildings, Wrexham, pleaded not guilty to stealing a gold wristle watch, value £12 10s., from Luther Middlesworth Boyer, a private in the American Forces.

Defendant was represented by Mr Dillwyn Ffoulkes Jones.

D.C.C. Philip Tomkins said that on Tuesday, May 2nd, the soldier visited Wrexham and met the defendant about 11 p.m. outside the Wynnstay Arms Hotel and walked with her to her home. They stood talking outside the house for some time and the soldier looked at his watch and found it had stopped. He asked the defendant for a cigarette and she said she had some in the house and offered to fetch one, at the same time saying she would take his watch and re-set it. Boyer gave defendant his watch and she went into the house but did not reappear. The soldier waited about for half an hour, and as the defendant had not come out he knocked on the door several times but got no response. Then he abandoned his efforts and went to report the matter to his own military police. The civil police were also informed and at 1.30 a.m. P.S. Barnard and P.C. Thomas, with the military police, approached the house where Boyer was still keeping watch. The soldier, in the presence of the defendant, said what had taken place and defendant replied, "I did not take it." She was questioned but persisted in her denials and invited the police to search her bedroom. That was done and nothing was found. Defendant still persisted in her denials of having taken the watch and suggested the soldier may have lost it outside the house. A search was then made outside but without result, and the police left shortly afterwards.

Wrexham Leader 19/5/16

THEFT FROM AMERICAN MILITARY POLICEMAN

CONVICTED MAN'S UNSUCCESSFUL APPEAL.

On February 28th last, the Wrexham Borough Magistrates' sentenced Reginald John Garside (40), of 20, Brandfort St., Lidget Green, Bradford, to three months' hard labour. They had found him guilty of stealing cigarettes, soap and razor blades, value 2s. 1d., the property of James Earl Callahan, a member of the American Military Police.

At Ruthin, on Thursday week, Garside appeared before the Appeals Committee of the Denbighshire Quarter Sessions (Mr. Aneurin Evans presiding), and appealed against the conviction.

Mr. J. Jones Roberts appeared for the appellants, and Mr. J. P. Elsden for the respondents.

Callahan and Garside were, according to the evidence, both staying at the Wynnstay Hotel in adjoining rooms. On February 21st, it was alleged, Garside was drinking with Callahan and his colleagues, who said they were going in to dinner. Instead Callahan went to his room, then along the corridor, and on his return, found Garside in the room. Garside said he had come to ask for some tobacco. On checking up Callahan found various articles missing. When the police were called Garside was in a corridor leading to the dining-room and was called, but continued into the dining-room and the police saw him throw something into the fire and which was not recovered. A packet of American cigarettes was found in his possession. Soap similar to that missing was found in his room, as also were razor blades, among others, similar to those missing.

Wrexham Leader 19/5/16

In court Pugh stated that the American had given her the watch in return for 'services rendered' and that she intended to give it to the Military Police when Boyer left the house. She also stated that he had torn her coat and made advances towards her, which she rejected. In addition she denied that she had already been reprimanded by P.C. Thomas earlier in the evening for 'making a noise' with another American serviceman. Later in the cross-examination she admitted that she had:

"… told some untruths to the police." (Wrexham Leader 19/5/44)

She was found guilty but a plea was put forward for a non-custodial sentence as she had three young children. The chairman stated that he was sorry to see:

"… a young married woman like the defendant who had created such a record for herself. She had family responsibilities and her husband was away doing his job (in the army). She had a good income and there was no reason at all for her running wild like she was instead of being at home looking after her children." (Wrexham Leader 19/5/44)

She was fined £10 and was warned that the magistrate did not want to see her there again.

There were a number of incidences in the Wrexham and Oswestry area of G.I.s being stolen from. On 28 February 1944 Reginald Garside of Bradford was convicted of stealing cigarettes, soap and razor blades to the value of two shillings and a penny from James Callahan, an American Military Policeman. Apparently both Garside and Callahan were staying at the Wynnstay Hotel in Oswestry and had been drinking together. Later, when Callahan returned to his room, he found Garside there. Garside made the excuse that he had come to the room to borrow tobacco, but when Callahan found the various items were missing from the room he called the police. By the time the police arrived Garside had already thrown something into the fire, but cigarettes, soap and razor blades were found in his possession. Garside protested his innocence but the fact that he had previous convictions went against him and he was convicted to three months hard labour.

In June 1944 Robert Millington of Wrexham pleaded guilty to stealing a bicycle from Richard Thomas and selling it to Corporal Edward Slade of the U.S. Army. Apparently the bike had been left by its owner in an alleyway by the Golden Lion Pub. A few weeks later it was found in the possession of the American soldier who explained that he had bought it from the accused for £3. The accused stated that he had bought it from a Royal Marine for £3, although earlier he had admitted that he had stolen it.

When found guilty Millington explained that he had recently been discharged from the army on medical grounds, his wife had left him and he was living with his mother. He stated that he had never done anything like this before and never would again. Unfortunately for him it was noticed that when he had arrived at court earlier he was wearing an overcoat that had been stolen from Clarkes Garage in York Street.

After first claiming that he had bought the coat he eventually admitted that he had stolen it. To make matters worse for him when his military records came to light it transpired that rather than being discharged from the army he had deserted. He was sentenced to three months imprisonment with hard labour.

WREXHAM MAN'S THEFT
CYCLE AND OVERCOAT OFFENCES

At a special sitting of Wrexham Borough Magistrates' Court Friday, before Messrs T. Lloyd Williams (presiding) and A. A. Gree Robert Millington (28), of 15, Pea bryn, Wrexham, pleaded guilty stealing a cycle, value £5 10s, the property of Richard Kenneth Thoms of 31, St. Giles' Crescent, Spri Lodge.

D.C.C. Tomkins said that at 2-1 p.m. on June 5th, Mr Thomas left h cycle in the entry by the Golden Lic Inn, High Street, and when he r turned at 3 p.m. he found it w missing. He reported the matter to the police, and inquiries were mad Later the cycle was seen in the po session of an American soldier, an was recognised by the owner. It w eventually found to have been sold t the accused to the American. T defendant was taken to the polic station, where he made a statemen This was to the effect that about fiv weeks ago he met a Royal Marin commando in High Street. Th marine approached him and asked hir if he wished to buy the cycle. H asked him how much he wanted for and he replied £2, whereupon h (accused) said he would give him 25 for it, to which the marine agreed He then took the cycle home and sol it later to the American soldier i question for £3. That morning, how ever, the accused had made anothe statement admitting having stolen th cycle from the entry near the Golde Lion, and that he had sold it to th American for £3. He said he had ha drink at the time, but they would hea that although he had had drink, th number on the cycle, which was th only identification mark the polic had, had been filed off. The polic were asking for the magistrates' assist ance, as a great number of cycles ha been stolen in Wrexham lately.

Wrexham Leader 23/6/44

CRASHED INTO MILITARY LORRY
LORRY DRIVER FINED FOR DANGEROUS DRIVING

At the Wrexham Bromfield Magistrates Court on Tuesday, Mr. E. A. Cross presiding, William Howell Jones (19), 8, Chapel Street, Ponciau, was charged with driving a motor lorry in a manner dangerous to the public, driving without due care and attention, and driving a motor lorry with faulty brakes. His employer, Thomas Jones, 49, Church Street, Rhos, was charged with permitting the above last offence.

Mr. Cyril O. Jones appeared for the defendants and pleaded "Not guilty."

D.C.C. Philip Tomkins, prosecuting, said defendant William Howell Jones was a collier, who drove the lorry in his spare time for a coal merchant. The charge arose out of an accident on the Ruabon to Wrexham main road outside the North Wales Power Company's offices on May 22nd, when a coal lorry driven by defendant came into collision with a military truck travelling in the same direction. There were only two vehicles on that 30-feet wide road at the time. Defendant said, after the accident, that he swerved and hit the military truck because another vehicle came to meet him, but he (D.C.C. Tomkins) thought the court would be satisfied after hearing the witnesses that there was no other vehicle. The accident occurred about 9.45 a.m., and the military lorry, an American one, with six passengers, was proceeding towards Wrexham, and when opposite the North Wales Power premises, the lorry driven by the defendant came from behind, crashed into the side of the military truck, and forced it on to the pavement, and it crashed into the wall.

Wrexham Leader 9/6/44

Also in June 1944, collier William Jones was charged with driving a lorry dangerously and hitting an American military vehicle. At around 9.45 a.m. on 22 May, on the Ruabon to Wrexham main road his coal lorry had been in a collision with a military truck that was travelling in the same direction. Jones stated that the accident was caused by him swerving to avoid another vehicle but witnesses stated that there were no other vehicles on the road.

American contingent in the Salute the Soldier Parade marching past saluting base (Wrexham Leader 5/6/44)

Review stand of Salute the Soldier Parade (on steps of old technical college in Regent Street). Salute taken by Major General Maitland Wilson, Colonel of the Royal Welsh Fusiliers. Front row (L-R): Philip Walters (Town Clerk), 2 U.S. Army Officers, Mrs Cyril Breese (Mayoress), Mrs Ethel Breese (Mayor), Major General Wilson, Sir Robert Williams-Wynn (Lord Lieutenant of Denbighshire), 2 U.S. Army Officers, Lady Williams-Wynn, Colonel James Rankin (W.A. Williams)

Salute the Soldier Parade (Wrexham Leader)

Alex Dawman, the driver of the military vehicle, explained that he was travelling around 20 miles per hour when the lorry crashed into the back of his truck, forcing it onto the pavement and injuring one of the six passengers. Two eyewitnesses, who were standing at the bus stop, corroborated his story. Jones was fined £10, ordered to pay costs of 6s/6d and disqualified from driving for six months. Charges against his employer, Thomas Jones, who had been charged with allowing the offence by not overhauling the vehicles, were dropped.

American military vehicles from the bases around Wrexham were involved in other road accidents. An enlisted man from Penley was killed in March 1945 when he was run over by one of the vehicles from the base. The driver was found to be not at fault.

As well as being seen in the courts and out socially in Wrexham, American servicemen from the nearby military bases were also regularly observed in Parades and Church Services. On 29 April 1944 soldiers from the 129th General Hospital at Penley took part in 'Salute the Soldier Parade' through Wrexham.

U.S. Guard of Honour posted at tomb of Elihu Yale (Wrexham Leader 16/6/44)

In June of that year there was a parade of American and British servicemen and a civic procession led by the Royal Artillery Band. The procession included some graduates from Yale University who were in Wrexham to celebrate Yale Commemoration Day. Although Elihu Yale (the founder of Yale University) had been born in Boston, Massachusetts, his family came from Plas Grono near Wrexham, and he spent the last twenty-two years of this life living between there and London. His tomb is in the Churchyard of Wrexham Parish Church.

The Parish church was full of contingents of British and American servicemen and outside there was a guard of honour posted at the tomb. The address was given by the Bishop of St. Asaph who started by saying:

> "We welcome you as brothers for we share a common tradition of faith and purpose. We welcome you as comrades in arms dedicated and pledged to defeat and overthrow the modern barbarism." (Wrexham Leader 16/6/44)

The service closed with the singing of the British, American and Welsh national anthems. Later in the day there was a reception at the Wynnstay Hotel to which some of the American officers, including Lieutenant Commander Yale (as a representative of the Yale family) were invited. The Colonel thanked the Mayor and British Council for their hospitality and stated that the members of the American forces greatly appreciated the warm welcome that had been given to them. He stated:

> "In this war the British and American soldiers wear different uniforms, but they fight as one army, and for the peace of the world." (Wrexham Leader 16/6/44)

American troops on parade in Guildhall Square as part of Yale Commemoration Day (Wrexham Leader 16/6/44)

In April 1945 Wrexham Parish Church was the venue for a more sombre occasion. The death of President Franklin D. Roosevelt was marked by flags flying at half mast from a number of public buildings in Wrexham, including the Guild Hall, which flew the Stars and Stripes at half-mast. The Union Jack was flown at half-mast at the Parish Church and both American and British flags were flown at half-mast at the Wrexham Borough Health Offices.

The Wrexham Leader reported that the Parish church was full to capacity:

> "Rarely has the accommodation at Wrexham Parish Church been taxed to a greater capacity." (Wrexham Leader 20/4/45)

A large contingent of American servicemen and nurses attended the service, which was conducted by the Vicar, Reverend Robert Davis, accompanied by the Lord Bishop of St Asaph (Dr.W.T. Harvard) and other religious dignitaries. Padre Ralph Crosby, who was attached to the U.S. Forces, read the lesson and the service was concluded with an address by the Bishop who said:

> "Our sincerest sympathies go out to the people of the United States of America. We share their grief. And this emotion of sorrow and loss has touched not only those in high places in this realm, it has moved the heart of the common man, even to the most humble of its ranks. … We and all mankind have lost one of the greatest and stoutest champions of law and liberty, of right and freedom." (Wrexham Leader 20/4/45)

The following month after the announcement of V.E. Day, there was a Victory Parade in Wrexham, culminating at the Parish Church, where the congregation included both British and American servicemen.

In July 1945, as the American forces began to leave the area, 400 officers, nurses and enlisted men from the 129th General Hospital at Penley, marched from Bodhyfryd to the Parish Church. At the gates they were met by civic dignitaries including the Mayor and Mayoress of Wrexham. During the short service the colour party presented the American flag that had been flying over the base at Penley and a brass plaque bearing the inscription:

> "Presented to the town of Wrexham with gratitude for its hospitality, 129th General Hospital, U.S. Army. Haec olim meminisse juvabit." [One day this will be pleasing to remember] (Wrexham Leader July 1945)

Colonel Blount, Commanding Officer of the 129th, stated in his speech that the flag had flown over 'a little bit of U.S. territory in Wales.' He added that the flag had seen nearly 10,000 battle casualties enter and leave Penley. (In 2005, due to the shabbiness of the flag, it was replaced by a new one presented by the U.S. Air Force.)

On the following Wednesday evening a similar ceremony was held at Penley Parish Church which was situated next to the hospital site. On this occasion Colonel Blount presented the church with an inscribed scroll on which was recorded the appreciation of the hospitality accorded to the U.S. Army by the people of Penley.

The last military parade in 1945 involving U.S. Servicemen in Wrexham was on 16 September 1945 when the U.S. Marine Corps flag was presented to the Parish Church. The U.S. Marine Corps had had historic links with the Royal Welsh Fusiliers dating back to 1900 when they fought side by side in the Boxer Rebellion in China.

The Marine Corps Commandant ordered that a set of Marine Colours was delivered with appropriate ceremony to the Royal Welsh Fusiliers whose regimental headquarters was located in Wrexham. A colour guard of four men was selected from a Marine Corps Detachment that was based in London under the command of Lieutenant Charles A. Godwin. (The unit was based in London to provide security for the Naval Radio Station and other key communications.)

Four Marines travelled to Wrexham where they paraded led by the band of the 2nd Battalion, Royal Welsh Fusiliers and a detachment of the 21st Holding Battalion under the command of Major W.R. Crawsham. At the church the colours were presented to Reverend Davies who accepted them to hang in a prominent position in the church to:

Wrexham Leader September 1945

"... remind the American people and our own of the time when they stood side by side in the fight for liberty." (Wrexham Leader September 1945)

The Mayor concluded the service by saying:

"Our two nations have been firmly united in war, may we now be firmly united in our endeavours to secure a prominent peace, to reconstruct Europe and the world so as to provide a decent standard of life for everyone, and to rid us of the terrible menace of war." (Wrexham Leader September 1945)

Chapter 16

A Superior Job Well Done

ON 12 April 1945 the 83rd General Hospital had the lowest patient census for its time at Llanerch Panna – 372. More patients arrived in the latter days of the war, the last convoy of patients being received on 8 May. By midnight of V.E. Day there were 848 patients. Some of the ward tents remained in use for storage at this time and some were used by the Information and Education Officer, 1st Lieutenant Edwin Patton (former Rehabilitation Officer). His new duties became an expansion of the activities he had already carried out in Rehabilitation. On the announcement on the base of V.E. Day the Commanding Officer Colonel Norbury, noted:

> "Another phase in the life history of the 83rd (U.S.) General Hospital ends with V.E. Day. It is more a matter of feeling of thankfulness that combat in this theatre is over more than anything else. The hospital is still on operational status. It is prepared to remain that way as long as need be. All of its personnel are determined to go on giving the best possible care to patients who come here. That has been the dominant thought in the minds of all since activation through the period of training and that of functional employment during the combat that is just closed." (A.R.C. 83 G.H. NARA)

The 83rd didn't celebrate V.E. Day with a party. The Red Cross unit recorded:

> "The only celebration we had was to pass out cider with the doughnuts brought by the clubmobile. Those girls served both on the wards and we served cider in the Recreation Hall in the evening." (A.R.C. 83 G.H. NARA)

After V.E. Day no additional convoys were received at the hospital but a small number of neurosurgical and orthopaedic patients were transferred in from other installations. On 21 May the hospital was notified that it was to revert to a 1000 bed hospital and on noon of that date word was received that it was closed for admission of patients from midnight. During the course of the afternoon other messages relative to closure, disposition of patients and procedures to be followed were received.

The hospital was alerted for movement on 23 May and by the 24th all patients had been transferred out. Most were sent to 129th General Hospital; some went to 168th General Hospital. On 25 May Colonel Norbury travelled to London to receive orders. At this point a number of officers were transferred to other hospitals and Reinforcement Depots. Equipment was sorted and classified and British property was returned. 'Marching Out' for buildings was held by the U.S. Area Engineer and representatives of the British D.C.R.S. on 30 and 31 May. The motor section moved to port for transportation on 10 June.

Colonel Norbury's report concluded on the 83rd's time at Llanerch Panna:

> "So, another chapter of the life history of the 83rd (U.S.) General Hospital is at a close. Slightly over fourteen months after taking over this installation known as Hospital Plant 4190, U.S. Army, a few days after the anniversary of D-Day, this command moves on for the next stage of its job. It is the feeling of this headquarters that the hospital has worked well at the job at this station. Consultants, inspectors and, most important of all, patients have given credit for that. While there have been, and will be, changes in personnel, the policy 'the patient comes first' has been, and will be carried out by this command." (A.R.C. 83 G.H. NARA)

The American Red Cross Assistant Field Director with the 83rd mused:

"As we prepare to walk out of here for the last time we think of the many personalities who have gone through these doors. Some are more vivid than others. For the more fortunate ones this whole war experience will be a memory. Others will carry permanent reminders in physical and nervous disabilities. … We feel privileged in our assignments and have tried to serve as they served." (A.R.C. 83 G.H. NARA)

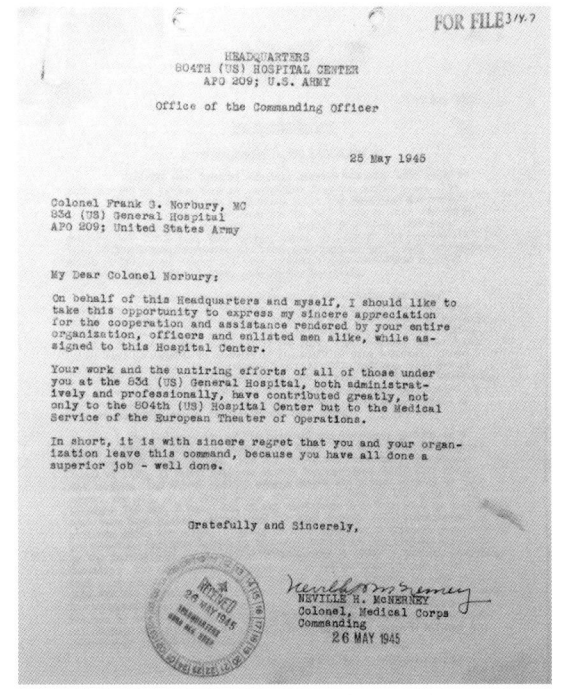

Letter sent to Colonel Norbury on closure of 83rd General Hospital at Llanerch Panna (NARA)

The 83rd left Llanerch Panna to open a hospital on the Continent near Reims in France.

The 68th General Hospital at Halston Hall also welcomed the news of Victory in Europe. On 7 May 100 German Prisoners of War arrived to be employed throughout the hospital just in time to hear the news of their country's surrender. Parties were held at all the clubs on the post on either 8th or 9th May to celebrate the Victory and both Catholic and Protestant services were held to offer prayers of thanks. The Assistant Field Director of the Red Cross unit attached to the 68th, Claire Sweeney, noted that V.E. Day:

> "… was mainly a day when we thanked God that one phase of the war was over and we reminded ourselves of our promise to see this to an end. There wasn't the hilarious celebration that one might have expected – the fellows didn't want that – too many of them have brothers and buddies fighting in the Pacific. We celebrated quietly with cakes, coffee and home-made cookies. These were made in our mess hall but the fellows said that they tasted like the kind mother used to make." (A.R.C. 68 G.H. NARA)

The 68th was also given notice for movement to the Continent and on 21 May a telephone call informed the Commanding Officer that all patients were to be transferred to the 137th General Hospital and the plant was to be closed. At 0150 on 13 June 1945 the 68th departed from Whittington Station bound for the South Coast and then France where they were to take over a hospital in Marmelon.

V.E. Day was celebrated on the base at Iscoyd Park; officers were also allowed to go into Whitchurch to celebrate with the local people. On 23 May 1945 the 82nd General Hospital ceased to function as a hospital and all patients were evacuated to other hospitals by 1800 hours on that day. The personnel prepared for movement to the Continent to take over the Hospital Plant at the Hospice Civil, Soissons that had previously been operated by the 230th General Hospital. This hospital opened to receive patients on 23 June and closed on 15 August 1945. On 27 August the 82nd moved to Hôpital Militair Gama, Toul, which was a medical installation that in turn had been used by French, German and U.S. Armies. Nurse Angela Weiss was given some opportunities for sightseeing during this time. She remembers being the only female in a photo of medical personnel taken in front of Versailles in June 1945.

Angela Weiss travelling in France at the end of the war (A. Weiss)

Meanwhile in Spring of 1945 Angela's husband's unit was moving around Germany. At one point it moved into billets that had been previously occupied by

German soldiers. They were amazed to see that one of the doors bore the name: Lt. Weiss (a name of German origin); naturally, he used that room. In July the 415th were ordered to report to Marseilles. Weiss understood that this meant that his unit would be preparing to travel to fight in the Pacific. One week later, the hydrogen bomb was dropped on Hiroshima and the unit was, instead, prepared to return to the U.S.

Angela Weiss was shipped home in November where she was sent directly to a military hospital in Atlanta, Georgia, due to her heart condition caused by the rheumatic fever contracted while with the 82nd General Hospital. The doctors told her that her heart was so badly damaged that having children would certainly kill her. The doctors were wrong and she went on to have three children, but later in life she was to suffer from the effects of the fever she had caught during the war.

Back in the U.K. at Oteley Deer Park, Tec. 5 McConkey had been given the task of planning the post-war training programme and on V.E. Day he was in Swindon carrying out work for the Information and Education Programme. He wrote home that classes were suspended for the day and the men were transported into town in trucks. McConkey was aware that he was very lucky not to have been one of the personnel from the 137th that was retrained as a replacement for a combat unit. After V.E. Day he wrote home:

> "I didn't mention it before so you wouldn't worry but during the past six months our outfit has been gradually giving up its personnel to the infantry and combat medics. Of course the war's end has bought this to a stop. About every four weeks a list of names would be posted, and with a great show of casualation, mixed with palpitating heart, we would rush over to the bulletin board to see if we were up to go. Since February the drafts came in earnest and almost daily I expected to be on the list, but fortunately my age or bad eyes and the Armistice all conspired to keep me here."

After V.E. Day McConkey was finally able to tell his family where he was stationed, as up to this point, it had been classified information.

There were no more convoys of patients for the 137th after V.E. Day but the hospital did start to admit Z.I. patients from other hospitals. The Red Cross reported that this group of patients were particularly difficult to keep occupied as they didn't understand why they couldn't be sent directly home from their previous hospital. Ironically after V.E. Day, when the patient census had dropped, facilities for the Red Cross improved and they were able

Outside the billets at Oteley Deer Park June 1945 T. McConkey on far right. (J. McConkey).

to move into a large roomy nissen hut where there were work benches, good lighting and room for wheelchairs.

After V.E. Day a number of American ex-Prisoners of War were still with the 137th. McConkey wrote home:

> "Some of them are almost as bad as the walking skeletons you see at the pictures. They are now getting back some of their normal weight."

Unlike the Z.I. patients the Red Cross noticed that these patients found being at the 137th a positive experience. They appreciated the fact that they could eat as much as they liked and also talk to different people. The Assistant Field Director, Doris Chatfield, noted:

> "Given any opportunity at all any R.A.M.P. (Released American Military Prisoner) will seat himself in the office and talk all afternoon or all evening. If we can listen so much the better; if we have to get out correspondence, answer telephone calls or balance books – a RAMP will go right on talking, content with an occasional nod from the audience." (A.R.C. 137 G.H. NARA)

Miss Chatfield also noted:

> "The acceleration of movement towards home seems to bring with it increased emphasis upon hasty marriages and upon plans for English wives and children to travel to the States." (A.R.C. 137 G.H. NARA)

Frank Billington of the 137th General Hospital on the way home to the U.S. on the R.M.S. Aquitania (J. McConkey)

Meanwhile, at Penley the tent extensions of the wards were taken down in April 1945 as the hospital numbers dropped. By 22 April the patient census was at 560, but the next day a trainload of 307 patients arrived of which 107 were litter and the rest ambulatory, 39 of these were liberated Allied P.O.W.s

V.E. Day was celebrated on the post on 9 May and on 13 May, five officers, ten nurses and fifteen enlisted men participated in a V.E. Sunday Parade held in Wrexham. By the end of July the 129th General Hospital had left Penley and the camp was put under the control of the War Office.

Epilogue

Gone, But Not Forgotten

AS THE U.S. troops moved out from the five hospitals in the cluster, plans were made for their post-war use. At first Penley and Llanerch Panna were temporarily used for demobbed British servicemen as a holding centre. After this three of the five hospitals were put aside to use as hospitals for detachments of the Polish Resettlement Corps. In August 1946 the hospital at Penley became known as Polish Hospital Number 3, Iscoyd Park – Number 4 Polish Tuberculosis Hospital and Llanerch Panna became Polish Hospital Number 11. Fortunately for the Poles the U.S.

View of the camp at Iscoyd Park from the water tower (B.B.C.)

View of camp at Iscoyd Park showing water tower (B.B.C.)

Army had left a considerable amount of their hospital equipment such as X-ray and operating equipment.

Originally the hospitals were staffed and equipped for the treatment of sick and injured Polish soldiers but in 1947 the hospitals were put into the hands of the Ministry of Pensions for the treatment of Polish families, not just those who had served in the military.

Penley, the largest of the three hospitals, also served as housing for doctors, nurses, auxiliary staff and their families. The camp had its own nursery, entertainment hall, clubroom with full-sized snooker table and a well-equipped cinema. One of the barracks was converted into a church which had a four foot high picture of the Saints behind the altar. Penley also had a maternity ward.

A lasting reminder of the Pole's stay at Penley is in Penley churchyard where there are rows of gravestones with Polish inscriptions, including a small group of graves for Polish children who died in the late 1940s-50s.

In 1949 the Polish hospital at Llanerch Panna closed down and the patients were transferred to the other two hospitals. There were plans to develop the site as an open prison or caravan park but these plans didn't come to fruition and the site at Llanerch Panna was left derelict until it was used for housing in the 1980s. The house at Lllanerch Panna has been modernised and is now known as Tudor Court.

View of camp at Iscoyd Park showing water tower (B.B.C.)

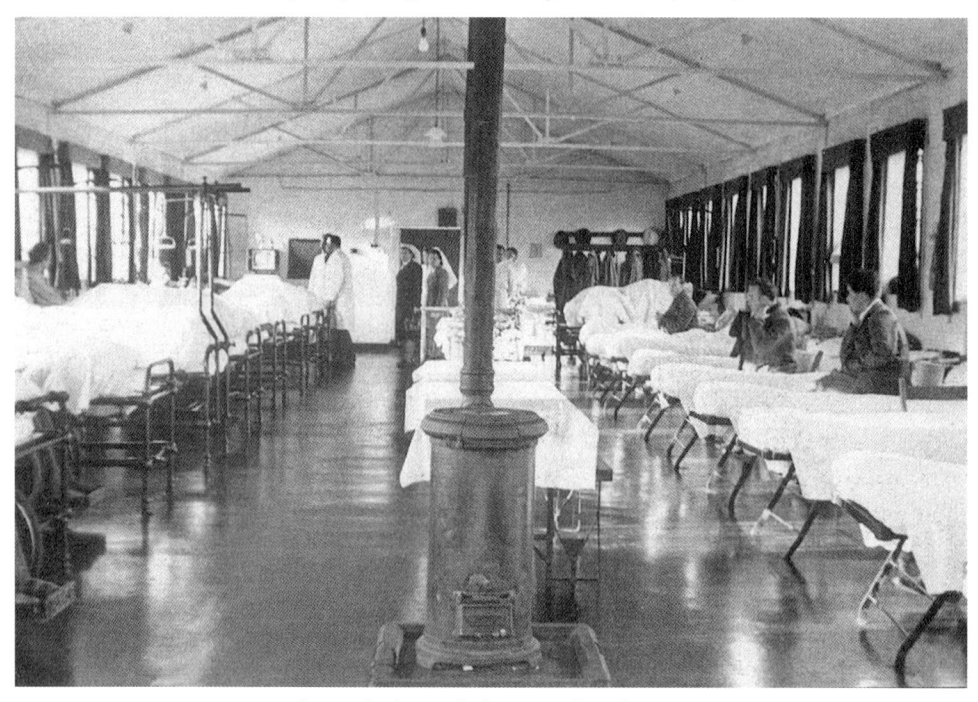

Ward at Penley hospital when in use by Poles (S.Pratt)

With the increased use of anti-biotics in the late 1940s and 50s the number of Tuberculosis cases at Iscoyd Park diminished and in 1956 the remaining T.B. patients, who could all speak English, were transferred to a Welsh sanatorium. Colonel Philip Godsal was able to return to his house at Iscoyd Park in 1946 but because of the Polish

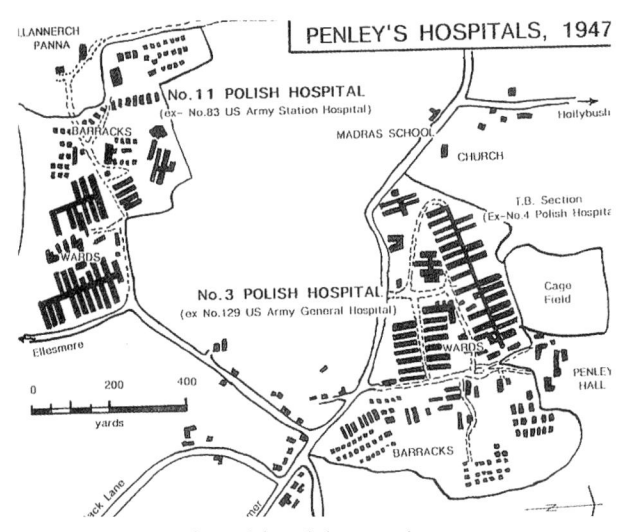

Map of two of the Polish Hospitals (S.Pratt)

Hospital he lived in a self-contained flat on the first floor in the Library wing. In 1957 the land was finally given back to the family and plans were made to demolish the remaining buildings in stages. Some nissen huts were sold to nearby farmers for their use. Today Iscoyd Park is run by the Godsal family as a scenic wedding venue.

In 1961 the hospital at Penley took on a new role, caring for old, disabled and chronically sick Poles. The last occupant of Penley Hall was the Dowager Lady Kenyon. The Gredington Estate was turned over to the Ministry of Works in 1964, which transformed the hall at Penley into a dining room and kitchens for senior staff in the hospital. When the Welsh Hospital Authority took over the hall it was left to deteriorate before being sold to a private developer in 1986, who demolished it the following year.

By 2002 the hospital at Penley had just one ward in use with six patients. It was

Skeleton of building at Llanerch Panna 1964 (S. Pratt)

not economically viable to keep the whole site open so in 2004 a new, smaller, purpose-built hospital was opened next to the original camp. The western most wards have now been converted for use as an industrial estate.

Halston Hall, site of the 68th General Hospital, was returned to the family after the war while at Oteley Deer Park the hall was demolished and the land returned to farming.

Derelict hut at Halston Hall (M. Collins)

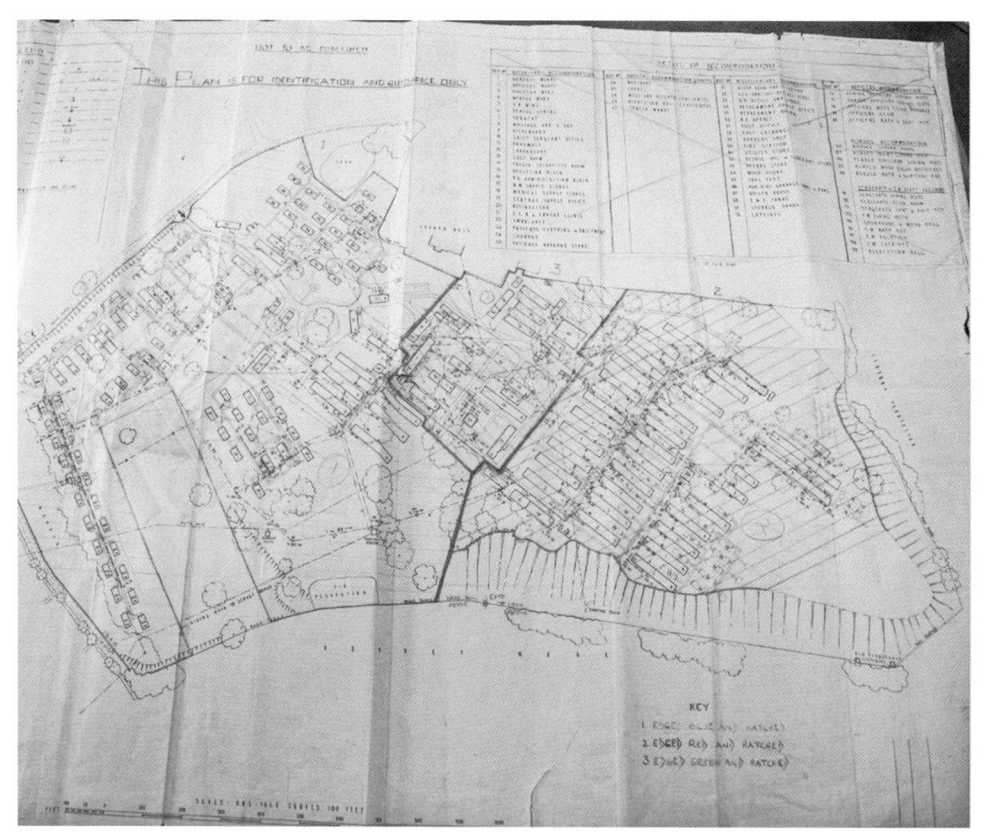

Map used to plan demolition of hospital buildings at Iscoyd Park (P. Godsal)

Wards used by Polish hospital at Penley (M. Collins)

GONE, BUT NOT FORGOTTEN

Covered walkways at Penley (M. Collins)

Iscoyd Park (M. Collins)

Purpose-built Polish hospital at Penley (M. Collins)

Abbreviations

A.F.D. – Assistant Field Director (Leader of the Red Cross at a base)
A.R.C. – American Red Cross
A.T.S. – Auxiliary Territorial Service
AWOL – Absent Without Leave
C.O. – Commanding Officer
D.O.P. – Detachment of Patients
E.E.N.T. – Eyes, Ears, Nose and Throat
E.N.S.A. – Entertainment National Service Association (U.K.)
E.T.O. – European Theatre of Operations
E.T.O.U.S.A. – European Theatre of Operations, United States of America
P.T.O. – Pacific Theatre of Operations
I. and E. – Information and Education service set up towards the end of the war to provide education that would help G.I.s in civilian life
H.Q. – Headquarters
M.P. – Military Police
N.P. – Neuro-Psychiatric
N.C.O. – Non-Commissioned Officer
Col. – Colonel
Cpl. – Corporal
Lt. – Lieutenant
Maj. – Major
Pfc. – Private First Class
Pvt. – Private
Sgt. – Sergeant
Tec. 4 – Technician 4th Grade
L.S.T. – Landing Ship Tank
O.R. – Operating Room
P.O.W. – Prisoner of War
P.X. – Post Exchange – (U.S. equivalent of NAAFI)
R.A.F. – Royal Air Force
R.A.M.C. – Royal Army Medical Corps (British)
R.A.S.C. – Royal Army Service Corps (British)
R.A.M.P. – Recovered American Prisoner of War
T/E – Table of Equipment
T/O – Table of Organization
U.S.A.A.F. – United States Army Air Force
U.S.O. – United Service Organisation (U.S.)
W.A.C. – Women's Army Corps (British)
W.V.S. – Women's Voluntary Service – British civilian voluntary organisation
Comm. Z. – Communication Zone – area behind the combat zone i.e. U.K.
Z.I. – Zone of the Interior (U.S.)

Glossary

Abreaction – the expression and consequent release of a previously repressed emotion, achieved through reliving the experience that caused it (typically through hypnosis or suggestion)

Affiliated Hospital – a hospital composed of staff from an existing hospital in the U.S.

Ambulatory – able to walk

Assigned – having permanent duties at a base

Attached – personnel attached to a hospital

Detached – personnel at hospital on temporary assignment

Limited Assignment – having temporary duties at a base

Class A Uniform – formal dress uniform

Litter – stretcher

Convalescent Hospitals – (C.H.) – Treated convalescing troops sent from station or general hospitals

General Hospital – (G.H.) – Hospitals with 1082 beds (although at times when the need arose this number was larger). Mainly intended for soldiers wounded during combat

Station Hospitals – (S.H.) – Hospitals with 834 beds serving the needs of troops in training. Often attached to a base

Hospital Center – Group of hospitals grouped together for administrative purposes under a Headquarters

Operation Overlord – Codename for Allied invasion of France.

Operation Bolero – Codename for the build up of troops in Britain in readiness for D. Day

Mess Hall – dining room on a military base

Motor Pool – Unit that repaired and maintained the vehicles attached to a unit

Replacement Depot – Transit camp for personnel awaiting assignment

Special Services – Education and Entertainment section responsible for the morale of troops on a base

Appendix 1: American Military Camps in Flintshire/Shropshire area during World War 2

With kind permission of Philip Grinton

30 September 1943
Llanerch Panna 304 Station Hospital, Headquarters, Medical Detachment
Atcham 6 Fighter Wing SP, HQ & HQ Squadron
Atcham 12 Station Complement Squadron
Atcham 18 Weather Squadron, Weather Detachment 342
Atcham 42 Service Group, 356 Service Squadron
Atcham 306 Dispensary
Atcham 333 Service Group, Group Headquarters Squadron
Atcham 526 Army Postal Unit
Atcham 1042 Signal Company (Service Group), Detachment A
Atcham 1148 Quartermaster Company (Service Group), Det A
Atcham 1258 Military Police Company (Aviation)
Atcham 1761 Ordnance Supply & Maintenance Company
Atcham 2906 Observation Training Group (Prov), HQ Squadron
Atcham 2908 & 2909 Flight Training Squadron (Provisional)
Atcham Finance Detachment 342
Market Drayton 5 Signal Radio Intelligence Team
Market Drayton 24 AW Comm Squadron, Detachment P
Shrewsbury 7 Chemical Depot Company
Wem 2 Finance Distribution Section
Wem 6 Medical Depot Company, Detachment D
Wem 187 Ordnance Depot Company, Detachment A
Wem 216 Signal Depot Company
Wem 244 Quartermaster Service Battalion (-), HQ & HQ Det, Company B, Medical Detachment
Wem 339 Quartermaster Depot Company
Wem 457 Engineer Depot Company
Wem 729 Railway Operating Battalion, Detachment F
Wem 756 Railway Shop Battalion, Detachment C
Wem 769 Military Police Battalion (ZI), Company A, Det C
Wem 980 Ordnance Depot Company
Wem General Depot G-16, Quartermaster, Chemical Warfare, Engineer, Medical, Ordnance, Signal, and Special Service Sections.

14 November 1943
Llanerch Panna 304 Station Hospital, Headquarters, Medical Detachment, Detachment of Patients
Atcham 12 Station Complement Squadron
Atcham 18 Weather Squadron, Weather Detachment 342
Atcham 42 Service Group, 356 Service Squadron
Atcham 306 Dispensary
Atcham 333 Service Group, Group Headquarters Squadron
Atcham Finance Detachment 342
Atcham 495 Fighter Training Group, HQ & HQ Squadron, 551 & 552 Fighter Training Sqdrn
Atcham 526 Army Postal Unit
Atcham 1042 Signal Company (Service Group), Detachment A
Atcham 1148 Quartermaster Company (Service Group), Det A
Atcham 1258 Military Police Company (Aviation)
Atcham 1761 Ordnance Supply & Maintenance Company
Atcham 2020 Engineer Fire Fighting Platoon
Market Drayton 24 A W Comm Squadron, Detachment P
Shrewsbury 7 Chemical Depot Company
Wem 2 Finance Distribution Section
Wem 6 Medical Depot Company, Detachments C & D
Wem General Depot G–16, Quartermaster, Chemical Warfare, Engineer, Medical, Ordnance, Signal, Special Services Sections
Wem 187 Ordnance Depot Company, Detachment A Shropshire
Wem 216 Signal Depot Company (-) Shropshire
Wem 244 Quartermaster Service Battalion (-), HQ & HQ Det, Company B, C, Medical Det
Wem 339 Quartermaster Depot Company
Wem 348 Ordnance Depot Company
Wem 457 Engineer Depot Company
Wem 557 Quartermaster Railhead Company
Wem 729 Railway Operating Battalion, Detachment F

APPENDIX 1

Wem 769 Military Police Battalion (ZI), Company D, Det C
Wem 1211 Fire Fighting Platoon Shropshire

31 December 1943
Llanerch Panna 304 Station Hospital, Detachment of Patients, Headquarters, Medical Detachment
Atcham 12 Station Complement Squadron
Atcham 18 Weather Squadron, Weather Detachment 342
Atcham 42 Service Group, 356 Service Squadron
Atcham 138 Army Postal Unit
Atcham 182 Medical Dispensary A
Atcham 333 Service Group Headquarters Squadron
Atcham 467 Service Squadron
Atcham 495 Fighter Training Group, HQ + HQ Sqdn, 551 & 552 Fighter Training Sqdn
Atcham 526 Army Postal Unit Shropshire
Atcham 1042 Signal Company (Service Group), Detachment A
Atcham 1148 Quartermaster Company (Service Group), Det A
Atcham 1258 Military Police Company (Aviation)
Atcham 1761 Ordnance Supply and Maintenance Company
Atcham 2020 Engineer Fire Fighting Platoon
Atcham Finance Detachment 342 S
Davenport House 373 Engineer General Service Regiment, 2 Bn, Co E
Gatacre Hall 373 Engineer General Service Regiment, 2 Bn, Co D
Kinlet 373 Engineer General Service Regiment, 1 Bn, Co B, Med Det, Det B
Loton Deer Park Chemical Warfare Service Depot C-900
Market Drayton 5 Signal Radio Intelligence Team
Market Drayton 24 A W Comm Sq, Det P Shropshire
Mawley Hall 373 Engineer General Service Regiment, 1 Bn, HQ Co, Med Det
Shrewsbury 7 Chemical Depot Company
Stanley Hall 373 Engineer General Service Regiment, 2 Bn, Co F
Sturt Common 373 Engineer General Service Regiment, 1 Bn, Co A, Med Det Co.A
Wem 1 Quartermaster Salvage Depot, Detachment D
Wem 2 Finance Distribution Section
Wem 6 Medical Depot Company, Detachment D
Wem 23 Quartermaster Truck Regiment, Company D
Wem 35 Bomb Disposal Squadron
Wem 187 Ordnance Depot Company, Detachment A
Wem 188 Signal Repair Company Shropshire

Wem 216 Signal Depot Company (-) Shropshire
Wem 244 Quartermaster Salvage Battalion, HQ & HQ Det, Medical Detachment, Company B, C
Wem 339 Quartermaster Depot Company
Wem 348 Ordnance Depot Company
Wem 457 Engineer Depot Company
Wem 557 Quartermaster Railhead Company
Wem 769 Military Police Battalion (ZI), Company D, Det C
Wem 1211 Fire Fighting Platoon
Wem 3013 Quartermaster Bakery Company
Wem General Depot G-16, Chemical Warfare Service, Engineer, Medical, Ordnance, Quartermaster, Signal, Special Services Sections
Whitchurch 29 Infantry Division, Military Police Platoon (-) Shropshire

21 February 1944
Llanerch Panna 304 Station Hospital, Headquarters, Medical Detachment, Detachment of Patients
Atcham 1 Gun Towed Target Flight
Atcham 12 Station Complement Squadron
Market Drayton 24 A W Comm Squadron, Detachment P
Market Drayton 1064 Military Police Company (Aviation), Detachment A
Mawley Hall 95 Engineer General Service Regiment (-), HQ, 1 Bn HQ & Hq Det, HQ & Serv Co.
Shrewsbury 7 Chemical Depot Company
Shrewsbury 373 Engineer General Service Regt, 1 Bn (-), HQ & HQ Det
Sturt Common 95 Engineer General Service Regt, 1 Bn, Company B
Sturt Common 95 Engineer General Service Regt, 1 Bn, Company B
Sturt Common 373 Engineer General Service Regt, 1 Bn, Company A
Wem 1 Quartermaster Salvage Depot, Detachment D
Wem 2 Finance Distribution Section
Wem 6 Medical Depot Company, Detachment D
Wem General Depot G–16, Quartermaster, Chemical Warfare, Engineer, Medical, Ordnance, Signal Special Service Sections
Wem 35 Bomb Disposal Squadron
Wem 216 Signal Depot Company
Wem 229 Quartermaster Salvage Collecting Company, Det E
Wem 244 Quartermaster Service Battalion (-), HQ & HQ Det, Co C&D, Med Det
Wem 308 Quartermaster Railhead Company
Wem 308 Quartermaster Railhead Company
Wem 339 Quartermaster Depot Company
Wem 348 Ordnance Depot Company

U.S. ARMY HOSPITAL CENTER 804

Wem 457 Engineer Depot Company
Wem 769 Military Police Battalion (Zone of Interior), Co D, Det C
Wem 1211 Engineer Comp Platoon (Fire Fighting)
Wem 3013 Quartermaster Bakery Company
Wem 3342 Quartermaster Truck Company
Whitchurch 29 Infantry Division, Military Police Platoon
Whitchurch 498 Medical Collection Company Shropshire
Heath Camp Field Force Replacement Depot 1, Casual Detachment 5

31 March 1944

Llanerch Panna 304 Station Hospital, Headquarters, Medical Detachment, Detachment of Patients
Trelogan 112 Infantry Regiment, Anti-Tank Company
Albrighton 196 Field Artillery Battalion (105mm), Headquarters, HQ Battery, Batteries A, B, C, Medical Detachment, Service Battery
Atcham 1 Gun Towed Target Flight
Atcham 12 Station Complement Squadron
Atcham 18 Weather Squadron, Weather Detachment 342
Atcham 42 Service Group, 356 Service Squadron
Atcham 182 Medical Dispensary (Aviation)
Atcham 331 Service Group (-), HQ & HQ Squadron
Atcham 333 Service Group (-), HQ & HQ Squadron
Atcham 495 Fighter Training Group, HQ & HQ Squadron, 551 & 552 Fighter Tng Squadrons
Atcham 526 Army Postal Unit
Atcham 793 Military Police Battalion (Zone of Interior), Co C, Det B
Atcham 1004 Signal Company (Service Group), Detachment A
Wem General Depot G–16, Quartermaster, Chemical Warfare, Engineer, Medical, Ordnance, Signal and Special Service Sections
Wem 216 Signal Depot Company
Wem 229 Quartermaster Salvage Collecting Company, Det E
Wem 244 Quartermaster Battalion, HQ & HQ Detachment, Medical Detachment
Wem 308 Quartermaster Railhead Company, Detachment A
Wem 339 Quartermaster Depot Company
Wem 348 Ordnance Depot Company
Wem 457 Engineer Depot Company
Wem 581 Quartermaster Battalion, Medical Detachment
Wem 769 Military Police Battalion (Zone of Interior), Co D, Det C

Wem 793 Military Police Battalion (Zone of Interior), Co C, Det A
Wem 1211 Engineer Fire Fighting Platoon
Wem 3013 Quartermaster Bakery Company
Wem 3263 & 3264 Quartermaster Service Company
Wem 3342 Quartermaster Truck Company
Whitchurch 2 Evacuation Hospital, Headquarters, Medical Detachment
Whitchurch 498 Collection Company
Whitchurch 581 Ambulance Company (Motorized)
Heath Camp Field Force Replacement Depot 1, Casual Detachment
Heath Camp 300 Replacement Company
Bryn-y-Pys 908 Field Artillery Battalion, Headquarters Battery, Batteries A, B, C, Medical Detachment, Service Battery
Gwernheylod Cam p329 Infantry Regiment, HQ, Anti-tank Co, Cannon Co, Med Det, Serv. Co
Iscoyd Park 82 General Hospital
Llanerch Panna 83 General Hospital, Headquarters, Med Det, Detachment of Patients
Llanerch 304 Station Hospital, Headquarters, Med Det, Det of Patients
Adderley 331 Infantry Regiment, Headquarters, 1 Batt A, B, C, D, Med Det
Albrighton 196 Field Artillery Battalion (105mm), Headquarters, HQ Batt, Batts A, B, C, Med Det, Serv Battery
Atcham 12 Station Complement Squadron
Atcham 18 Weather Squadron, Weather Detachment 342
Atcham 42 Service Group, 356 Service Squadron
Atcham 182 Medical Dispensary (Aviation)
Atcham 333 Service Group HQ & HQ Squadron
Atcham 334 Finance Detachment
Atcham 495 Fighter Training Group, HQ & HQ Squadron, 551 & 552 Fter Tng Sqn
Atcham 526 Army Postal Unit
Atcham 793 Military Police Battalion (ZI), Company C, Det B
Atcham 1004 Signal Company (Service Group), Detachment A
Atcham 1148 Quartermaster Company (Service Group), Det A
Atcham 1275 Military Police Company (Aviation), Det A
Atcham 1761 Ordnance Supply & Maintenance Company
Atcham 2020 Engineer Fire Fighting Platoon (Aviation)
Coton Hall 90 Quartermaster Company
Coton Hall 358 Infantry Regiment, 1 Battalion, HQ Co, 1 Batt Cos A, B, C, D, Headquarters
Coton Hall 603 Quartermaster Graves Registration Company, 3 Plt

170

APPENDIX 1

Coton Hall 790 Ordnance Light Maintenance Company
Claverley 445, 642 and 647 Quartermaster Trp T Companies
Davenport House 90 Infantry Division Artillery, Medical Detachment
Davenport House 315 Engineer Combat Battalion, Company A
Davenport House 343 Field Artillery Battalion (105mm), Headquarters, HQ Batt, Batts A, B, C, Med Det, Serv Batt
Davenport House 344 Field Artillery Battalion (105mm), Headquarters, HQ Batt, Batts A, B, C, Med Det, Serv Batt
Davenport House 345 Field Artillery Battalion (155 Gun), Headquarters, HQ Batt, Batts A, B, C, Med Det, Serv Batt
Davenport House 915 Field Artillery Battalion (105mm), Headquarters, HQ Batt, Batts A, B, C, Med Det, Serv Batt
Gatacre Hall 315 Medical Battalion, Company A, Med Batt, Company D, Combat Batt Co. B
Gatacre Hall 357 Infantry Regiment, 1 Battalion, Headquarters, HQ Co, Cos A, B, C, D
Kinlet 357 Infantry Regiment, Headquarters, Headquarters Co
Kinlet 357 Infantry Regiment, 2 Battalion, Headquarters, HQ Co, Companies E, F, G, H
Kinlet 357 Infantry Regiment, 3 Battalion, Headquarters, HQ Co, Cos I, J, K, L, M
Kinlet 357 Infantry Regiment, Anti-Tank Company, Cannon Co, Med Det, Serv Co
Kinlet 373 Engineer General Service Regt, Medical Det, Det B Shropshire
Loton Deer Park 66 Chemical Depot Company
Loton Deer Park 228 Chemical Base Depot Company
Loton Deer Park Chemical Warfare Service Depot C–900
Loton Deer Park 3342 Quartermaster Truck Company, 1 Platoon
Mawley Hall 1310 Engineer General Service Regt, 2 Bn (-), HQ & HQ Det, Co. D
Merrington 308 Medical Battalion, Companies A, B
Merrington 308 Engineer Combat Battalion, Companies A, B
Merrington 1310 Engineer General Service Regt, 1 Bn, Company B
Oteley Deer Park 15 General Hospital, Med Det Headquarters
Shavington 308 Engineer Combat Battalion (-), Headquarters, HQ & Serv Co., Med Det
Shrewsbury 7 Chemical Depot Company
Shrewsbury 373 Engineer General Service Regt, 1 Bn (-), HQ & HQ Det
Stanley Hall 447 & 448 Quartermaster Trp T Companies
Stanley Hall 3200 & 3201 Quartermaster Service Companies
Sturt Common 315 Medical Battalion, Company B
Sturt Common 358 Infantry Regiment, Headquarters
Sturt Common 358 Infantry Regiment, 2 Battalion, Headquarters, HQ Co, Companies E, F, G, H
Sturt Common 358 Infantry Regiment, 3 Battalion, Headquarters, HQ Co, Companies I, K, L, M
Sturt Common 358 Infantry Regiment, Anti-Tank Co, Cannon Co, Med Det
Styche Hall 308 Medical Battalion, Company C
Wem 2 Finance Distribution Section
Wem 6 Medical Depot Company, Detachment D
Wem General Depot G–16, Quartermaster, Chemical Warfare, Engineer, Med, Ordnance, Signal, Special Services Sections
Wem 53 Bomb Disposal Squadron
Wem 216 Signal Depot Company
Wem 229 Quartermaster Salvage Collecting Company, Det E
Wem 244 Quartermaster Battalion, HQ & HQ Detachment, Med Det
Wem 308 Quartermaster Railhead Company, Det A
Wem 339 Quartermaster Depot Company S
Wem 348 Ordnance Depot Company
Wem 457 Engineer Depot Company
Wem 484 Quartermaster Refrigeration Company (M), 3 Platoon
Wem 578 Signal Depot Company
Wem 581 Quartermaster Battalion, Medical Detachment
Wem 613 Quartermaster Depot Company S, 2 Platoon
Wem 793 Military Police Battalion (ZI), Company C, Det A
Wem 1211 Engineer Fire Fighting Platoon
Wem 3013 Quartermaster Bakery Company
Wem 3263 Quartermaster Service Company
Wem 3264 Quartermaster Service Company
Wem 3342 Quartermaster Truck Company
Whitchurch 2 Evacuation Hospital, Headquarters, Med Det
Whitchurch 498 Collection Company
Whitchurch 581 Ambulance Company (Motorized)
Heath Camp Field Force Replacement Depot 1, Casual Detachment 5
Heath Camp 36 Replacement Battalion, Headquarters, HQ Det, Med Det
Heath Camp 297, 298, 299, 300 Replacement Companies

31 May 1944
Bryn-y-Pys 11 Replacement Depot, Casual Detachment 29

U.S. ARMY HOSPITAL CENTER 804

Bryn-y-Pys 67 Replacement Battalion, Headquarters
Bryn-y-Pys 215, 216, 350, 489 Replacement Companies
Flint 204 Quartermaster Laundry Platoon (Hospital)
Gwernheylod Camp 1 Medical Concentration Center, 12 Med Hosp Center Convalescence Camp
Iscoyd Park 82 General Hospital, Headquarters
Llanerch Panna 83 General Hospital (-), Headquarters
Llanerch Panna 542 Ship Hospital Platoon
Llanerch Panna 30 Ship Hospital Platoon
Adderley 68 Replacement Battalion, Headquarters
Adderley 339 Replacement Company
Albrighton 196 Field Artillery Battalion (105 How), Headquarters
Aston 83 Infantry Division Artillery, Headquarters
Atcham 18 Weather Squadron, Weather Detachment 342
Atcham 42 Service Group, 356 Service Squadron
Atcham 182 Medical Dispensary (Aviation)
Atcham 333 Service Group (-), HQ & HQ Squadron
Atcham 495 Fighter Training Group, Headquarters, 551 & 552 Fighter Tng Sqns
Atcham 526 Army Postal Unit
Atcham 793 Military Police Battalion (ZI), Company C, Det
Atcham 1004 Signal Company (Service Group), Detachment A
Atcham 1148 Quartermaster Company (Service Group), Det A
Atcham 1761 Ordnance Supply & Maintenance Company
Atcham 2020 Engineer Fire Fighting Platoon (Aviation)
Babbinswood 329 Infantry Regiment, 2 Battalion, Headquarters, HQ Co, Companies E, F, G, H
Bridgnorth 447 & 448 Quartermaster Trp T Companies
Bridgnorth 3201 Quartermaster Service Company
Calverhall 308 Engineer Combat Battalion, Company B
Calverhall 3933 Quartermaster Gasoline Supply Company
Catherton Common 463 Anti-Aircraft Artillery AW Battalion (M), HQ
Coton Hall 90 Quartermaster Company
Coton Hall 358 Infantry Regiment, 1 Battalion, Headquarters, HQ Co, Cos A, B, C, D
Claverley 445 Quartermaster Trp T Company
Claverley 642 Quartermaster Trp T Company
Claverley 3918, 3919, 3920 Quartermaster Gasoline Supply Companies
Davenport House 90 Infantry Division Artillery, Headquarters
Davenport House 315 Engineer Combat Battalion, Company A
Davenport House 343, 344, 345 Field Artillery Battalions (105 How), Headquarters
Davenport House 915 Field Artillery Battalion (105 How) Shropshire
Gatacre Hall 357 Infantry Regiment, 1 Battalion, Headquarters, HQ Co, Companies A, B, C, D
Halston Hall 68 General Hospital, Headquarters
Halston Hall 212 Quartermaster Laundry Platoon (Hospital)
Hawkstone Park 7 Disciplinary Training Center
Kinlet 315 Engineer Combat Battalion, Company B
Kinlet 315 Medical Battalion, Company D
Kinlet 357 Infantry Regiment (-), Headquarters
Kinlet 373 Engineer General Service Regt, Medical Det, Det B
Loton Deer Park Chemical Warfare Service Depot C–900
Loton Deer Park 3342 Quartermaster Truck Company (TC), 1 Platoon
Ludlow 18 Field Artillery Group (Motorized), HQ & HQ Battery
Ludlow 47 Ordnance Battalion, HQ & HQ Detachment
Ludlow 99 Infantry Battalion, Headquarters
Ludlow 174 Field Artillery Battalion (155 Gun), Headquarters
Ludlow 204 Field Artillery Battalion (155 How), Headquarters
Ludlow 258 Field Artillery Group (Motorized), Field Artillery (155 Gun) Headquarters
Ludlow 300 Ordnance Maintenance Anti-Aircraft Company
Ludlow 514 Ordnance Heavy Maint Field Artillery Company
Ludlow 544 Ordnance Heavy Maint Field Artillery Company
Ludlow 690 Field Artillery Battalion (105 How), Headquarters
Ludlow 744 Tank Battalion (Light), HQ & HQ Co.
Ludlow 991 Field Artillery Battalion (155 Gun), Headquarters
Mawley Hall 221 Signal Depot Company
Merrington 11 Replacement Depot, Casual Detachment 30
Merrington 212 & 349 Replacement
Oswestry 83 Armored Field Artillery Battalion, HQ Battery Oswestry 322 Field Artillery Battalion (105 How), Headquarters Shropshire
Oswestry 323, 324 & 908 Field Artillery Battalions (105 How), Headquarters
Oswestry 1310 Engineer General Serv Regt, 2 Bn HQ & HQ Det, Company

APPENDIX 1

Oteley Deer Park 15 General Hospital, Headquarters
Oteley Deer Park 213 Quartermaster Laundry Platoon (Hospital)
Oteley Deer Park 544 Ship Hospital Platoon
Shrewsbury 7 Chemical Depot Company
Shrewsbury 66 & 288 Chemical Base Depot Companies
Stanley Hall 3200 Quartermaster Service Company
Stoke on Tern 83 Reconnaissance Troop (Mechanized)
Stoke on Tern 783 Ordnance Light Maintenance Company
Sturt Common 358 Infantry Regiment, Headquarters
Wem 2 Finance Distribution Section
Wem General Depot G–16, Quartermaster Section
Wem 53 Bomb Disposal Squadron
Wem 103 Finance Distribution Section
Wem 216 Signal Depot Company
Wem 229 Quartermaster Salvage Collecting Company, Det E
Wem 240 Quartermaster Depot Company S, Detachment B
Wem 244 Quartermaster Battalion, HQ & HQ Detachment
Wem 308 Quartermaster Railhead Company
Wem 339 Quartermaster Depot Company S
Wem 348 Ordnance Depot Company
Wem 457 Engineer Depot Company
Wem 484 Quartermaster Refrigeration Company (M), 3 Platoon
Wem 567 Quartermaster Battalion, HQ & HQ Detachment
Wem 578 Signal Depot Company
Wem 784 Base Depot Company (Transportation Corps), Det A
Wem 793 Military Police Battalion (ZI), Company C, Det A
Wem 1211 Engineer Fire Fighting Platoon
Wem 1230 Engineer Fire Fighting Section
Wem 3013 Quartermaster Bakery Company (Mobile)
Wem 3263 Quartermaster Service Company
Wem 3264 Quartermaster Service Company
Wem 3277 Ordnance Base Depot Company
Whitchurch 2 Evacuation Hospital, Headquarters
Whitchurch 11 Replacement Depot, Headquarters
Whitchurch 114 Anti-Aircraft Artillery Group, Headquarters Battery

30 June 1944
Bettisfield 11 Replacement Depot Casual Detachment 32
Flint 204 Quartermaster Laundry P1 H
Hanmer 11 Replacement Depot Replacement Detachment O19-A, X21-F
Iscoyd Park 82 General Hospital, Headquarters
Iscoyd Park 4192 Hospital Plant
Overton 11 Replacement Depot Casual Detachment 29
Overton 11 Replacement Depot Replacement Detachment U20-B, U20-D, X21-C, X22-B, X23-C
Gwernheylod 12 Medical Hospital Center Convalescent Camp
Overton 67 Replacement Battalion Headquarters
Llanerch Panna 83 General Hospital, Headquarters
Overton 215, 216, 350 & 489 Replacement Companies
Overton 571 Ambulance Company (Motorized) Flintshire
Llanerch Panna 4190 Hospital Plant Flintshire
Gwernheylod 6810 Med HP Center Flintshire
Adderley 11 Replacement Depot Casual Detachment 33 Shropshire
Adderley 11 Replacement Depot Replacement Detachment O16-C, X21-A, X22-D
Adderley 68 Replacement Battalion Headquarters
Adderley 339 Replacement Company
Atcham 12 Station Complement Squadron
Atcham 42 Service Group, 356 Serv Sqn
Atcham 182 Medical Dispensary A
Atcham 333 Service Group (-) HQ & HQ Squadron
Atcham 495 Fighter Training Group, 551 & 552 Fighter Tng Squadrons & HQ
Atcham 526 Army Postal Unit
Atcham 793 Military Police Battalion ZI, Company C, Det B
Atcham 1004 Signal Company (Service Group), Detachment A
Atcham 1148 Quartermaster Company (Service Group), Det A
Atcham 1385 Military Police Company (Aviation), Detachment A
Atcham 1761 Ordnance S M Company
Atcham 2020 Engineer Fire Fighting Platoon (Aviation)
Bridgnorth 447 & 448 Quartermaster Trp T Companies
Bridgnorth 999 Field Artillery Battalion (8 Inch How)
Bridgnorth 3201 Quartermaster Service Company
Catherton Common 463 Anti-Aircraft Artillery AW Battalion M HQ
Coton Hall 93 Signal Battalion HQ & HQ Company
Coton Hall 3255 Signal Service Company
Chyknell 3918 Quartermaster Gasoline Supply Company
Claverley 642 & 647 Quartermaster Trp T Companies

U.S. ARMY HOSPITAL CENTER 804

Claverley 3919, 3920, 3933 Quartermaster Gasoline Supply Companies
Halston Hall 212 Quartermaster Laundry Pl H
Hawkstone Park 7 Disciplinary Training Center
Heath Camp 863 Ordnance Heavy Auto Maintenance Company
Loton Deer Park 3342 Quartermaster Truck Company TC, 1 Platoon
Loton Deer Park Chemical Warfare Service Depot C-900
Ludlow 18 Field Artillery Group (Motorized) Headquarters
Ludlow 174 & 204 Field Artillery Battalions (155 Gun) Headquarters
Ludlow 300 Ordnance MAA Company
Ludlow 544 Ordnance Heavy Maintenance FA Company
Ludlow 991 Field Artillery Battalion (155 Gun), Headquarters
Mawley Hall 221 Signal Depot Company
Merrington 11 Replacement Depot Casual Detachment 30
Merrington 11 Replacement Depot Replacement Detachment O19-B, U20-C, X22-C
Merrington 212 & 349 Replacement Companies
Oteley Deer Park 15 General Hospital Headquarters
Oteley Deer Park 213 Quartermaster Laundry P1 H
Oteley Deer Park 4189 Hospital Plant
Shrewsbury 7 Chemical Depot Company
Shrewsbury 66 Chemical Base Depot Company
Shrewsbury 228 Chemical Depot Company
Sturt Common 167 Engineer Combat Battalion
Wem 2 Finance Distribution Section
Wem 53 Bomb Disposal Squadron
Wem 103 Finance Distribution Section
Wem 240 Quartermaster Depot Company S, Detachment B
Wem 244 Quartermaster Battalion
Wem 308 Quartermaster Railhead Company
Wem 339 Quartermaster Depot Company S
Wem 457 Engineer Depot Company
Wem 520 & 567 Quartermaster Battalions M TC, HQ & HQ Det
Wem 578 Signal Depot Company (-) Shropshire
Wem 581 Quartermaster Battalion, Medical Detachment
Wem 613 Quartermaster Depot Company S, 2 Platoon
Wem 785 Base Depot Company TC, Detachment A
Wem 793 Military Police Battalion ZI, Company C, Det A
Wem 1211 & 1230 Engineer Fire Fighting Platoons
Wem 3013 & 3062 Quartermaster Bakery Company M
Wem 3264 Quartermaster Service Company
Wem 3277 Ordnance Base Depot Company
Wem 3342 Quartermaster Truck Company TC
Wem General Depot G-16 Shropshire
Whitchurch 11 Replacement Depot Headquarters
Whitchurch 114 Anti-Aircraft Artillery Group, Headquarters
Whitchurch 131 Army Postal Unit

31 August 1944
Gwerheylod Camp 930 & 663 Ship Hospital Platoon
Iscoyd Park 82 General Hospital
Iscoyd Park Detachment of Patients 4192 HP
Llanerch Panna 22 Hospital Trains
Llanerch Panna 83 General Hospital Flintshire
Overton 505 Replacement Company
Llanerch Panna Detachment of Patients 4190 HP
Gwernheylod 6810 Medical HP Center
Penley 129 General Hospital
Penley Detachment of Patients 4191 HP
Alberbury Chemical Warfare Service Depot C–900
Atcham 12 Station Complement Squadron
Atcham 72 Mobile Training Unit
Atcham 182 Medical Dispensary (Aviation)
Atcham 185 Mobile Training Unit
Atcham 333 Service Group
Atcham 356 Service Squadron
Atcham 495 Fighter Training Group
Atcham 551 & 552 Fighter Training Squadrons
Atcham 1148 Quartermaster Company (Service Group)
Atcham 1761 Ordnance Supply & Maint. Company (Aviation)
Atcham 2020 Engineer Fire Fighting Platoon (Aviation)
Davenport House 135 Engineer Combat Battalion
Oteley Deer Park 137 General Hospital
Loton Deer Park 195 Chemical Depot Company
Loton Deer Park 239 Chemical Base Depot Company
Merrington 4285, 4286, 4288, 4289 Quartermaster Railhead Companies
Merrington 4394 Quartermaster Railhead Company
Oteley Deer Park Detachment of Patients 4189 HP
Stanley Hall 5, 26, 122 Quartermaster Battalions M
Stanley Hall 642 Quartermaster Trp T Company
Sturt Common 166 & 167 Engineer Combat Battalions
Wem General Depot G–16
Wem 457 Engineer Depot Company
Wem 578 Signal Depot Company
Wem 3191 & 3212 Quartermaster Service Company
Wem 3212 Quartermaster Service Company
Whitchurch 1 Medical Conc Center

APPENDIX 1

Whitchurch 18 Hospital Trains
Whitchurch 29, 506, 520, 533, 543, 544, 557, 560, 597, 599, 609 Ship Hospital Platoons

31 October 1944
Iscoyd Park 82 General Hospital
Iscoyd Park 164 General Hospital
Iscoyd Park Detachment of Patients 4192 Hospital Plant
Llanerch Panna 83 General Hospital
Overton 505 Replacement Company Flintshire
Llanerch Panna Detachment of Patients 4190 Hospital Plant
Gwerhnheylod 6810 Medical Hospital Center
Penley 129 General Hospital
Penley Detachment of Patients 4191 Hospital Plant
Alberbury 195 Chemical Depot Company
Alberbury 239 Chemical Base Depot Company
Alberbury Chemical Warfare Service Depot C–900
Atcham 12 Station Complement Squadron
Atcham 182 Medical Dispensary (Aviation)
Atcham 185 Mobile Training Unit
Atcham 333 Service Group
Atcham 356 Service Squadron
Atcham 495 Fighter Training Group
Atcham 551 & 552 Fighter Training Squadrons
Atcham 1148 Quartermaster Company (Service Group)
Atcham 1761 Ordnance Supply & Maint Company (Aviation)
Atcham 2020 Engineer Fire Fighting Platoon (Aviation)
Oteley Deer Park 137 General Hospital
Oteley Deer Park Detachment of Patients 4189 Hospital Plant
Wem General Depot G–16
Wem 457 Engineer Depot Company
Wem 3095 Quartermaster Supply Section
Wem 4404 Quartermaster Service Company
Whitchurch 1 Medical Demons Platoon
Whitchurch 1 Medical Concentration Center
Whitchurch 118 Finance Distribution Section
Whitchurch 209 Army Postal Unit Type F
Whitchurch 504, 534, 542, 543, 545, 549, 556, 558, 578, 581, 582, 601, 711, 712, 720, 874, 900, 914, 927, 975 Ship Hospital Platoons

25 November 1944
Iscoyd Park 82 General Hospital
Iscoyd Park Detachment of Patients 4192 HP
Llanerch Panna 83 General Hospital
Llanerch Panna Detachment of Patients 4190 HP
Penley 129 General Hospital
Penley Detachment of Patients 4191 HP
Alberbury 195 Chemical Depot Company
Alberbury 239 Chemical Base Depot Company
Alberbury Chemical Warfare Service Depot C–900
Atcham 12 Station Complement Squadron
Atcham 182 Medical Dispensary (Aviation)
Atcham 185 Mobile Training Unit
Atcham 333 Service Group
Atcham 356 Service Squadron
Atcham 495 Fighter Training Group
Atcham 551 & 552 Fighter Training Squadrons
Atcham 1148 Quartermaster Company (Service Group)
Atcham 1761 Ordnance Supply & Maint Company (Aviation)
Atcham 2020 Engineer Fire Fighting Platoon (Aviation)
Oteley Deer Park 137 General Hospital
Oteley Deer Park Detachment of Patients 4189 HP
Wem General Depot G–16
Wem 295 Ordnance Heavy Maint Field Artillery Company
Wem 367 Ordnance Maintenance Anti-Aircraft Company
Wem 457 Engineer Depot Company Shropshire
Wem 1349 Engineer General Service Regiment
Wem 3464 Ordnance Medium Auto Maintenance Company
Whitchurch 1 Medical Conc Center
Whitchurch 1 Medical Demons Platoon
Whitchurch 6 Hospital Group (Provisional)
Whitchurch 118 Finance Distribution Section
Whitchurch 209 Army Postal Unit Type F
Whitchurch 504, 549, 558, 578, 581, 711, 720, 874, 900, 914, 927, 975 Ship Hospital Platoons
Whitchurch 6810 Medical Hospital Center

16 December 1944
Iscoyd Park 82 General Hospital
Iscoyd Park 4192 HP Detachment of Patients
Llanerch Panna 83 General Hospital
Llanerch Panna 4190 HP Detachment of Patients
Penley 129 General Hospital
Penley 4191 HP Detachment of Patients
Alberbury 195 Chemical Depot Company
Alberbury 239 Chemical Base Depot Company
Alberbury 900 Chemical Warfare Service Depot C–900
Atcham 12 Station Complement Squadron
Atcham 182 Medical Dispensary (Aviation)
Atcham 185 Mobile Training Unit
Atcham 333 Service Group
Atcham 356 Air Service Squadron
Atcham 495, 551 & 552 Fighter Training Groups
Atcham 1148 Quartermaster Company (Service Group)
Atcham 1761 Ordnance Supply & Maint. Company (Aviation)

U.S. ARMY HOSPITAL CENTER 804

Atcham 2020 Engineer Fire Fighting Platoon (Aviation)
Oteley Deer Park 137 General Hospital
Hawkstone Park 1274 Engineer Combat Battalion
Heath Camp 897, 898 & 899 Field Artillery Battalions (105 How)
Oteley Deer Park 4189 HP Detachment of Patients
Wem 16 General Depot G–16
Wem 295 Ordnance Heavy Maint. Field Artillery Company
Wem 367 Ordnance Maintenance Anti-Aircraft Company
Wem 457 Engineer Depot Company
Wem 1469 Engineer Maintenance Company
Wem 1666 Engineer Utilities Detachment
Wem 3464 Ordnance Medium Maintenance Company
Whitchurch 1 Medical Conc Center
Whitchurch 1 Medical Demons Platoon
Whitchurch 118 Finance Distribution Section
Whitchurch 209 Army Postal Unit Type F
Whitchurch 504, 549, 558, 578, 711, 720, 874, 900, 914, 927, 975 Ship Hospital Platoons
Whitchurch 6810 Hospital Center Shropshire

2 May 1945
Iscoyd Park 82 General Hospital
Iscoyd Park 275 Medical Mess Detachment
Iscoyd Park 455 Military Police Patrol Detachment
Iscoyd Park 3973 Signal Switchboard Detachment
Iscoyd Park Detachment of Patients 4192 HP
Llanerch Panna 276 Medical Mess Detachment
Llanerch Panna 423 Military Police Patrol Detachment
Llanerch Panna 1131 Army Postal Unit Type A
Llanerch Panna 3974 Signal Switchboard Detachment
Llanerch Panna 83 General Hospital
Llanerch Panna Detachment of Patients 4190 HP
Penley 129 General Hospital
Penley 277 Medical Mess Detachment
Penley 424, 425 Military Police Patrol Detachments
Penley 1132 Army Postal Unit Type A
Penley 1361 Labor Supv Company
Penley 3975 Signal Switchboard Detachment
Penley Detachment of Patients 4191 HP
Alberbury 223 Chemical Base Depot Company
Alberbury Chemical Warfare Service Depot C–900
Oteley Dee Park 137 General Hospital
Halston Hall 68 General Hospital
Halston Hall 421 & 422 Military Police Patrol Detachments
Halston Hall 1130 Army Postal Unit Type A
Halston Hall Detachment of Patients 4188 HP
Hawkstone 1021 Labor Supv Company
Oteley Deer Park 278 Medical Mess Detachment
Oteley Deer Park 426 Military Police Patrol Detachment
Oteley Deer Park Detachment of Patients 4189 HP
Wem 457 Engineer Depot Company
Wem 3143 Quartermaster Service Company
Whitchurch 118 Finance Distribution Section
Whitchurch 121 Medical Mess Detachment
Whitchurch 122 Medical Mess Detachment
Whitchurch 123 Lbr Supv Center
Whitchurch 155 Medical Service Detachment
Whitchurch 175 Medical Auto Maintenance Detachment
Whitchurch 199 Medical Ambulance Detachment
Whitchurch 209 Army Postal Unit Type F
Whitchurch 230 & 231 Medical Supply Detachments
Whitchurch 315 & 316 Medical Maintenance Detachments
Whitchurch 456 Military Police Patrol Detachment
Whitchurch 804 Hospital Center
Whitchurch 826 Ship Hospital Platoon

29 December 1945
Iscoyd Park 455 Military Police Patrol Detachment
Whitchurch 826 Ship Hospital Platoon

Appendix 2: Military Camps in Shropshire during World War 2

With kind permission of Adrian Pearce

Adderley Hall Camp, Audlem (SJ654399)
Reinforcement camp to be occupied by 3 Corps in the event of an invasion of the UK. Capacity 1,000 personnel. Known to have been occupied at some time by Black American soldiers and later used as a Prisoner of War camp for captured Italians.

Albrighton Camp, RAF Cosford (SJ796055)
Air Ministry Works Department (AMWD) Repair Depot based at RAF Cosford. There was also a US Army Camp nearby with a capacity of 720 personnel.

All Stretton Camp, Church Stretton (SJ4695)
Army basic training camp with 50th Anti-Tank Training Regiment.

All Stretton Vehicle Depot, Church Stretton (SO465950)
Army vehicle depot. Vehicles were probably camouflaged from aerial observation.

Apley Castle Camp, Wellington (SJ656132)
US Army staging camp. Capacity 3,600 personnel.

Aston Park Camp, Wem (SJ525298)
US Army camp. Capacity 1,560 personnel. Units based there were No 83 Ordnance Sub-Depot, 3264th Quartermaster Service Company, General Stores Depot G-16 and 20th Hospital Train.

Central Ammunition Depot, Nesscliffe (SJ354192)
CAD Nesscliffe was opened by the War Office in 1941. In order to service the extensive property, the War Office took over the virtually defunct Shropshire and Montgomeryshire Railway and built extensive additional service tracks along the 8¾ miles of railway line from Maesbrook to the former Ford and Crossgate railway station. Like a typical ammunition depot, the site was laid out over an extensive area to avoid total destruction should an accidental explosion occur, or the site be attacked by enemy. The depot was made up of five separate sites at:
Kinnerley (SJ354192), Pentre (SJ374170), Ford (SJ408139), Argoed (SJ327217), Loton Park (SJ357137).
The first four sites were capable of storing around 55,000 tons of shells. Loton Park was used for storage of both incendiary ammunition and chemical weapons shells from 1943. This was one of only two Chemical Warfare depots operated in co-operation with and guarded by the United States Army Air Force, specifically 7th US Chemical Depot Company. Locomotives and train drivers were provided by the Royal Engineers, who also maintained the extensive network. Their main servicing depot for rolling stock was on the stub-junction of the former branchline to Criggion. Ammunition storage on site officially stopped in 1959.

Central Ordnance Depot, Donnington (SJ700141)
The Central Ordnance Depot (COD) at Donnington was opened by the Royal Army Ordnance Corps in 1940 to hold non-vehicle technical stores

Chyknell Camp, Claverley (SO777932)
Army summer camp. Capacity 1,302 personnel. Also home to US Army 3918th Quartermaster Gasoline Supply Company.

Cluddley Camp, Wellington (SJ631103)
US Army staging camp. Capacity of 300 Black American soldiers. Later used as Prisoner of War Camp.

Coton Hall Camp, Alveley (SO772862)
US Army summer camp. Capacity 1,302 personnel.

Criggion Radio Station, Criggion (SJ283144)
Established in the Second World War to intercept foreign wireless signals and pass these to Bletchley Park for decoding. It acted as a back-up unit for the larger Rugby Radio Station and took over the latter's traffic for a short period in 1943 following a fire.

Davenport House Camp, Worfield (SO753954)
US Army summer camp. Capacity 2,604 personnel.

Draycott Weapon Training School (SO812928)
Training centre that was used as a Home Guard Weapon Training School.

Duddleston Heath Supply Depot, Duddleston Heath (SJ38203600)
Supply depot which became Elson Industrial Park.

Ebury Hill Tank Park/l Vehicle Testing Station, Haughton (SJ546164)
The station was established to test small semi-armoured personnel vehicles fitted with a Bren gun and known as Universal or Bren carriers. Prior to the Normandy landings in 1944 these vehicles had to be modified so that they could be driven through water. The site comprises a series of concrete roads, barrack blocks, offices and stores. In the northern part of the quarry within the hillfort is a pool of water into which a concrete ramp descends. The number of military buildings suggests that the site was used both to test vehicles after modification and to train drivers before they were sent overseas.

Edgerley Ammunition Store, Wilcott (SJ353193)
Site of ammunition store at Acksea Farm.

Gatacre Hall Camp, Claverley (SO792902)
US Army summer camp. Capacity 1,302 personnel.

Hawkstone Hall, Weston (SJ577301)
US Army Disciplinary Training Centre No 7.

Kinlet Hall, Highley (SO706814)
Army summer camp. Capacity 2,604 personnel.

Ludford Park Camp, Overton (SO51457230)
RAF Training Depot and US Army camp.

Market Drayton PLUTO Pumping Station (SJ64943300)
The PLUTO (Pipeline Under The Ocean) line was used for delivering fuel to the Allied Army after D-Day from Britain to Cherbourg. A pipeline was constructed in 1944 from the refinery at Ellesmere Port to Fawley in Hampshire and then across to Shanklin on the Isle of Wight. A pumping station on the pipeline was constructed at Fordhall Farm and this is still in fair condition. The cross-Channel pumping operations ceased at the end of July 1945.

Meole Brace Vehicle Depot, Shrewsbury (SJ485110)
Army vehicle depot.

Merrington Green Camp, Bomere Heath (SJ465208)
US Army summer camp. Capacity 1,302 personnel. After the war it was used as a prisoner of war camp.

Park Hall Barracks, Oswestry (SJ3031)
Former 1st World War camp and hospital for the Royal Welsh Fusiliers, reactivated in July 1939 and divided into Birch, Butler, Milne and Wingate Lines. There was a hutted camp near Park Hall Rugby Club (SJ304310), another at Park Hall (SJ310315) and one for officers at Park Crescent (SJ310317). A batch of 2,500 Royal Artillery recruits was installed, learning basic skills and gunnery instruction. It was also the home for No 1 Plotting Officers' School. To assist the movement of troops, a small station called Park Hall Halt had been built in the early 1920s. This was re-opened and was in regular use throughout the war.

Prees Heath Camp, Prees Heath (SJ564375)
Army Camp replaced by RAF Tilstock.

Racecourse Camp, Ludlow (SO493775)
US Army camp.

RAF Bridgnorth (SO743924)
A basic recruit training camp for RAF personnel from 1939-63. During WWII it was called Nos 4 & 7 Recruits Centres and Nos 18, 19, 50 & 81 Initial Training Wings. There was also a hospital there during the Second WWII.

Royal Naval Armament Depot Ditton Priors (SO616886)
The depot was established in 1939, South-East of Ditton village on land made available by Lord Boyne. The depot had 25 magazines and four stores for naval mines and made use of the Ditton Priors Light Railway, which had sidings in the depot

Sheriffhales Camp, Sheriffhales (SJ758114)
Army transit camp later used as a Prisoner of War Camp.

Stanley Hall Camp, Astley Abbotts (SO714964)
US Army summer camp. Capacity 1,302 personnel.

Stokesay Court Training School No 3, Onibury (SO44447864)
Training centre that was used for tactics and leadership instruction for Home Guard units.

Sturt Common Camp, Wyre Forest (SO725773)
US Army summer camp. Capacity 1,302 personnel.

Styche Hall Camp, Market Drayton (SJ644358)
US Army camp. Capacity 200 personnel.

Ternhill Camp, Stoke Heath (SJ6431)
US Army Detachment 'P', 24th Airways Communications Squadron.

Whitchurch Radio Station (SJ54144202)
Established in the Second World War to intercept foreign wireless signals and pass these to Bletchley Park for decoding. It was run by the Army and based at the Old Rectory in Whitchurch. The station itself was based in Nissen huts but the Hollies Hotel (SJ53794195) was requisitioned for sleeping accommodation.

Appendix 3: US Army Hospitals in UK, August 1944

Plant No.	Site	Hospital Unit	Plant No.	Site	Hospital Unit
4100	Truro	314SH	4154	Blockley	327SH
4101	Tavistock	115SH	4155	Moreton	
4102	Moretonhampstead ?		4156	Fairford	
4103	Newton Abbot	124GH	4157	Salisbury	152SH
4104	Exeter	36SH	4165	Tyntesfield	74GH
4105	Barnstaple	313SH	4166	Bristol	117GH
4106	Bishops Lydeard	185GH	4167	Stoneleigh	307SH
4107	Norton Manor	101GH	4168	Bromsgrove	123GH
4108	Taunton	67GH	4169	Wolverley	52GH
4109	Axminster	315SH	4170	Bewdley	297GH
4110	Yeovil, Houndstone	169GH	4171	Bewdley	114GH
4111	Yeovil, Lufton	121GH	4172	Blackmore Park	93GH
4112	Sherborne	228SH	4173	Blackmore Park	155GH
4113	Frome St Quintin	305SH	4174	Malvern Wells	96GH
4114	Blandford	22GH	4175	Malvern Wells	53GH
4115	Blandford	119GH	4176	Malvern Wells	55GH
4116	Blandford	125GH	4177	Leominster	135GH
4117	Blandford	131GH	4178	Foxley	123GH
4118	Blandford	140GH	4179	Foxley	156GH
4119	Wimborne	106GH	4180	Kington	122GH
4120	Ringwood	104GH	4181	Kington	107GH
4121	Netley	110SH	4182	Abergavenny	279SH
4122	Winchester	38SH	4183	Rhyd Lafar	81GH
4123	Stockbridge	34GH	4184	Carmarthen	232SH
4124	Odstock	158GH	4185	Lichfield	33SH
4125	Grimsdith	250SH	4186	Shugborough	312SH
4126	Warminster	216GH	4187	Sudbury Derby	182GH
4127	Tidworth	3SH	4188	Whittington	68GH
4128	Perham Downs	103GH	4189	Oteley Deer Park	137GH
4129	Everleigh	187GH	4190	Overton	83GH
4130	Devizes	141GH	4191	Penley	129GH
4131	Devizes	128GH	4192	Iscoyd Park	82GH
4132	Erlestoke Park	102GH	4193	Saighton	109GH
4133	Bath	160SH	4194	Clatterbridge	157GH
4134	Falfield	94GH	4195	Stockton Heath	168SH
4135	Malmesbury	120SH	4196	Davey Hulme	10SH
4136	Lydiard Park	302SH	4197	Glasgow	316SH
4137	Swindon	154GH	4198	Harrogate	115GH
4138	Chiseldon	130SH	4199	Harrogate	116GH
4139	Marlborough	347SH	4200	Mansfield	184GH
4140	Hermitage	98GH	4201	Nocton Hall	7GH
4141	Checkendon	306GH	4202	Allington	348SH
4142	Kingwood	304GH	4203	Thorpe North	303SH
4143	Wheatley	97GH	4204	Diddington	49SH
4144	Headington	91GH	4205	Cambridge	163GH
4145	Middleton Stoney	318SH	4206	Newport	280SH
4146	Ramsden	317SH	4207	Braintree	121SH
4147	Burford	61GH	4208	Acton, Suffolk	136SH
4148	Fairford	186GH	4209	Redgrave Park	65GH
4149	Cirencester	188GH	4210	Wymondham	231SH
4150	Cirencester	192GH	4211	North Mimms	1GH
4151	Daglinworth	111GH	4212		
4152	Stowell Park	160GH	4213	Packington	77SH
4153	Ullenwood	110GH	4261	London	16SH

Appendix 4: Army Hospital Centers

Hospital Center	Hospital Group	Place
12	5	Malvern
15	4	Cirencester
801	1	Taunton
802	2	Blandford
803	3	Devizes
804 (Originally 6810 provisional-activated June 1944)	6	Whitchurch
805	7	Newmarket

N.B. Hospital Groups designated October 1944
Hospitals in Shropshire and Flintshire came under the jurisdiction of the 6810 Hospital Center at Whitchurch.

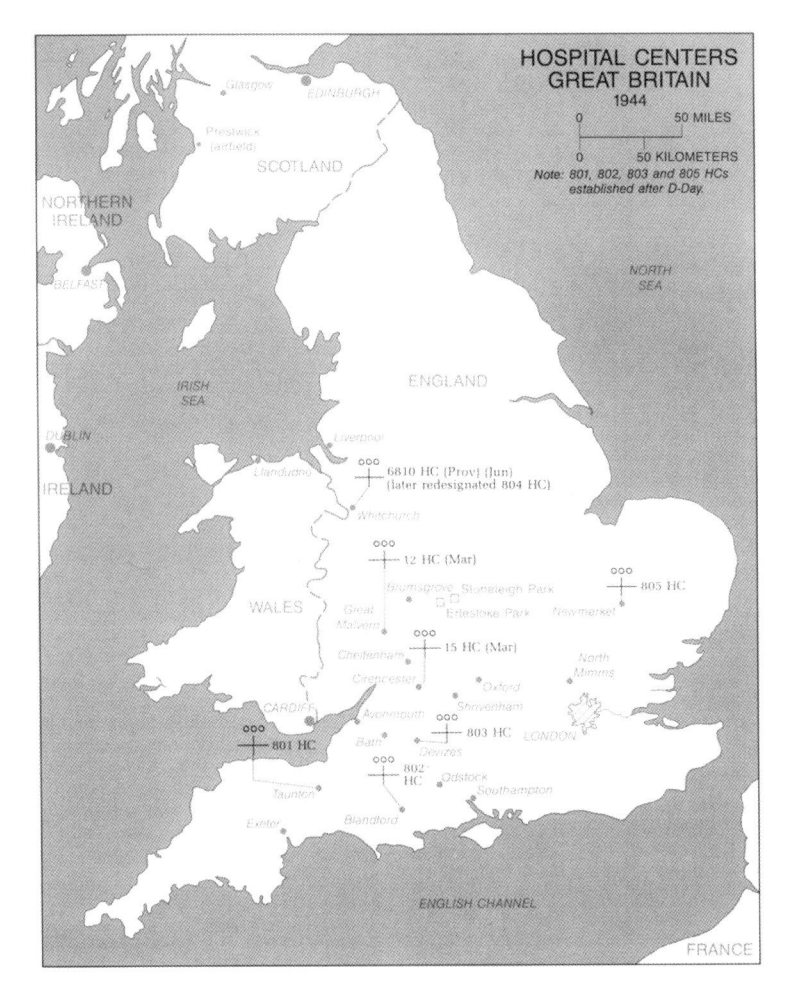

Map showing Medical Centers in the U.K. (U.S. Military archives)

Appendix 5: Hospital Trains

With kind permission of Adrian and Neil Turley

Hospital train railheads in the Shropshire/Flintshire group:
   Ellesmere
   Overton-on-Dee
   Malpas

Known hospital train movements to the above:

1 May 1944 Oxford to Malpas
4 May 1944 Salisbury to Malpas Train 59
3 June 1944 Oxford to Malpas Train 64
17 June 1944 Swindon to Ellesmere Train 14
18 June 1944 Axminster to Malpas Train 11
20 June 1944 Marlborough to Ellesmere Train 14
24 June 1944 Newbury to Ellesmere Train 12
8 July 1944 Newbury? to Ellesmere Train 12
10 July 1944 Swindon to Malpas Train 14
12 July 1944 Winchester to Ellesmere Train 14
9 August 1944 Newbury to Malpas Train 12
12 August 1944 Newbury to Ellesmere Train 12
14 August 1944 Newbury to Malpas Train 12
28 Sept 1944 Netley to Malpas Train 11
29 Sept 1944 Sherborne to Malpas Train 14
2 Oct 1944 Chiseldon to Overton-on-Dee Train 65
4 Oct 1944 Swindon to Ellesmere Train 4
16 Oct 1944 Chiseldon to Ellesmere Train 14
4 Nov 1944 Chiseldon to Ellesmere Train 14
18 Nov 1944 Netley to Ellesmere Train 14
3 Dec 1944 Chiseldon to Overton-on-Dee Train 1
11 Dec 1944 Southampton to Overton-on-Dee Train 2
27 Dec 1944 Chiseldon to Ellesmere Train 1

Acknowledgements

We are indebted to:

Muriel Engelman for sharing her memories and photos of her time as a nurse at the 16th General Hospital.

Jill McConkey, daughter of Tec. 4 Thomas McConkey for sharing with us her late father's photos and numerous letters.

Dennis Nicola, son of Lt. Col Quintus Nicola (Executive Officer at the 82nd General Hospital), for providing us with a number of black and white and colour photos and letters belonging to his late father.

Reverend Paul Osaphl for sharing memories and photos of his father, Chaplain Carl Osaphl of the 304th Station Hospital.

Alice Weiss, daughter of Nurse Angela De Gioia (Weiss) of the 82nd General Hospital, for sharing with us photos and information about her late mother.

J.D. Wilson for sharing memories and photos of his father, Lieutenant Sharia Wilson of the 304th Station Hospital.

Also in grateful acknowledgement of the following contributors to the book:

Gary Bedingfield, P. Curtis, Philip Grinton, Margery Jones, Steve Mackreth, Dave Moore, Shirley Pratt, Gordon Richards, Ann Trevor, Neil and Adrian Turley, Donna Ulloa.

Also in acknowledgement of the following organisations and publications:

Letters of Tom Morrisey

Army Medical Department (AMEDD)

Jill Burton (Editor of Overton Chronicle)

ACKNOWLEDGEMENTS

David Broad and Judith Hoyle of Whitchurch Heritage Centre

Janet Miller (Whitchurch History and Archaeology Group)

Phil Godsal Jr and Philip Godsal Sr from Iscoyd Park

Med.dept.com and Ben Major

Adrian Pearce and shropshirehistory.com

National Archives and Records Administration (NARA) Washington D.C.

Viv Davies and The Welsh Assembly

Owen Mostyn Owen from Rednal Airfield

English Heritage

National Museum of Health and Medicine (NMHM)

Wrexham Archives

Wrexham Leader

Wrexham Advertiser and Star

By the same authors

Letters for Victory, ISBN 978-1-85858-016-6, £10.95

Somewhere in The Midlands, ISBN 978-1-85858-119-4, £6.95

They Also Serve Who Stand And Wait, ISBN 978-1-85858-204-7, £9.95

Camp Foxley, ISBN 978-1-85858-285-6, £10.95

Blackmore Park in World War Two, ISBN 978-1-85858-428-7, £10.95

Return to Duty, ISBN 978-1-85858-454-6, £10.95

The Friendly Invasion of Leominster, ISBN 978-1-85858-493-5, £10.95

Bridging The Gap, ISBN 978-1-85858-525-3, £10.95